IMAGES
of America

THE OSBORN

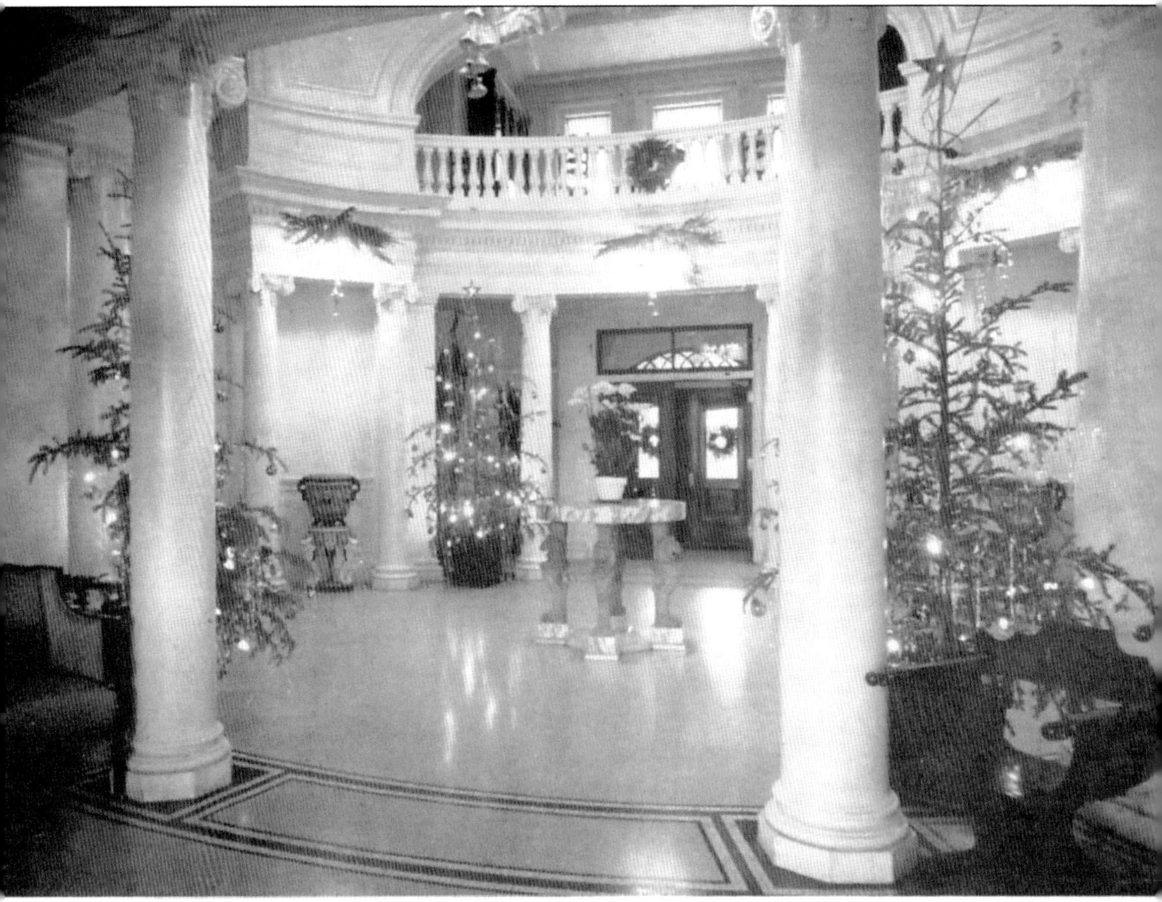

ROTUNDA OF THE OSBORN BUILDING—OPENED IN 1908 JOHN GASS

This Christmas card was created for The Osborn's 50th anniversary. The view is toward the front door. The sentiment of the card is enduring, "With sincere good wishes and with the hope that the coming year may bring health and happiness to you and to all other friends of The Osborn Home."

On the cover: Brightly shining in the noonday sun, the first building on The Osborn campus was completed in 1908 as a home for aged gentlewomen in needy circumstances and the culmination of Miriam Osborn's dream. Over the past century, other buildings have been added and countless women and men have come to live in them surrounded by lush and tranquil grounds and cared for by a staff dedicated to Miriam's vision. (Courtesy of The Osborn collection.)

IMAGES
of America

THE OSBORN

Mark R. Zwerger, Janet M. Malang,
and Andrew F. Horn

ARCADIA
PUBLISHING

ISBN 978-0-7385-5535-5

Published by Arcadia Publishing
Charleston SC, Chicago IL, Portsmouth NH, San Francisco CA

Printed in the United States of America

Library of Congress Catalog Card Number: 2007931491

For all general information contact Arcadia Publishing at:
Telephone 843-853-2070
Fax 843-853-0044
E-mail sales@arcadiapublishing.com
For customer service and orders:
Toll-Free 1-888-313-2665

Visit us on the Internet at www.arcadiapublishing.com

We dedicate this book to Miriam Osborn,
founder and benefactor of the Miriam Osborn Memorial Home,
to all the residents who have called it home and graced its halls,
and to all those who cared so well for them over the years.

Contents

ACKNOWLEDGMENTS

The authors would like to thank the following for their support and help with this project: the board of trustees and Jack Miller, board chairman; the book group, Michael Freddino, Rosann Catania, Kathy Briotte, Marie Vize, Denise Stroh, Anne Kelsey, and Sue Seitz of the board of managers; and Debra Curcio, Ana Maria Lopez, Susan Keating, Matt Anderson, Jane Fox, and Lew Cox for their technical assistance. An invaluable resource then and now is Helen Adams, who had the wisdom to preserve the memories of her 60-year association with The Osborn Home. Unless otherwise noted, all images are from The Osborn collection.

INTRODUCTION

In 1908, one woman's dream that had become one man's passion became a reality when The Miriam Osborn Memorial Home opened. The result of years of careful planning, The Osborn Home became a world-class institution that over the past century has cared for thousands of deserving aged citizens from the Greater New York area. As part of the centennial celebration of The Osborn Home, now called The Osborn, this book recounts the remarkable history and legacies of Miriam Osborn, John Sterling, and the countless people touched by their vision and their generosity.

By all accounts, Miriam was a kind soul who lived the life of a wealthy New Yorker but conducted herself with the demure gentility and grace of a true Southern lady. Born Miriam Adelaide Trowbridge in 1840 in Augusta, Georgia, she was sent to New York to be formally educated. In 1858, she wed Charles Osborn, one of a cadre of successful Wall Street speculators in the late-19th-century era of Rockefeller, Vanderbilt, Carnegie, Morgan, and Gould. In this setting they met John Sterling, one of New York's most prominent attorneys and cofounder of the prestigious law firm Shearman and Sterling.

As was the custom of wealthy New Yorkers of that era, Charles and Miriam decided to build a grand summer home on the shore of Long Island Sound in Mamaroneck. They retained the legendary Stanford White to design Tahoma. Shortly after taking occupancy, Charles took ill and died, leaving Miriam and their son, Howell.

While Miriam's widowhood was eased by the fortune Charles bequeathed her, she saw many women of her generation struggle when left on their own as they aged. Thus the dream of establishing a memorial home to care for aged gentlewomen in needy circumstances was born and appropriate instructions left in her will. Upon her death in 1891, the Miriam Osborn Memorial Home Association was established by the New York State legislature.

As executor, John Sterling implemented Miriam's dream with characteristic zeal and attention to detail, addressing such minutiae as the order of premeal prayers and the qualifications of the first residents. Sterling rejected Miriam's idea of using Tahoma for the home. He acquired hundreds of acres on Theall's Hill in Rye and hired respected New York architect Bruce Price. During construction, Sterling visited the site regularly by train from his office at 55 Wall Street in New York. The result is the magnificent redbrick Georgian structure that is still occupied today.

Sterling served as chairman of the home's board of trustees until his death in 1918. In his will, Sterling donated funds for the construction of two buildings and approximately 500 acres of land in nearby Harrison (later the home's trustees formed Rye Ridge Realty to develop the property into single-family homes). The Strathcona building, named to honor his friends Donald Alexander Smith (Lord Strathcona) and George Stephen (Lord Mount Stephen), was constructed in 1928 to house the infirmary. The building's most remarkable features were the two grand dining rooms with their ornate plaster trim work and gold chandeliers. In 1934, the Sterling Building, designed by esteemed architect James Gamble Rogers, was constructed. The building was named in honor of Catherine Sterling, John's mother, whose portrait is prominently displayed above the fireplace in the Sterling Lounge today. The Sterling Building was a remarkable architectural achievement. Highlighted by the 10-story Sterling Tower and adorned with etched glass windows and art deco light fixtures designed by Rogers himself, it houses the stately Sterling Theater and Lounge, which can accommodate gatherings of up to 500 people.

John Sterling put the "ship" of Osborn to sail with a fixed rudder that stayed on course during the next seven decades. During those years at The Osborn Home, as it was called, incoming residents paid a nonrefundable admission fee of $500 (later increased to $1,000) and assigned all their worldly possessions to the home in exchange for care for the remainder of their lives. The last "assignment" resident still lives at The Osborn today, having moved in during 1975. After that date, New York State ended the practice.

In the period from 1950 to 1970, the board sold off landholdings to generate funds for operations. Much of the property surrounding the present 56-acre campus was sold to companies, including ITT/Continental Baking, Chrysler, and Pitney Bowes. Property to the north was sold for single-family homes while a parcel at the corner of Boston Post Road and Osborn Road was sold to the school district, which built the Osborn Elementary School.

Although prudently managed by capable leaders R. Eugene Curry and Harold O. Mawhiney, the home's destiny in the second half of the 20th century was altered by fiscal woes and a series of external events. These events revolutionized aging services. Titles XVIII and XIX of the Social Security Act established the Medicare and Medicaid programs and the regulations governing the establishment and operation of nursing homes. In 1969, The Osborn Home in its entirety came under the jurisdiction of the New York State Department of Health as a licensed nursing home. Over the next two decades, regulations governing nursing homes became more complex and stringent.

Additional forces gradually made The Osborn Home obsolete. These included the evolution of attitudes and consumer behavior among seniors and a revolution in the care of the mentally ill that shifted care for those with Alzheimer's disease to the chronic care system. Additionally, changes in workforce demographics, the growth of health care unions, and increasingly costly government oversight of operations would dramatically increase the cost of operating the home. Eventually the increases in the cost of labor, employee benefits, and energy combined with a massive commitment to charity care would cripple the home's financial integrity.

In 1988, the board brought in Mark R. Zwerger to lead the effort to restore the institution to fiscal health and create a sustainable operation to continue to fulfill Miriam Osborn and John Sterling's vision. By the time he took the helm as chief executive officer, occupancy had dwindled to 115 residents with 60 residents fully supported financially by the home. After three years of study, the board adopted a comprehensive plan to restore The Osborn to its original mission and create a sustainable charity into perpetuity. This plan, titled Pathway 2000, called for renovating and expanding the facility to become a continuing care retirement community. It was officially adopted by the board on May 14, 1991.

Simultaneously, a task force chaired by Jack Bowen determined what intermediate actions could be taken while Pathway 2000 was being planned. Immediate steps taken to bolster occupancy included improving the deteriorating decor and launching a successful petition to the courts to allow the admission of men. The more complex problem of operating a retirement continuum under a nursing home license began to be addressed in 1993 when the New York State Department of Health approved the "decertification" of the Sterling Building from a nursing home to an independent living residence. Marketing initiatives included a new logo, a streamlined admission process, and a contemporary name—The Osborn.

The plan called for the construction of 26 new buildings, including 20 duplex garden homes, 3 multistory apartment buildings, a natatorium, a gatehouse, and a new skilled nursing facility,

The Osborn Pavilion. Architectural firm Ellerbe Beckett of Minneapolis was retained to create a master plan for the campus. Chief architect Frank Neimeth and health care specialist Dale Tremain had worked on projects of similar scope and visibility for Notre Dame University and the Mayo Clinic. Development attorney Frank McCullough and local land use planner Mike Divney were hired to secure local approval of the site plan.

This was the largest construction project ever in the city of Rye. It was submitted to the city planning commission in November 1992 and approved in June 1993, a timetable heretofore unheard of for a project of this magnitude. This reflected the thoroughness of the plan, its sensitivity to potential opposing issues, and the professionalism of the development team. Essential to convincing the stakeholders of the plan's urgency was for everyone to understand that status quo at the home was unacceptable.

Four major hurdles remained before the new facilities could be constructed, including approvals by the New York State Department of Health of the new skilled nursing facility and licensed home health agency, state attorney general of the Sterling Park entrance fee apartments and garden homes, and State Dormitory Authority and letter of credit banks of the needed tax exempt bond financing. Finally marketing to secure the necessary number of deposits or "presales" was a prerequisite. The first building constructed was the sales and information center in what is now garden home 5001/5002. This impressive center was instrumental in the successful sellout of the project.

During this time period, the leadership team was strengthened with Jack Bowen elected chairman of the board, the addition of chief financial officer Nate Soffio (1992), medical director William Martimucci, M.D. (1991), and human resources director Elizabeth Rossi (1994). On a crisp, windy autumn day, November 6, 1994, the official groundbreaking ceremonies took place. Congresswoman Nita Lowey and many of the incoming Sterling Park residents attended.

Shortly thereafter, Phase I commenced, including The Osborn Pavilion skilled nursing facility with its state-of-the-art cluster design, 13 of the total of 20 duplex garden homes, the 54-unit Sterling Park 2000 apartment building, the new gatehouse, and a natatorium housing the pool and spa. Scully Construction of White Plains completed needed renovations where the new buildings connected to existing ones. This resulted in the creation of the rehabilitation facilities and Westchester Medical Group clinic on the east connection and the Marketplace and activity room at the west connection.

While the first winter of construction, 1994–1995, was mild, the second winter was one of the worst in Rye's 435-year history. Thirteen major snowstorms were recorded. By spring, the construction was delayed and the development team was weary. Its extraordinary efforts nonetheless resulted in the 2000 building and garden homes opening on June 6, 1996, in time for the "spring 1996" promised opening. The pavilion opened one month later. Two more key members joined the management team in 1996: Janet M. Malang to manage Sterling Park and Kathy Lonergan to oversee home care and business development. In 1997, the first phase was awarded the prestigious Design for Aging Award by the American Institute of Architecture. By year-end 1996, the new buildings were fully occupied by a remarkable group of seniors. Early in 1997, they formed the Sterling Park Residents Association.

The original buildings were then renovated in phases from 1997 to 1999. The project was overseen by local Rye architects Anderson LaRocca Anderson. Every effort was made to restore the facilities to their original condition while insuring that the resulting accommodations were desirable for future residents. In 1998, the remaining 12 garden homes were constructed, and in 1999, the Betty Neagle Perennial Garden was created with generous donations from grateful resident families.

The final phase of Pathway 2000 commenced in January 2000 with the successful marketing, financing, design, and construction of the remaining two Sterling Park apartment buildings, which opened in July 2001. Designed by Perkins Eastman Architects, the project included the Bistro dining room and kitchen and Cinema 3000, a high-tech screening room. By the completion of the project, the management team was expanded to include a new home care director Eileen

Killeen (1997), facilities manager Paul Mackey (1998), skilled nursing facility administrator Matthew Anderson (1998), and marketing director Jane Fox (2002). This exceptional team continues to lead The Osborn to this day.

On September 28, 2002, The Osborn officially dedicated Pathway 2000 in a glorious ceremony that featured New York City mayor Rudolph Giuliani. The evening included a tribute to Mike Pirraglia, The Osborn construction project manager. Days before the event, The Osborn became the first continuum of care in downstate New York to be accredited by the Continuing Care Accreditation Commission. The ceremonies concluded with the unveiling of the dedication plaques and a fabulous fireworks display on the south lawn.

In late May 1996, without prior warning or discussion, the City of Rye assessor revoked The Osborn's century-old real estate tax exemption. This placed the entire property on the tax roll at an annual cost in excess of $1 million. Despite The Osborn's efforts to negotiate a settlement, this dispute resulted in 10 years of protracted litigation that cost The Osborn and the taxpayers of Rye dearly. On December 30, 2006, the Westchester Supreme Court ruled that The Osborn, despite its unchallenged status as a 501(c)(3) charity, was entitled to a 16 percent partial exemption because its licensed nursing home is considered a hospital for real estate tax purposes. The court completed the case on June 5, 2007, ruling that the city assessor had overassessed the property by about $4.5 million for the period 1997–2006, resulting in a refund to The Osborn of nearly $5 million and a reduction in the tax burden on the property going forward in excess of 50 percent. As of spring 2008, the matter remains under appeal, pending a negotiated settlement.

In 1996, upon the opening of the first facilities, Sterling Home Care, The Osborn's licensed home care services agency, was established. Today the agency, renamed Osborn Home Care, provides over $7 million annually in exceptional home care both on the campus and in the community. The Osborn Pavilion admits 300 patients a year and has become the preferred rehabilitation facility for seniors in the region. Now home to 430 senior citizens, The Osborn holds an investment grade rating from Standard and Poor's and has achieved the financial sustainability that was the key motivation for Pathway 2000. In 2006, Jack Bowen retired as chairman and was succeeded by Jack Miller.

Given their dreams for a memorial home for aged gentlewomen, Miriam Osborn and John Sterling would be proud to know that today The Osborn is widely recognized as the finest facility of its kind in the nation.

One

Beginnings

The Miriam Osborn Memorial Home Association was formed on March 5, 1892, by an act of the New York State legislature, approved by Gov. Roswell Pettibone Flower, and signed and sealed by Secretary of State Frank Rice. Those named as members of the association, in addition to John Sterling, were William C. Whitney, a Yale graduate who served as secretary of the navy and corporation counsel of New York, and William Steinway, the son of the piano master builder who served with the group that planned the New York subway system. He founded the Long Island division of the Daimler Motor Company. LaGuardia Airport is located on land he developed as a resort. Others included Cornelius N. Bliss, who served as United States secretary of the interior and declined to be vice presidential candidate with William McKinley; Chauncey M. Depew, a Yale graduate and United States senator from New York; Frederic P. Olcott, a New York State comptroller; and James W. Husted, a Yale graduate who served as president of the Village of Peekskill, president of the Peekskill Bank, and United States congressman. All were successful, imaginative men possessing leadership qualities. Then, three years after the death of Miriam Osborn, the search for a suitable site for The Osborn Home began after a meeting of the board of trustees on January 9, 1894. Neither the Osborn estate, Tahoma, nor the Mitchell place, acquired and favored by Miriam Osborn, was deemed suitable. Tahoma was the childhood home of Miriam's niece Olive, and the Mitchell place was not fireproof, and the house was too small. A Professor Wheeler of Yale University, who lived in Rye, suggested Theall's Hill in the village of Rye, totaling 21.7 acres. John Sterling, the trusted family attorney and advisor, came to envision a handsome building in the center of parklike land, larger than imagined by Miriam Osborn, and so he commenced to purchase many plots contiguous to the site for the home. Step by careful step, The Osborn, only an idea at first, was taking shape.

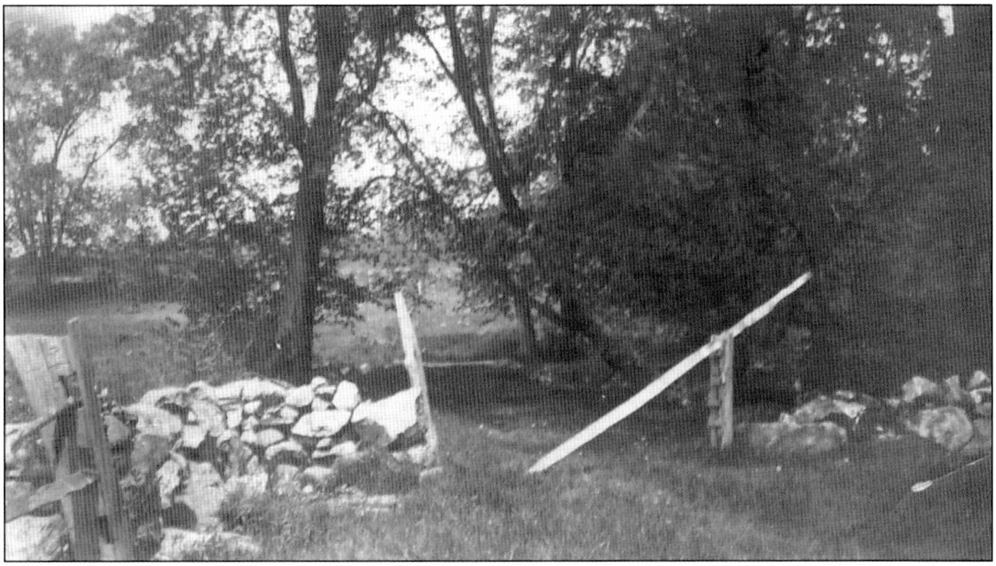

This view of the building site in 1894 from Purdy Lane opposite the southwest entrance shows the undeveloped property.

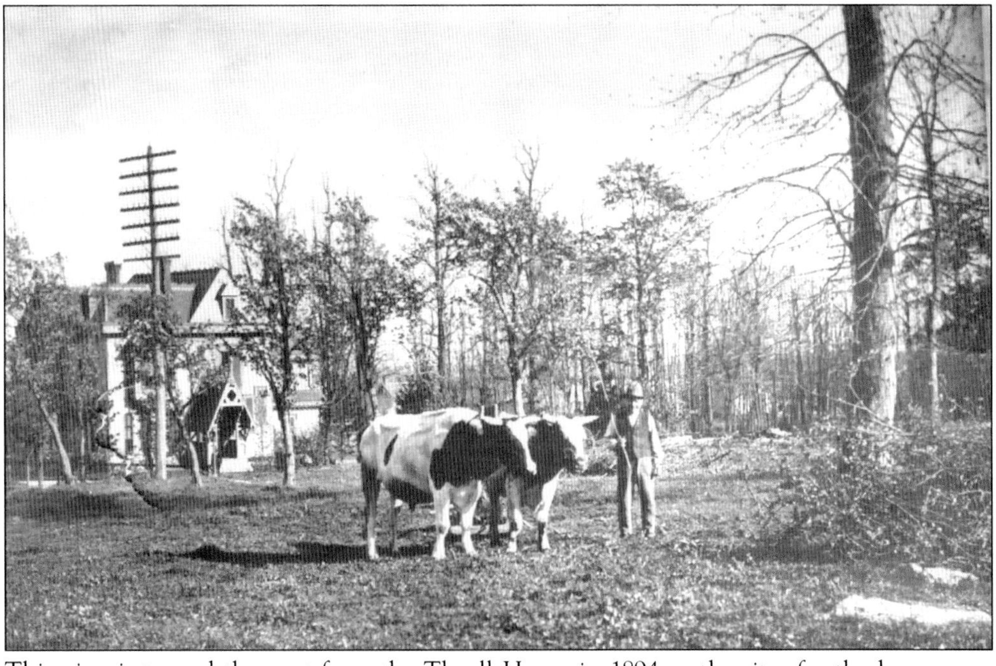

This view is toward the west from the Theall House in 1894 as the sites for the home were being purchased.

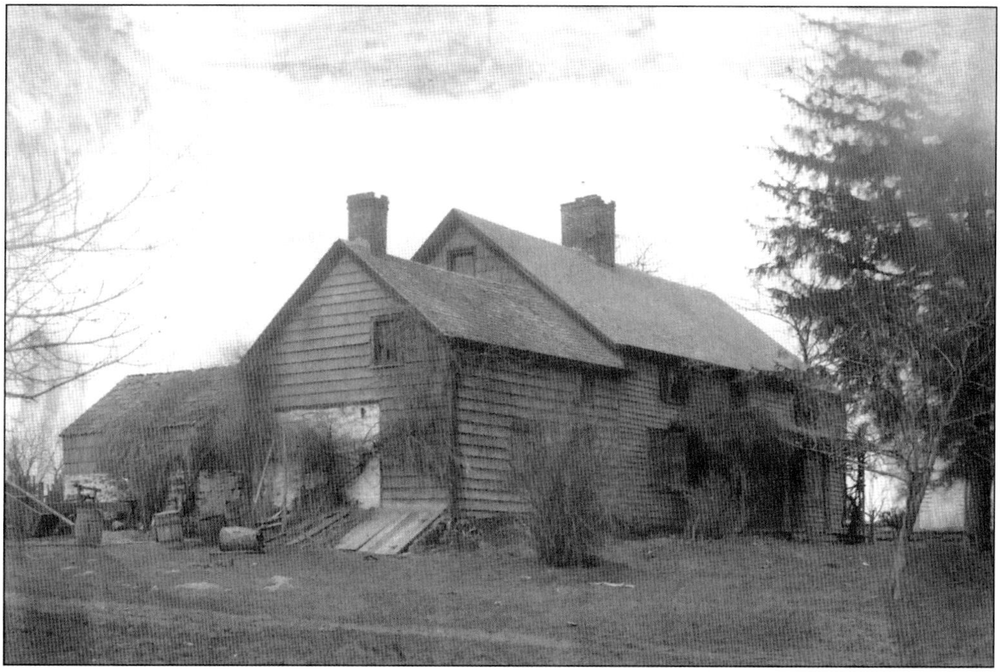

The Purdy House, located on the building site south of Boston Post Road, was demolished on May 4, 1900, shortly after this photograph was taken. The Purdy, Theall, and Mead families were early Rye settlers. Members of the Purdy family were early supervisors and constables of Rye. Daniel Purdy most likely built this house for son Joshua about 1740.

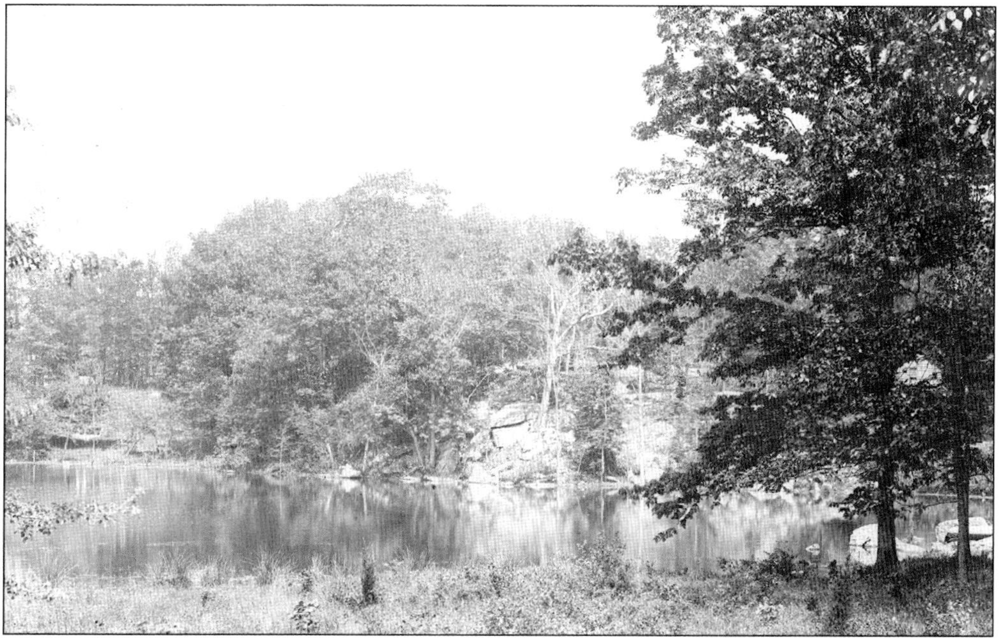

Mead Pond was a favorite ice-skating place. After John Sterling bought the Mead property, he had Mead Pond, near the corner of North Street and Railroad Avenue, dredged and the muck saved for spreading on the lawns. A stone wall was laid around the pond and a substantial dam built to control the water level. It was renamed Lake Miriam for a while.

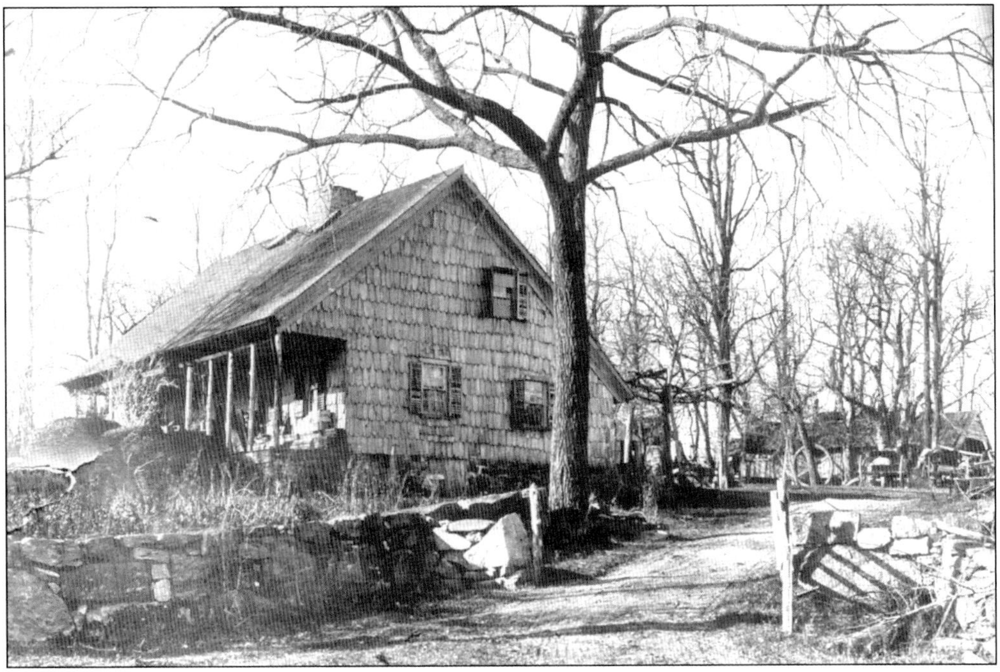

The Mead farmhouse, built in 1681, occupied land purchased by John Sterling for the home. Capt. Joseph Theall and his grandson Charles Theall, a King George loyalist, were early occupants. About 1815, Joseph Bonaparte, ex-king of Spain, sought a home in America. He negotiated for land on Theall's Hill but, unlike John Sterling, was unable to secure enough contiguous land. Adjacent sites acquired by Sterling included plots as far as North Street, on both sides of Railroad Avenue (now Theall Road), on both sides of the Old Post Road and Boston Post Road, and land south of the home site, beyond Osborn Road, then Rye Beach Avenue. Sterling's will named these the Rye Lands. In the photograph below by George S. Olmstead, Sterling had restored Mead Cottage. When demolished, it was over 250 years old.

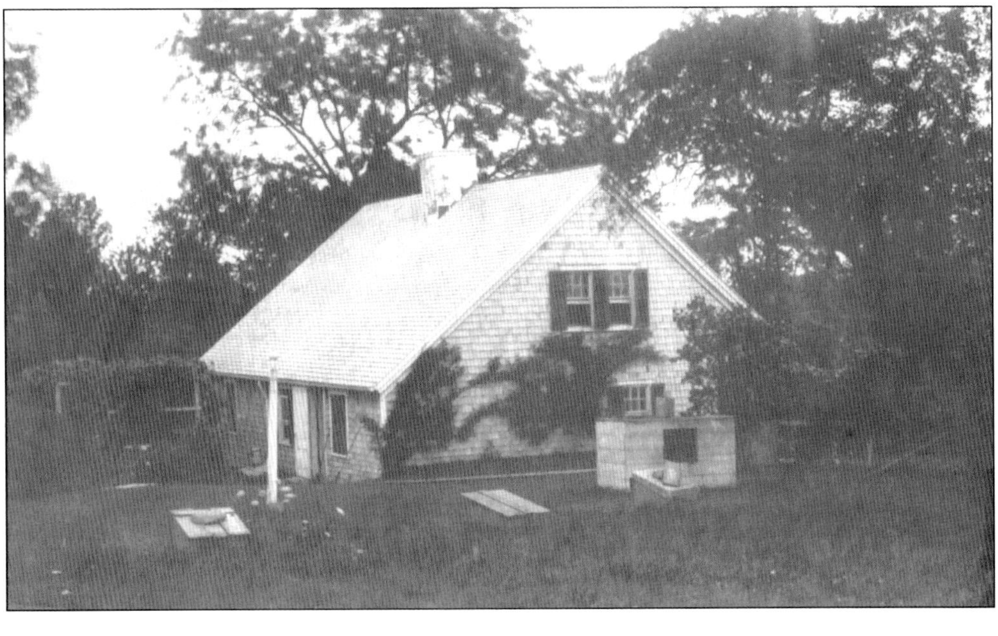

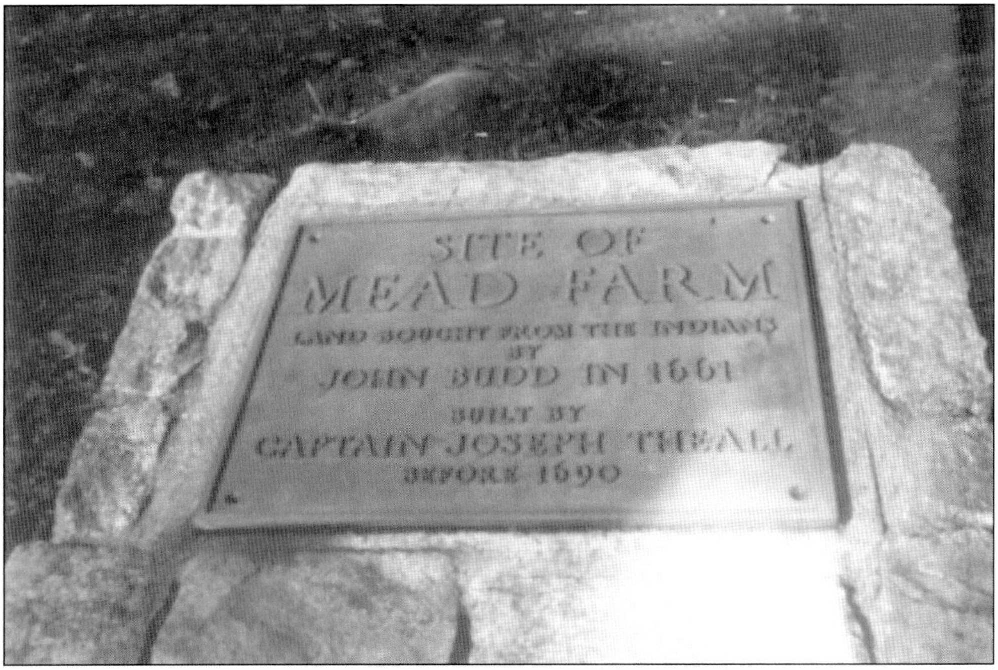

John Budd purchased the land later known as Theall's Hill from Chief Peningo and the Mohawk Indians in 1661 for "8 cotes, 7 shirts and 15 fathoms of wampone," according to Helen Adams's papers. Franklin C. Odell designed the site marker that is near the present-day skilled nursing pavilion, seen behind the trees. It commemorates the site of Mead Farm. The historical society reported the Mead house, perhaps the oldest house in Rye, had no historical interest. The society did not advise its repair. It was in poor condition, being infested with termites. No records were found to support local opinion that it had been used as George Washington's headquarters. The chimney was left standing when the house was demolished because it was among the first authentic chimneys built in Rye.

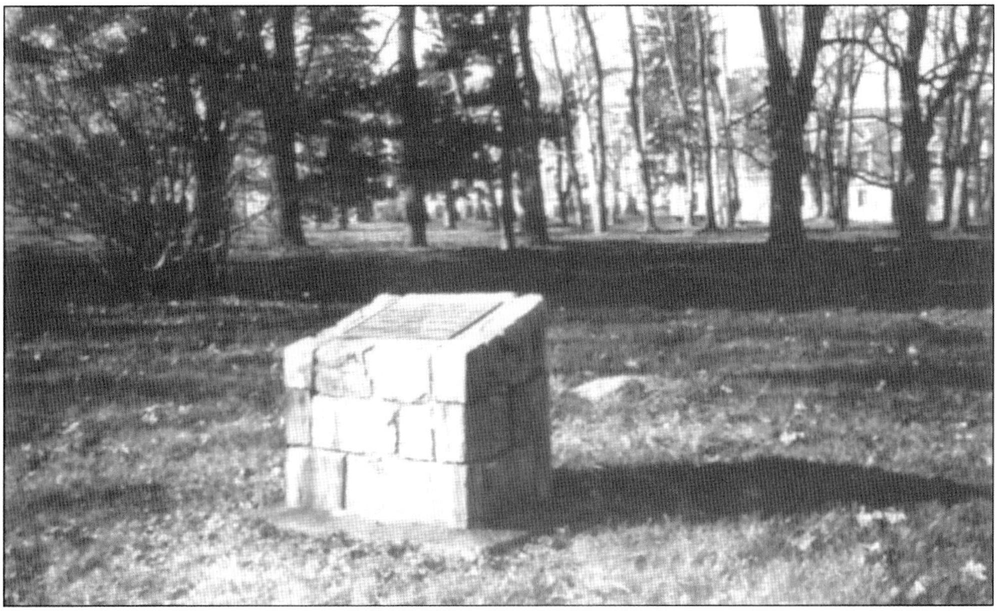

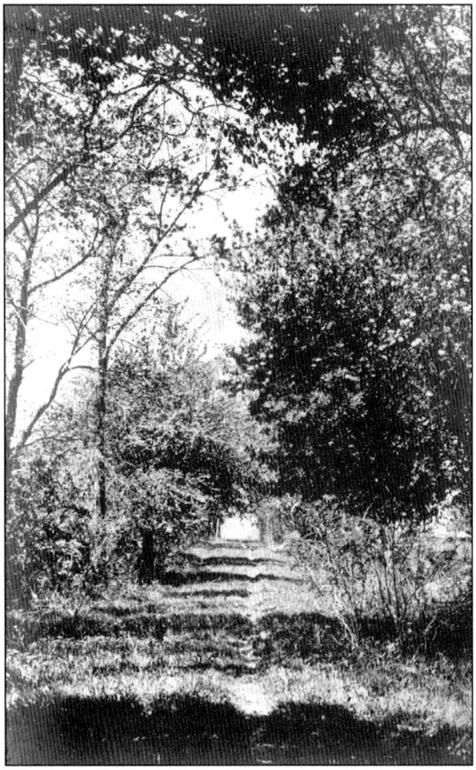

This 1894 view of the site is Cornell Farm and Cornell Lane, also called "the Old Lane," leading to the home. Consideration was given to sites in Manhattan, the Bronx, New Jersey, and Rye and Tuckahoe in Westchester County. Bruce Price, the architect who designed the recitation hall at Yale University, enthusiastically endorsed the site on the crest of Theall's Hill. The site was 114 feet above the level of Long Island Sound. The home paid $38,000 for the land. By 1900, excavations began for the main building and masons had started the cement footings.

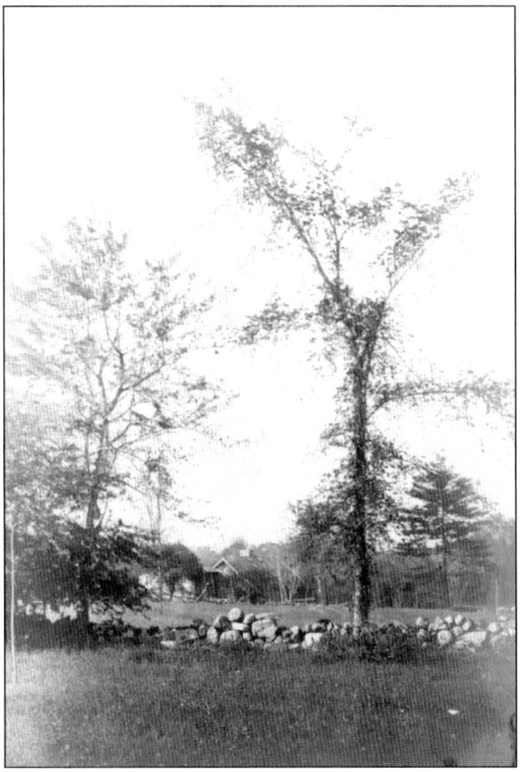

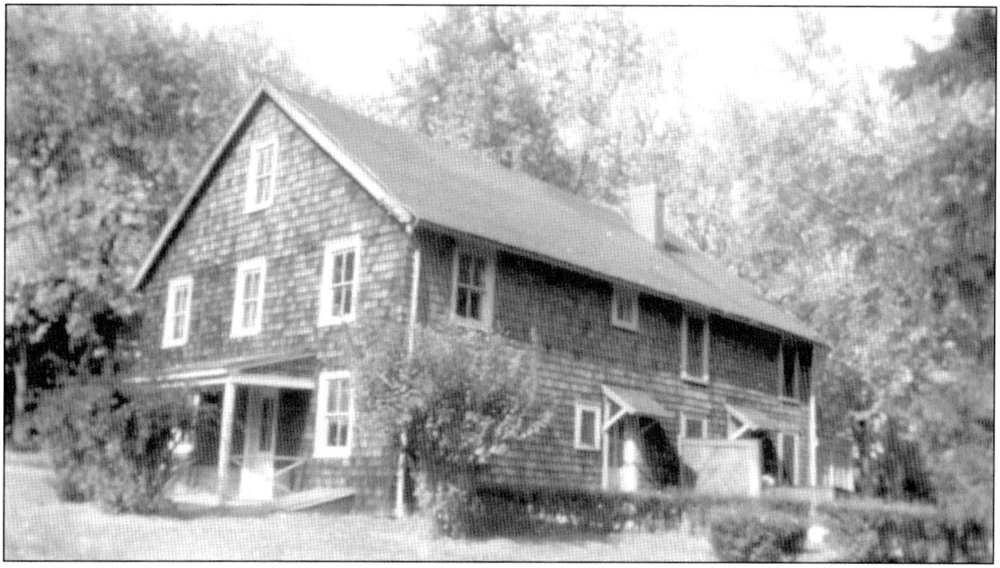

The buildings on the Rye Lands were repaired to provide staff housing. The green office building (above) with an apartment for the coachman, the green horse barn, the honeymoon cottage (pictured below), the Daniels House demolished after a fire, and the Purdy House and the Octagon House, both once occupied by the Billipps, are examples. The green office building was the home for Walter Branch and the gardener, and their families.

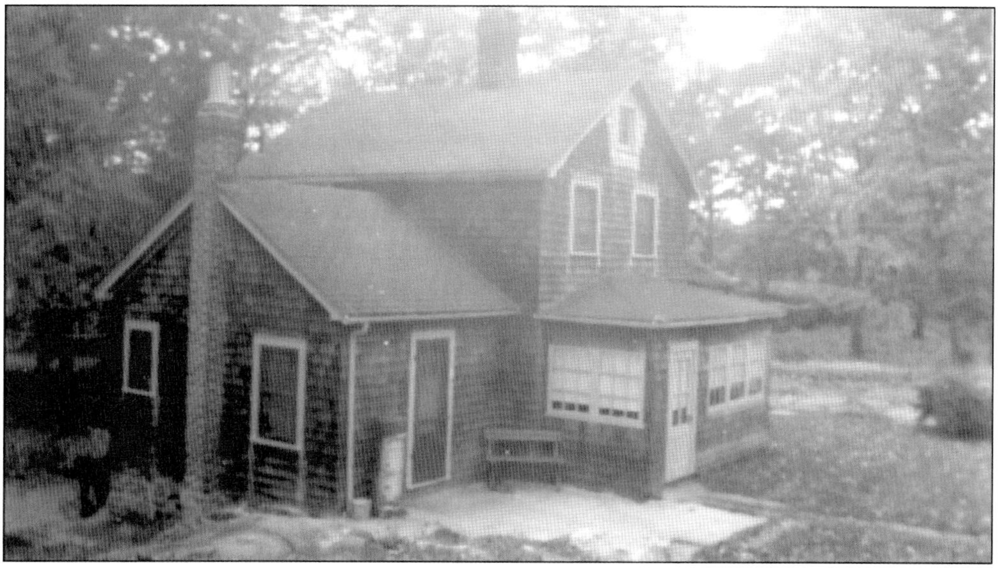

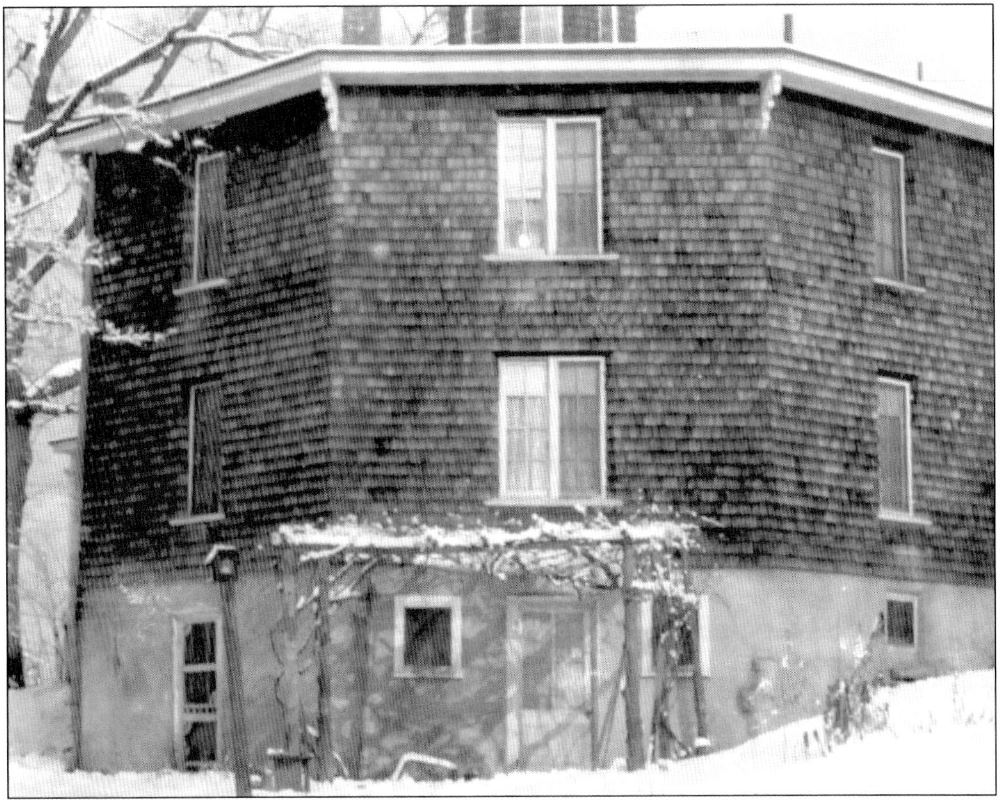

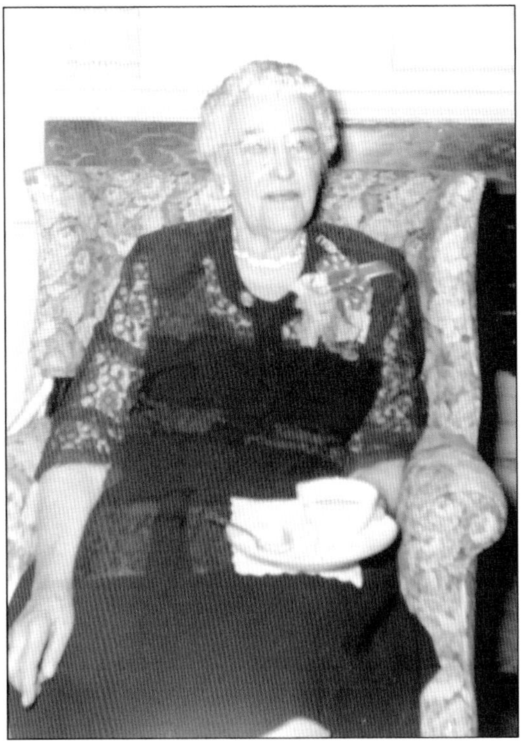

The Octagon House (above), located at the corner of North Street and Railroad Avenue, was demolished in 1940. Pauline E. Billipp (left) occupied it from October 1913 until then. Billipp met John Sterling for the first time in the green office building. After reassuring him she could spell, he hired her for a two-week trial before giving her a contract for one year. She earned $12 a week in 1913. Sterling rented the Octagon House to the Billipp family as a convenience, and for 50 years, Pauline worked for the home as secretary and cashier and lived on the grounds with her sister.

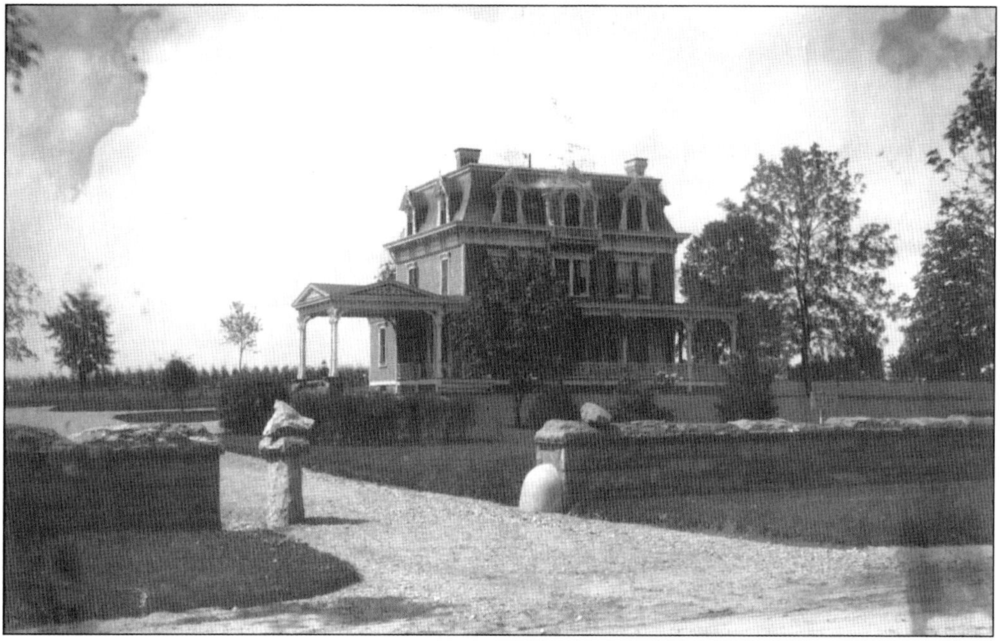

The new house of the late William Purdy was located on Boston Post Road, south of the southern line of the Theall Farm. Sterling added the piazzas, porte cochere, and butler's pantry in 1901. He also added the stone walls. George S. Olmstead took the photograph above in August 1902. The sign outside the house reads, "For rent, furnished." Today the Purdy House is the home of the chief executive of The Osborn. The photograph on the right shows the property before the landscaping and stone wall improvements.

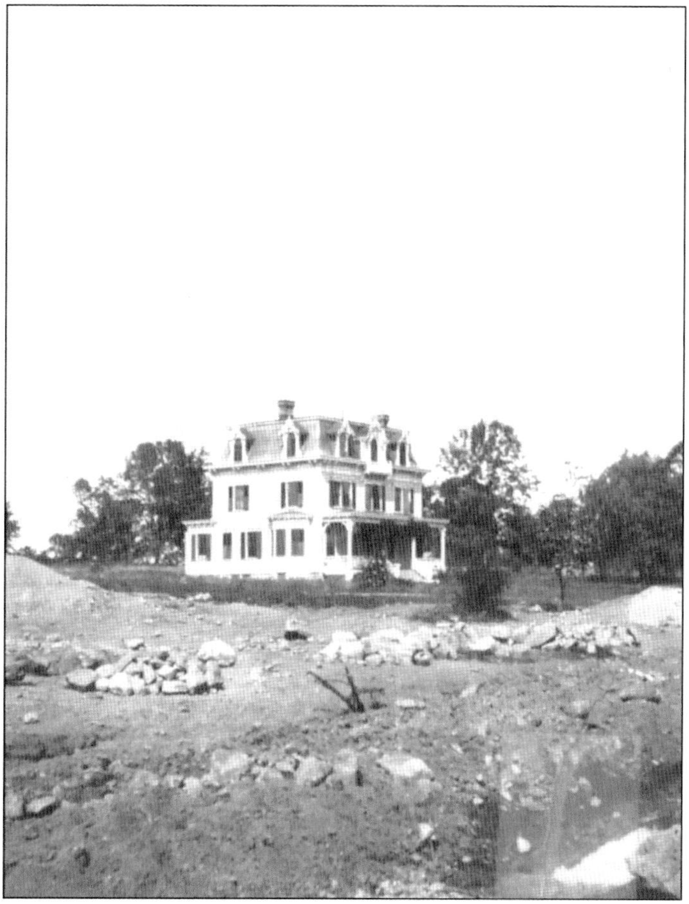

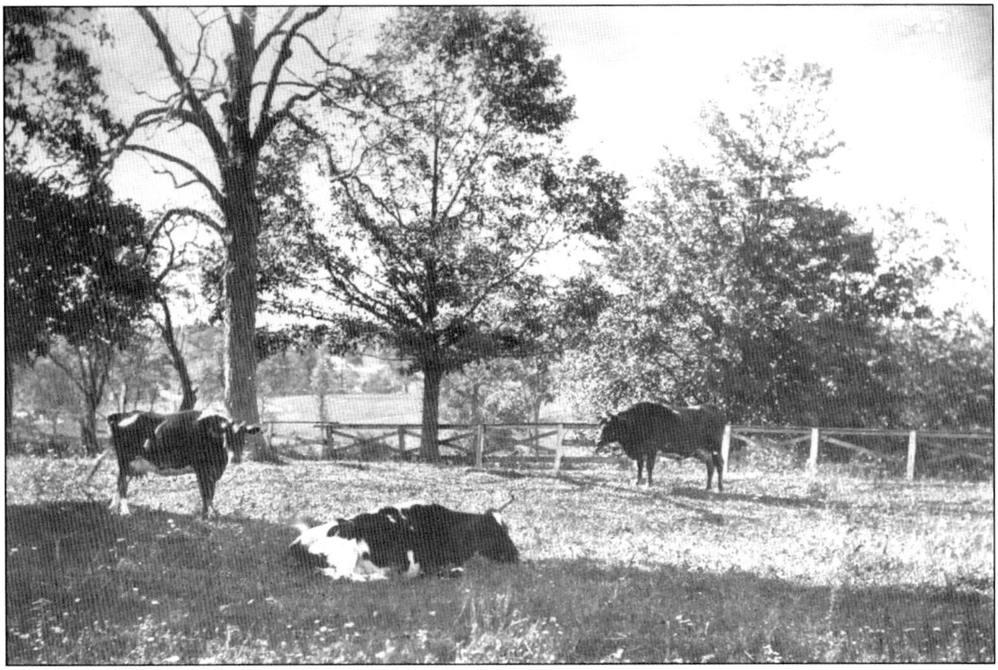

John Sterling thought the hillside west of the railroad was perfect for the dairy he planned. Beaver Swamp Brook that flowed through it had sufficient water for the eight Guernsey cows, seven calves, and one award-winning Holstein bull he purchased. He instituted a milk route with a distribution station at Silver Lake, north of White Plains. Seen in 1893, Railroad Avenue now is Theall Road.

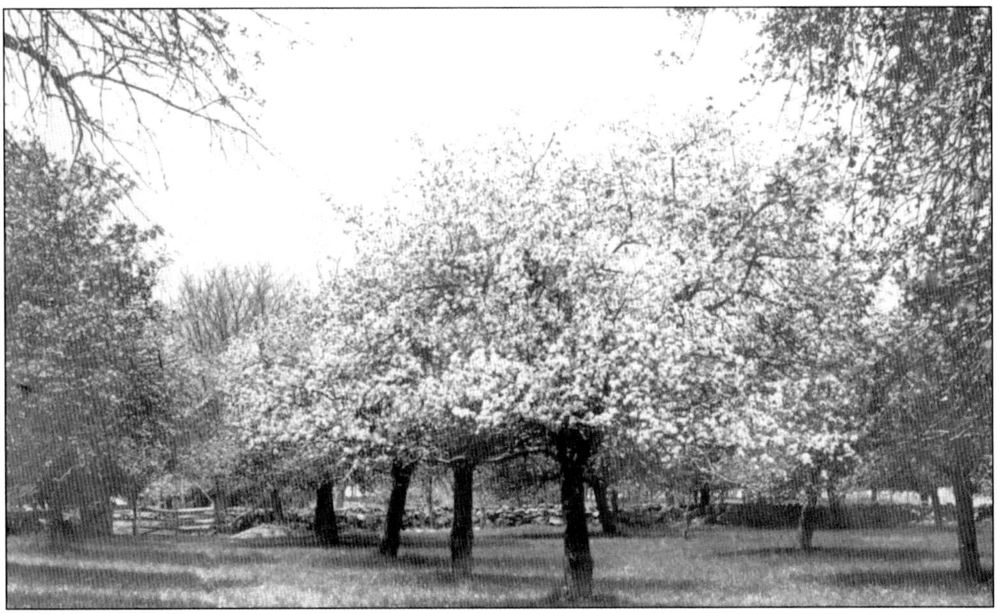

Many berry bushes and 280 fruit trees, purchased by Sterling some years before, were brought from the farm at Mamaroneck. Useless growth was cleared from the land. Sterling purchased a large assortment of trees and shrubs, intending to plant at least one tree of each variety suitable for the latitude. In all, 2,258 trees were planted.

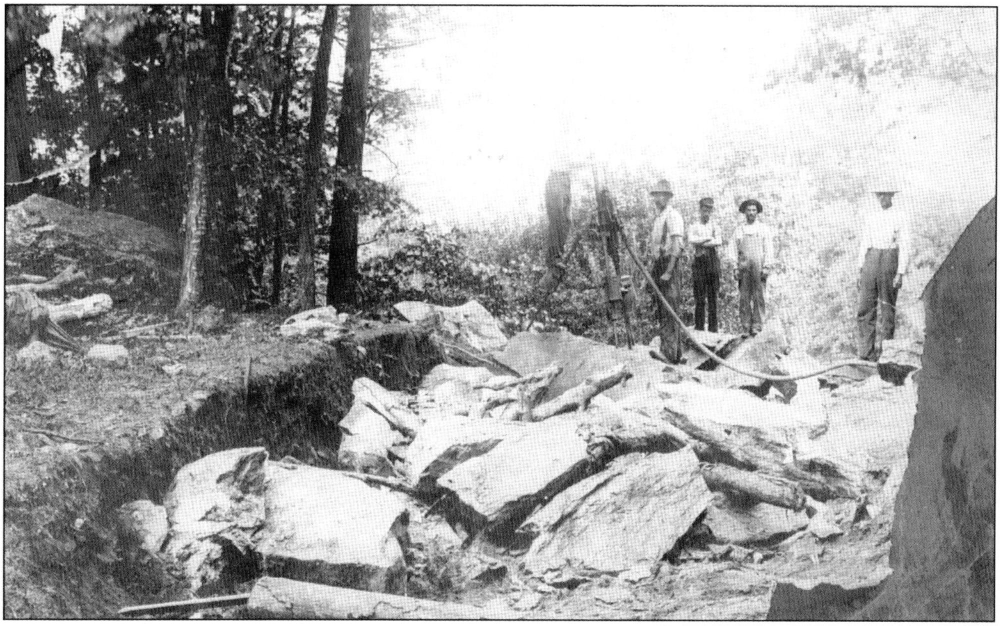

A laborer stands atop a drill, as work on the home grounds gets underway in August 1897. A good supply of stone from Harrison donated to the home by Joseph Park ended when Park died. Transporting the stone from J. W. Buckley in Port Chester became too expensive. After a period of searching, Sterling found and purchased three lots in Rye that had massive ledges of hard, blue stone that contained an inexhaustible supply.

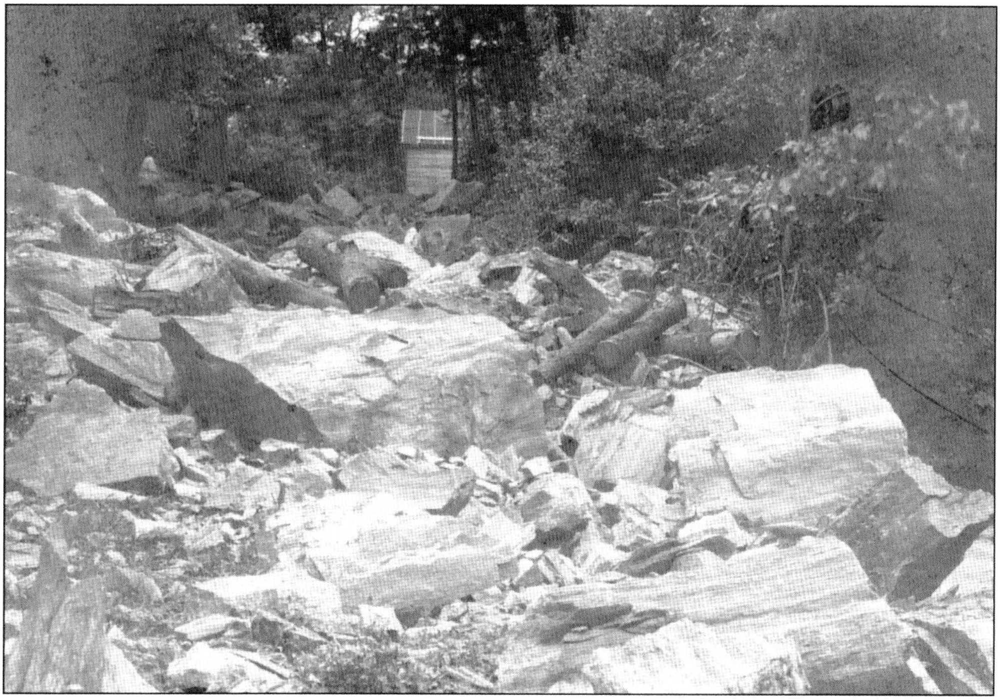

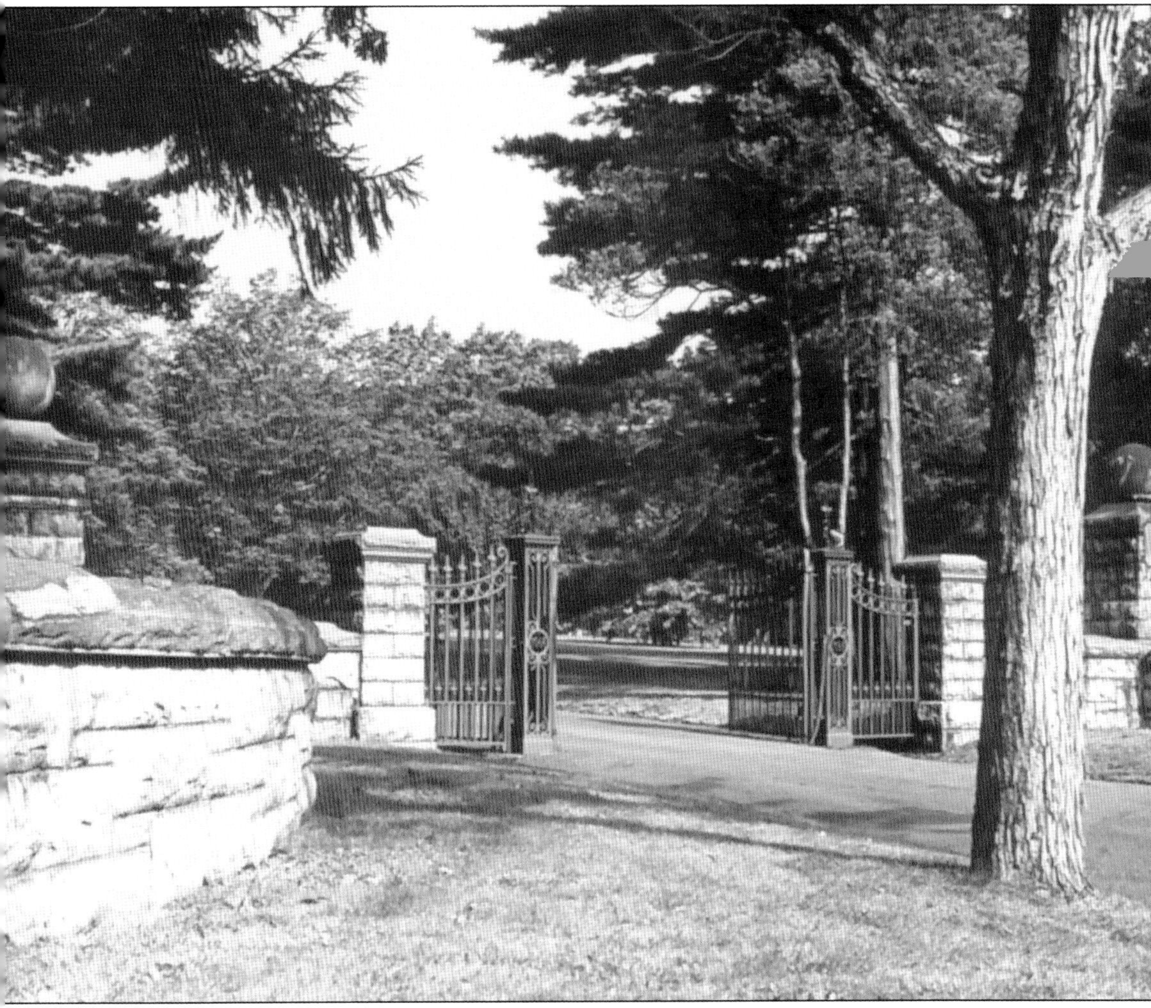

Thomas Dimond made the iron gates that were set between granite piers at the entrance to the grounds. The entire property was enclosed by stone walls or galvanized iron pipe fence. The gates welcomed residents into a special place where the security they represented was a substantial element of Miriam Osborn's vision.

Two

The Founders

The Osborn, named for the woman who envisioned it long before ground was broken, is a fine architectural structure with details as imposing as the individuals who turned a dream into reality. The founders, guided by a code of excellence and dedication to its residents, created a legacy, durable as The Osborn's structure, which sustained it for 100 years.

Miriam Osborn's concerns for aged widowed women resulted from her worry for her acquaintances because of how easily fortunes could be lost in the financial markets where her husband worked. After her husband died, she consulted his attorney John Sterling and began planning her own legacy. She envisioned a home where women, raised like she, without self-sustaining work, could live out their lives.

John Sterling, a New York attorney with well-known clients like Jay Gould, James Fisk, the National City Bank, and Standard Oil, and founding partner in the firm of Shearman and Sterling, supported Miriam Osborn's idea and became an active participant in advancing it. After her death, he dedicated himself to the actualization of her plan, from selection of the site, land acquisition, and selection of master craftsmen and materials to supervising the operation. The Osborn would not exist without his drive to make it happen and his expectation for excellence.

Sterling surrounded himself with staff who shared his keen observation skills and love of the home. More than any other, Helen Adams was the embodiment of the talent he hired. She began work for Sterling at the age of 25 in 1904, as the temporary replacement for his beloved longtime secretary "Miss Agnes" C. Branagan. Loaned for a time to Sterling by George H. Church, Adams notes in unpublished writings, "That time never seemed to come." She worked for Sterling for the rest of his life. She eventually served The Osborn as its executive superintendent, treasurer of the association, and trustee, retiring in 1947, 39 years after the home opened. She died in 1967, a resident of the home, and is buried in The Osborn cemetery. A granite obelisk dedicated to the founders rises above her grave.

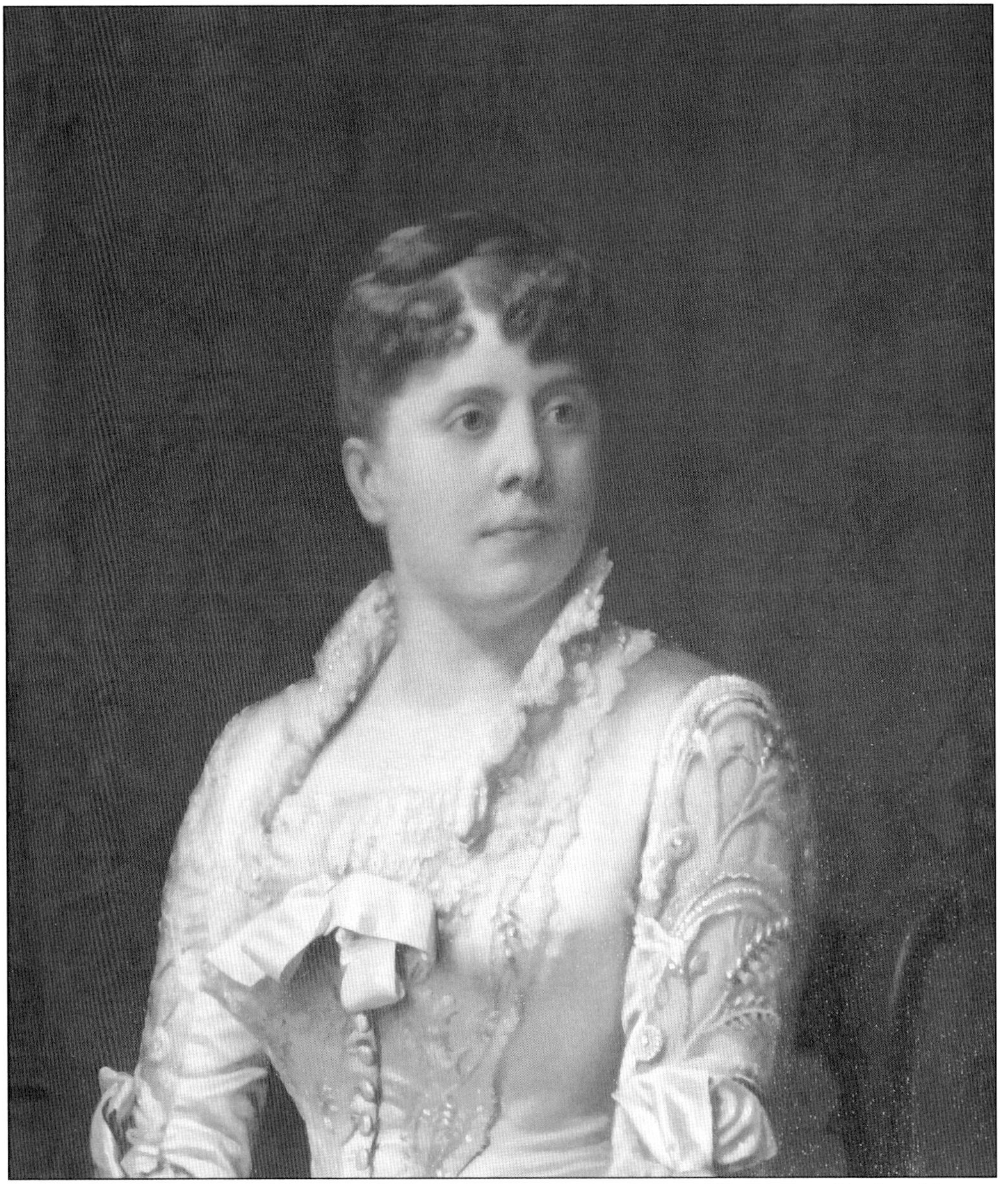

Miriam Adelaide Osborn was born on April 15, 1840, in Augusta, Georgia, to Evalina Francis Trowbridge and Nelson Clement Trowbridge, prominent citizens of that city. Miriam's maternal grandmother and the grandmother of Pres. Theodore Roosevelt were sisters. Miriam was the oldest of five children; her siblings were Leila, Mary, Clement, and Grace. Miriam was sent to New York to complete her education at a fashionable boarding school on Madison Avenue near 29th Street run by Madame Chegarey. While in New York, she met Charles James Osborn, and they were married in 1858, when she was just 18 years old. Charles found working as a clerk in the Spruce Street leather business for his stepfather, William P. Miller, too mundane. He proved highly successful from the start, however, as a Wall Street broker, managing large blocks of stock for many of the great figures of the business world, such as J. P. Morgan. Charles died in November 1885 at the age of 45 from Bright's disease and pneumonia. Miriam died about six years later, on March 14, 1891, from stomach cancer.

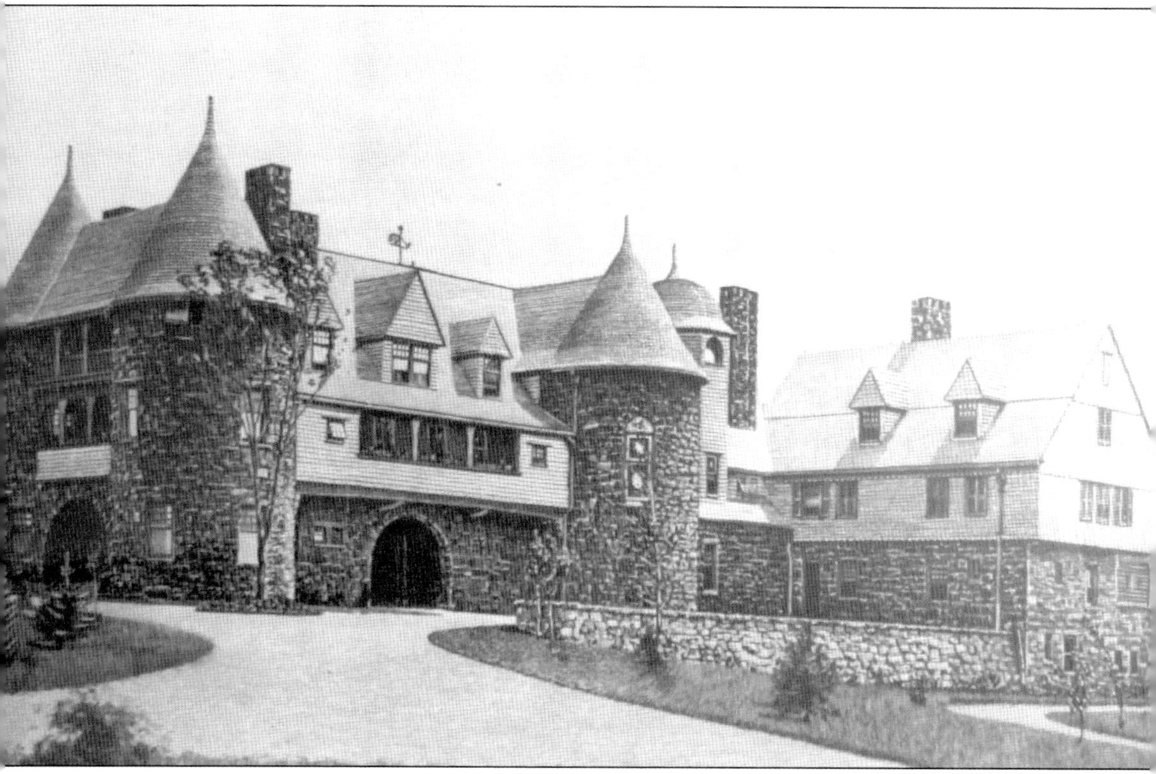

The Native American name of the 12.6 acres in Rye Neck bordered by the Mamaroneck River and Long Island Sound was Ahomat. When purchased in 1883 by Charles Osborn for his home with Miriam, they renamed it Tahoma. They chose Sanford White as the architect. According to John Sterling's records, Tahoma's cost was $750,000. The complete estate included stables and a carriage house so that it was considered a possible site for The Osborn Home after Miriam's death. Shortly after it was completed, Charles died in November 1885. Reportedly a damp environment was to blame. Tragedy struck again four months later when Miriam's brother, Clement, died. He had lived at Tahoma and stayed on with his young daughter Henrietta Olive after his wife, Henrietta, died giving birth to Olive. Tahoma remained the home of Henrietta Olive Trowbridge until the home association sold it in 1924 for use as a yacht club before being sold again to the Shubert brothers of Broadway fame.

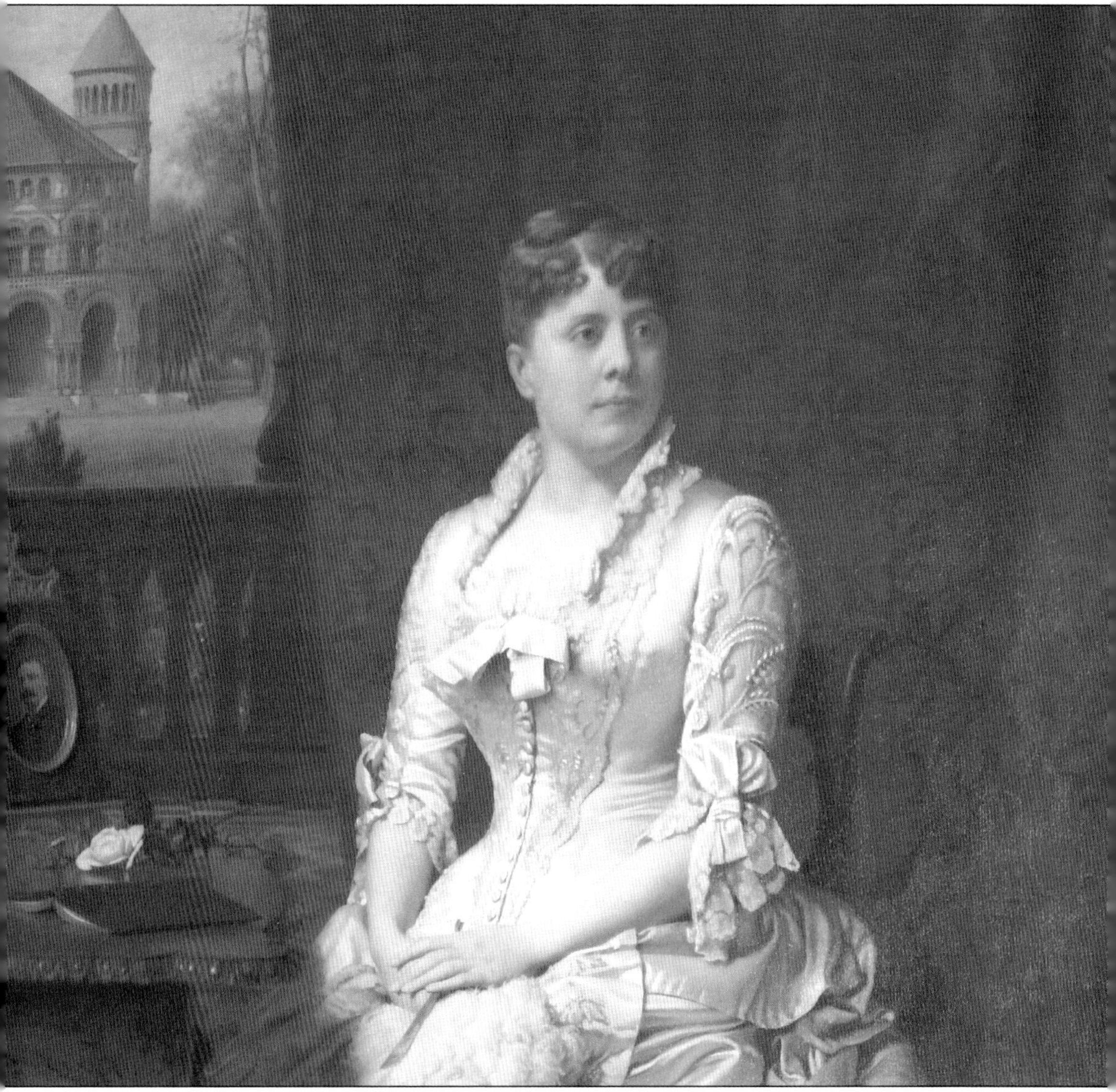

John Sterling commissioned this portrait of Miriam Osborn by Seymour J. Guy. It shows her with a background photograph of her husband, Charles, and her memorial to him, Yale University's Osborn Recitation Hall. Architect Bruce Price, also chosen as the architect for The Osborn, designed the recitation hall. It was thought to be Yale's most beautiful building. Miriam formed a lasting friendship with Yale's president Dr. Timothy Dwight II and his wife during the building's planning. Dr. Dwight delivered Miriam's eulogy. He commented that the recitation hall at Yale satisfied her desire for it to be an ornament to the college grounds and to the city. The beauty of The Osborn Home, in keeping with this sentiment, would have pleased her as well.

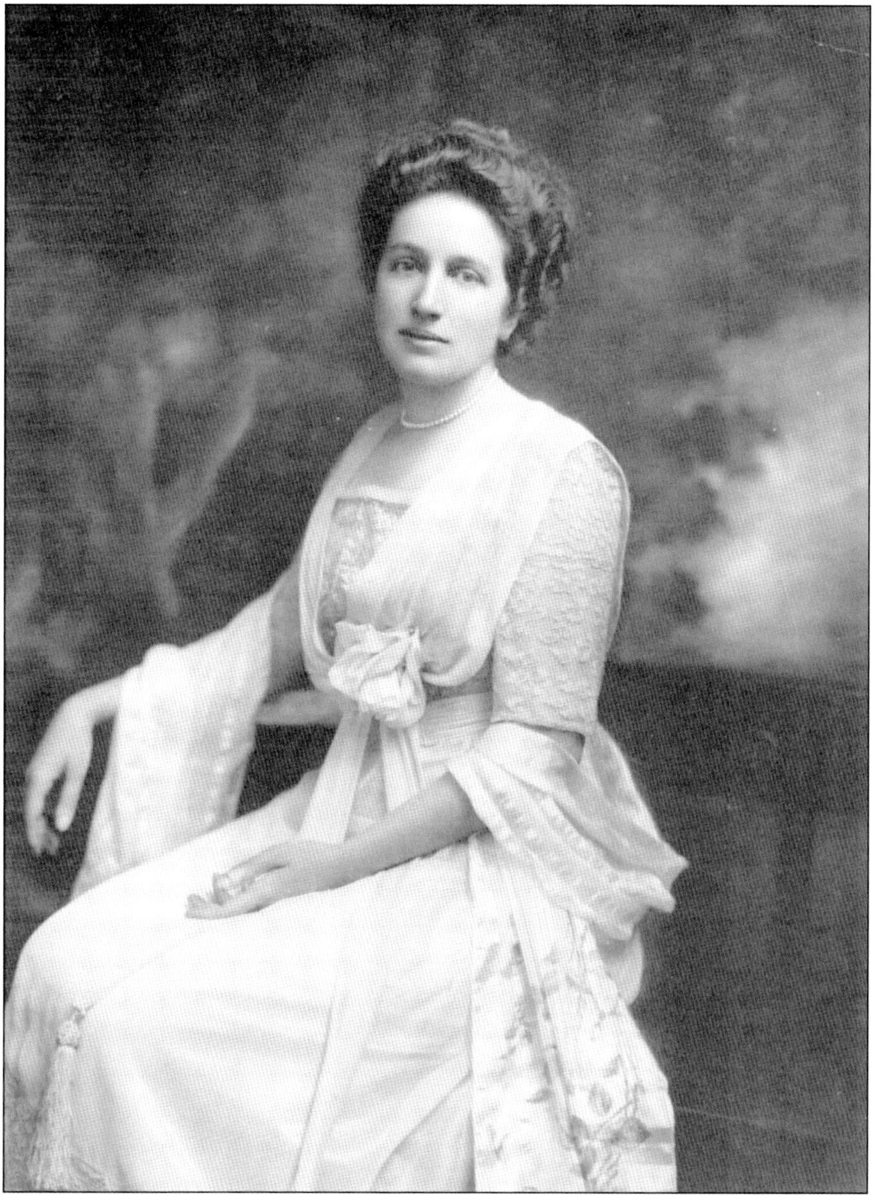

Henrietta Olive Trowbridge, born in June 1883, was the daughter of Miriam Osborn's brother, Clement, and his wife, Henrietta. Olive's mother died in childbirth, and her father died when she was three, leaving her care to Miriam. Childhood friend Hopeton Atterbury Quaid described Olive as handsome, with heavy blonde hair, gray eyes, and a lovely complexion that she protected from the bright sun with a veil. Miriam was extremely fond of Olive in contrast to her son, Howell, whom she considered headstrong. An accomplished pianist, Olive practiced daily for hours. Olive disliked her companion Eleanor Agnew, a fine but strict woman. Upon the death of Miriam, John Sterling became Olive's guardian. She continued to live at Tahoma until 1923. In 1911, marriage was on her mind as she considered Frank C. Littleton, who worked for the Morris Plan Bank in New York. They were married on February 10, 1912, at Tahoma. Olive descended the grand staircase escorted by Sterling. She was instrumental in opening The Osborn Home, serving on its first board of lady managers.

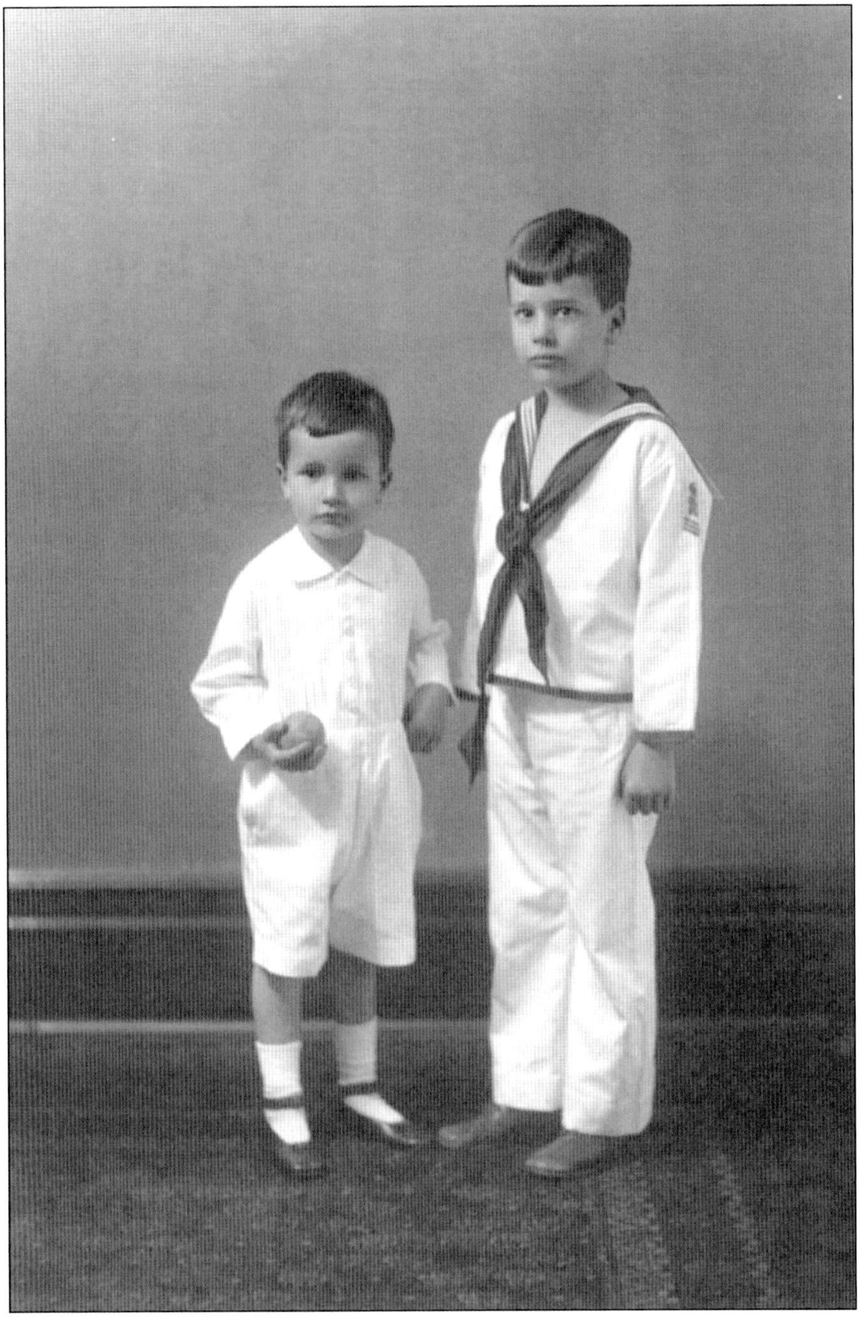

The Littletons had two sons, Frank C. and Trowbridge, but tragedy struck the younger Trowbridge after a fall from his pony. Paralysis caused by encephalitis lasted seven years before his death. In spite of Frank C. Littleton's business ventures raising violets and carnations in the Tahoma greenhouses, by 1922 the upkeep of Tahoma became too expensive. The home association paid Olive $60,000 plus the furnishings of the house to relinquish her right to live at Tahoma. The Littletons moved to Virginia to Oak Hill, a home once owned by Pres. James Monroe. The new home was decorated graciously with items from Tahoma and articles left behind by the Monroe family. Olive died one year later at the age of 41, on July 12, 1924.

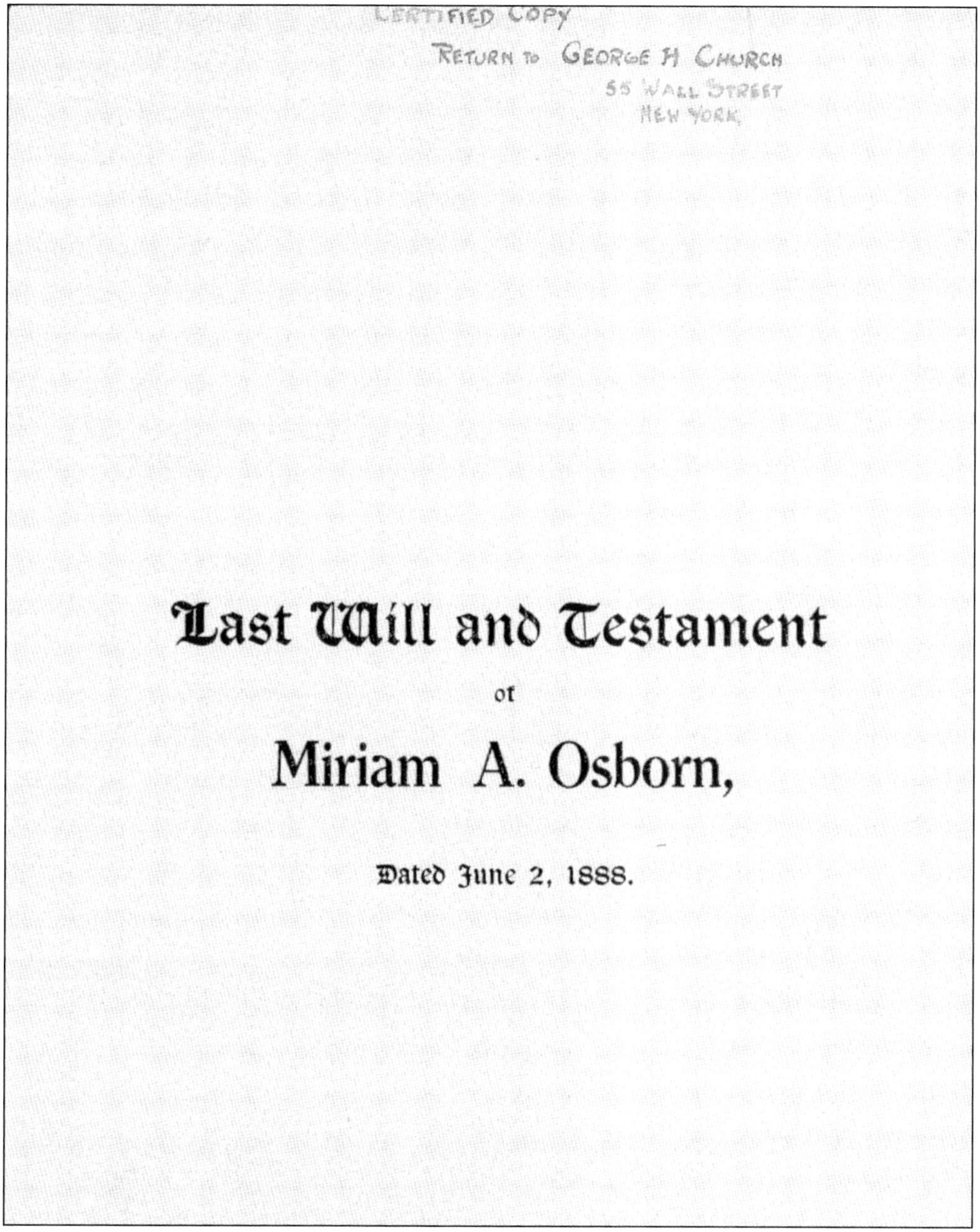

Certified Copy

Return to George H Church
55 Wall Street
New York

Last Will and Testament

of

Miriam A. Osborn,

Dated June 2, 1888.

Miriam Osborn's will made liberal provisions for her son, Howell, her eight-year-old niece Olive, and her longtime servants. She also named her two sisters, Leila O. Henriques and Mary A. Mason, her niece Leila O. Neame (née Henriques), and a devoted friend, Minnie A. Garson. Additionally, she left approximately $645,000 to the Association for the Relief of Respectable, Aged, Indigent Females, known as the "Association Home." On his visit to the home, April 15, 1942, the anniversary of Miriam's birth, Cortlandt Betts spoke of meeting Miriam Osborn for business at her home, 587 Fifth Avenue. He told his audience of her grace, charm, and poise. He also told the amusing story of an error made by a typesetter on the charter document for the home that he was given to proofread. The document named the home, "Home for Respectable, Aged, *Indignant* Females."

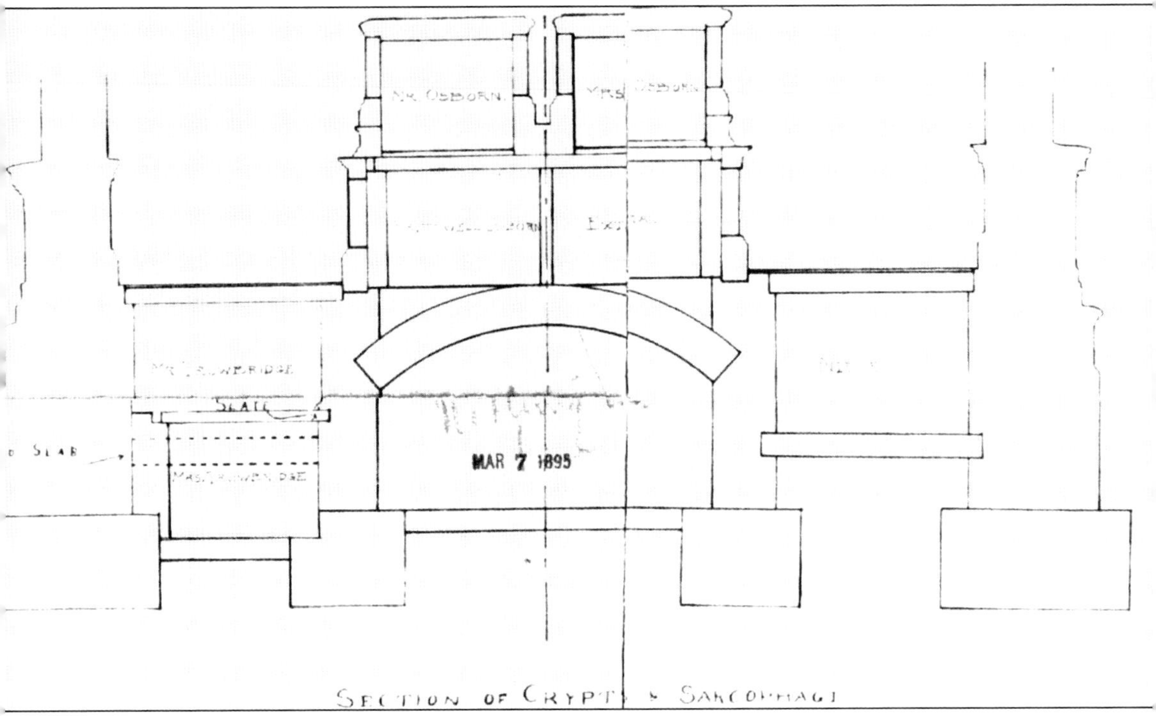

Miriam Osborn and John Sterling purchased three plots in Woodlawn Cemetery in 1889 in the area called Brookside. After Miriam Osborn died, Sterling asked Sanford White of McKim, Mead and White to design a mausoleum with foundation walls 20 inches thick and a dome roof of Gaustavino tile, similar to that used in Grand Central Station. Instructions called for it to be waterproof and fireproof. The exterior of the roof is specified as Milford pink granite to be sheathed with copper or bronze tile. The interior walls are a combination of granite, enameled brick, and terra-cotta friezes. The doors are two-inch-thick bronze, the dado around the top is pink Knoxville marble, and the floor is one and a half inches thick of pink granite, pink Knoxville marble, and white marble. The cost for this beautiful structure was $20,000. Clement and Henrietta Trowbridge, Miriam and Charles Osborn, and the Osborns' son, Howell, are interred there.

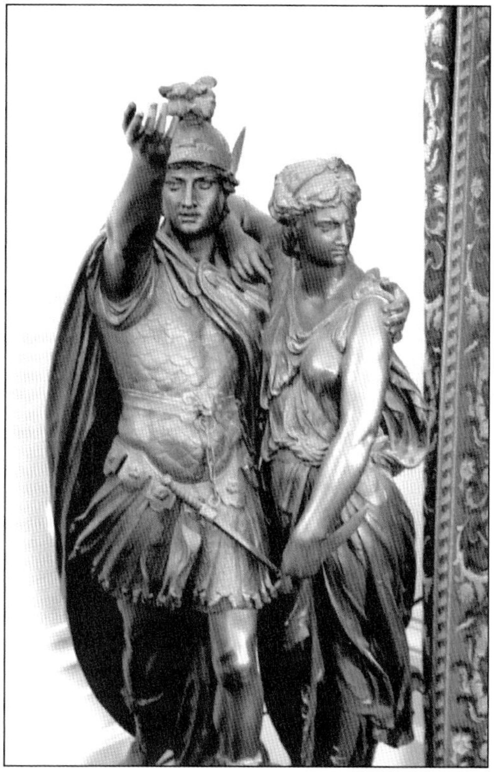

Bronze statues of Aeneas and Dido (right) and Perseus and Andromeda (below) by Jean-Louis Gregoire belonged to Miriam Osborn and were loaned to Howell for his Paris apartment. Eventually they were returned to The Osborn, where they remain. Howell, born on August 21, 1859, died on February 6, 1895, at age 35. Caught in a snowstorm while on a hunting trip in January, it took seven hours to travel 14 miles to shelter. Suffering from diabetes, he did not recover. His companion, Broadway star Fay Templeton, was appearing in *Evangeline* at the 14th Street Theater. They lived together at Sixth Avenue and 52nd Street. In spite of a shaky relationship, Templeton cared for Howell through his final days. Actress Irene Manning portrayed Templeton in the 1942 movie *Yankee Doodle Dandy*.

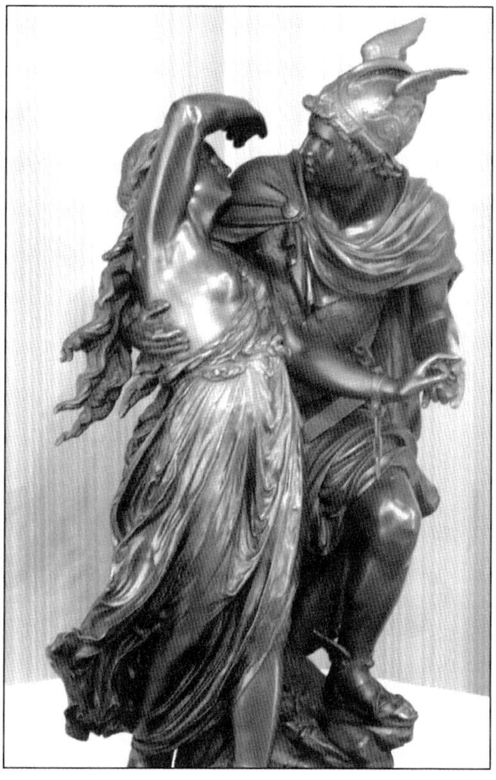

Fay Templeton's Death Recalls Interesting Bit of History

The death of Fay Templeton, great American actress of the past century, has an interesting side-light to residents of this section.

It is noted that she was married to Howell Osborn, son of Charles H. Osborn, one of the greatest financiers of his day, whose vast fortune was inherited by his wife, the late Miriam Osborn.

Miriam Osborn had a strong antipathy to actresses and provided in her will that her estate should go toward the founding of a Home should her son and only heir marry a member of the theatrical profession. Howell Osborn married Fay Templeton, which resulted in the erection of the Miriam Osborn Memorial Home in Rye.

Many referred to Howell Osborn and Fay Templeton as husband and wife, but because Miriam Osborn did not approve of actresses, they may have kept the marriage secret. An unknown publication implying that Miriam Osborn knew about Templeton's marriage to Howell, redirecting his legacy to the home, is inaccurate. Miriam Osborn's will provided well for Howell. After Howell's death, however, the funds Miriam left him reverted to The Osborn. Miriam's sisters contested Howell's will and his intention to leave material goods to Templeton and others. Court documents reveal that Howell, like his father Charles, did not have good relationships with his aunts.

Port Chester Item

Oct. 7, 1939.

Fay Templeton Death Recalls HomeFounding

Actress Of Past Era Was Daughter-In-Law Of Miriam Osborn

The death Wednesday of Fay Templeton, famous American actress of the Gay Nineties, recalled to some old residents of this section that she was the wife of Howell Osborn, son of Charles J. Osborn, financier, whose wife, Miriam Osborn, left her husband's fortune for the most part for the founding of the home which bears her name.

Contrary to popular belief that Mrs. Osborn left all her money to the home project because she had objections, as did many persons of that period, to actresses, she endowed the home out of philanthropic reasons. At the same time she provided a large trust fund for her only son and heir, Howell. In her will she provided that after his death, the money revert to the home and this cut off his wife, Fay Templeton.

The Miriam Osborn Memorial Home was erected in Rye after her death by the late John W. Sterling, her executor, and it has served since the early part of the century as the haven for Protestant gentlewomen in their declining years.

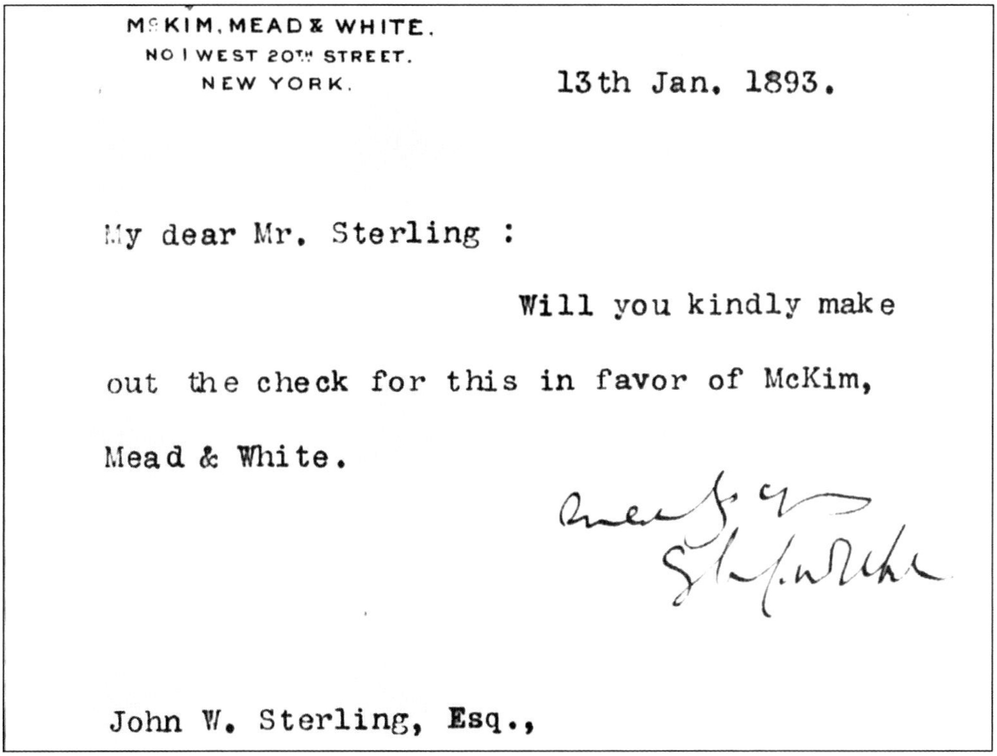

McKIM, MEAD & WHITE.
NO 1 WEST 20TH STREET.
NEW YORK.

13th Jan. 1893.

My dear Mr. Sterling :

Will you kindly make out the check for this in favor of McKim, Mead & White.

[signature]

John W. Sterling, Esq.,

The note signed by Sanford White to John Sterling is most likely regarding the Osborn mausoleum. It is located in the area of Brookside next to the Sterling mausoleum. The 1904 map below shows the location of the Osborn mausoleum; other grave sites in the vicinity were Jay Gould and R. H. Macy. White was the most noted architect of the Gilded Age. He also designed the old Madison Square Garden, where he was shot to death by Harry Thaw, the jealous husband of Evelyn Nesbit, noted as "the Girl on the Red Velvet Swing," in a movie of the same name. White also designed the Washington Square Arch in New York City.

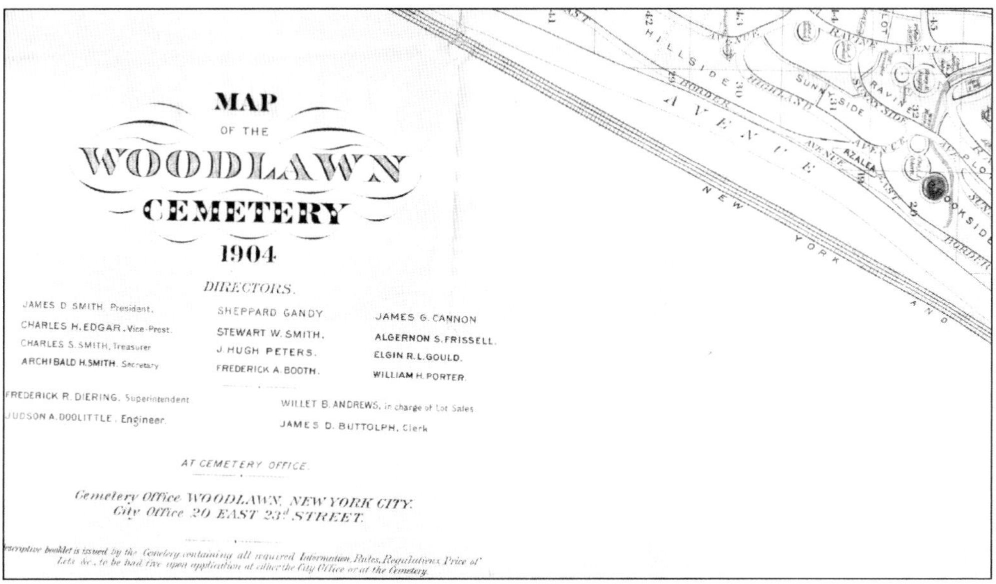

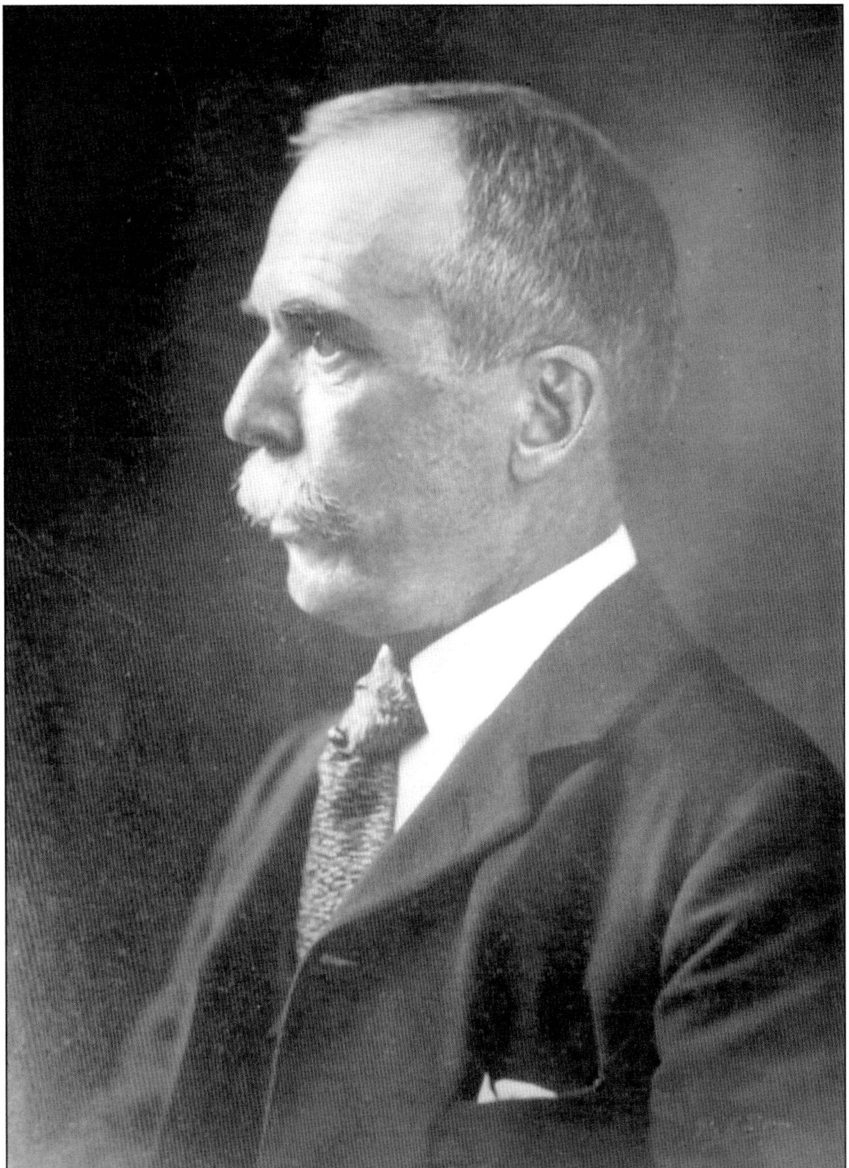

John Sterling, born in Stratford, Connecticut, on May 12, 1844, was destined to become a noted attorney. His professional relationship with Charles and Miriam Osborn was fundamental in the creation of The Osborn. He was the youngest of three children of John William Sr. and Catherine Tomlinson Plant Sterling. His sisters were Cordelia and Catherine. John's father was captain of the *Splendid*, one of the largest clipper ships. His maternal grandfather was David Plant, a Connecticut state senator and lieutenant governor. Helen Adams, in unpublished writings, described John as possessing "his father's energy, boldness, leadership, and surpassing executive and business ability, but not his love of the sea." He never traveled abroad. He did love the land, however, and spent hours working on the grounds of family properties. He graduated as valedictorian from each of these schools he attended: Stratford Academy, Yale University, where he was a member of Phi Beta Kappa, Alpha Delta Phi, and Skull and Bones, and Columbia Law School. At Yale, he earned a master of arts degree in 1869 and a doctor of laws degree in 1893.

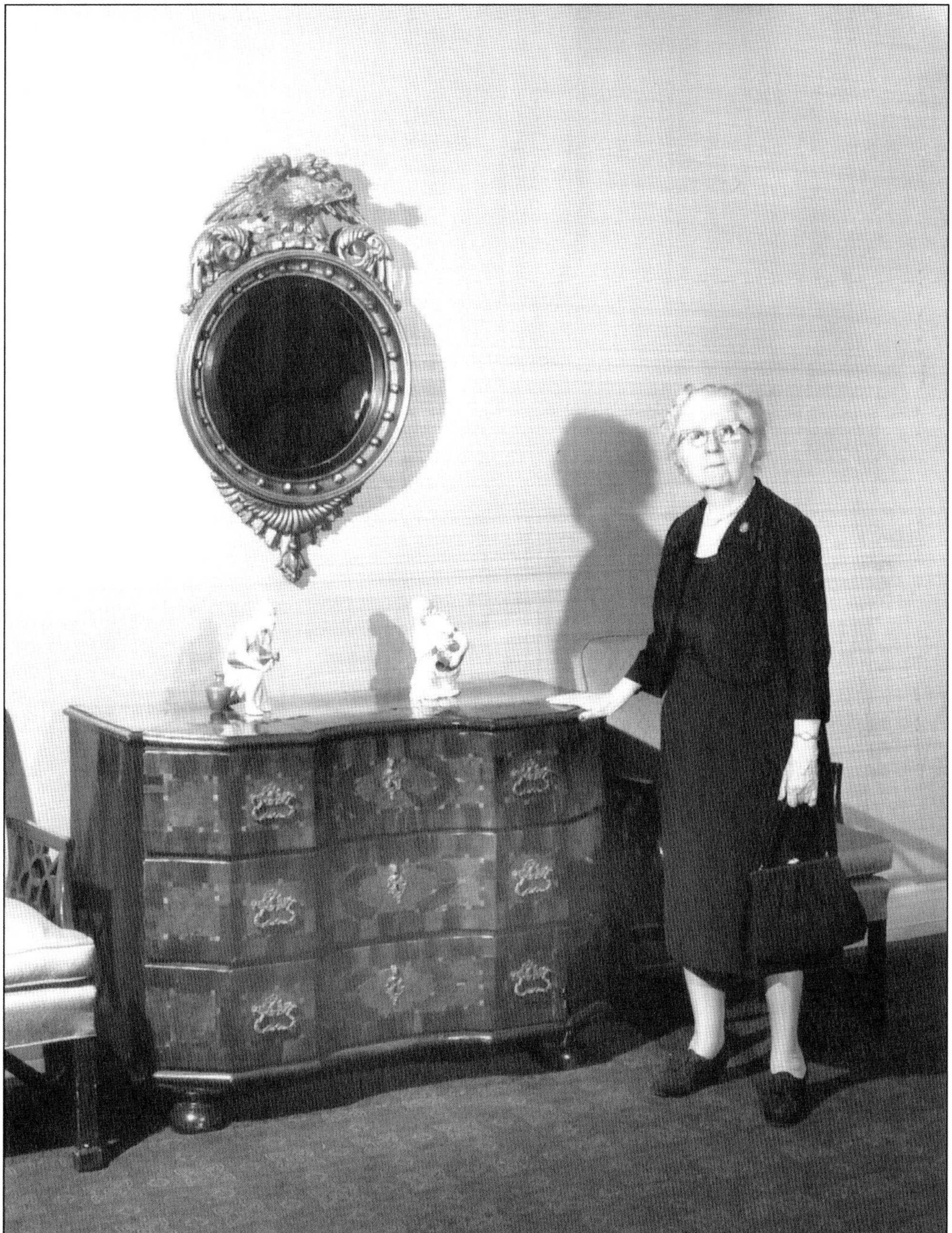

Helen Adams nurtured the new home and supported its growth as a parent guides a child from infancy to maturity. Adams's father was a descendent of the Massachusetts Adams family. He was one of the country's first electrical engineers but died young, leaving his wife and baby to support themselves. Adams's mother taught herself to type, and Adams began teaching at age 16. Her ambition was to be an actress, and for a while, she was a dancer and a member of the Floradora Viennese Quartet. In 1904, she temporarily worked for Sterling, while working in the office of George H. Church, an accountant who after Sterling's death became the executor of his will. Her temporary assignment lasted the length of her career.

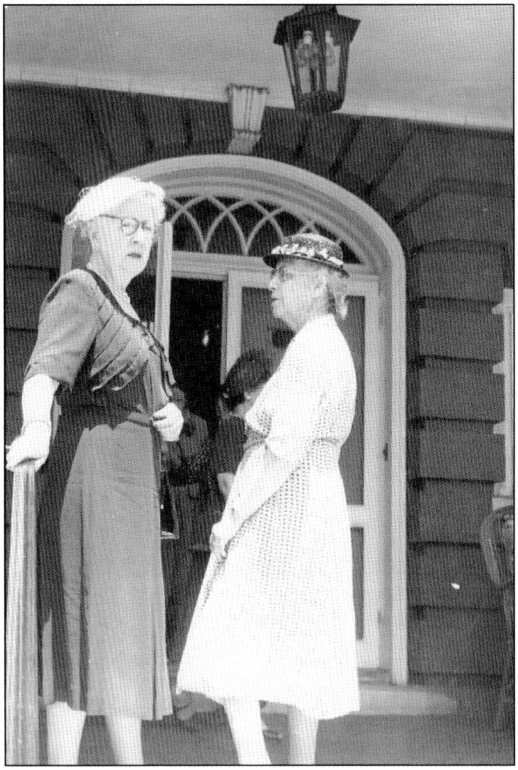

Helen Adams, on the left of the picture, was noted for excellent financial judgment, eventually becoming executive superintendent and secretary/treasurer for the association with responsibility for the home's executive duties. She was "the key figure." She was the first woman trustee in 1937. Adams retired in 1947. She became a resident in 1962 and died on March 30, 1967. She led the home into an era of enlightened care for the aged. She planned the Sterling and Strathcona buildings to have different levels of care. She helped establish and publish the standards of care for the aging in the Welfare Council of New York City. Below, Adams and Walter Branch pose on June 6, 1961, by the mounting block John Sterling had cut by masons working on the lands 60 years before. It commemorates when horses and cattle lived on the lands.

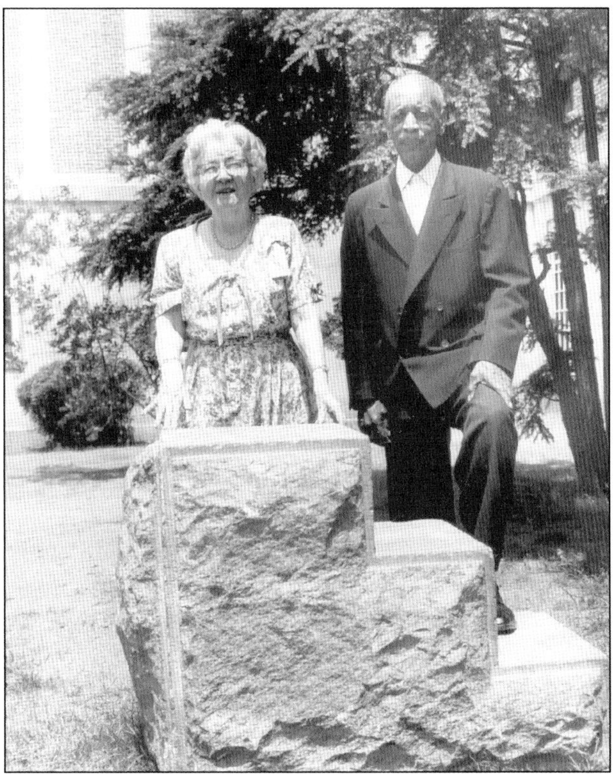

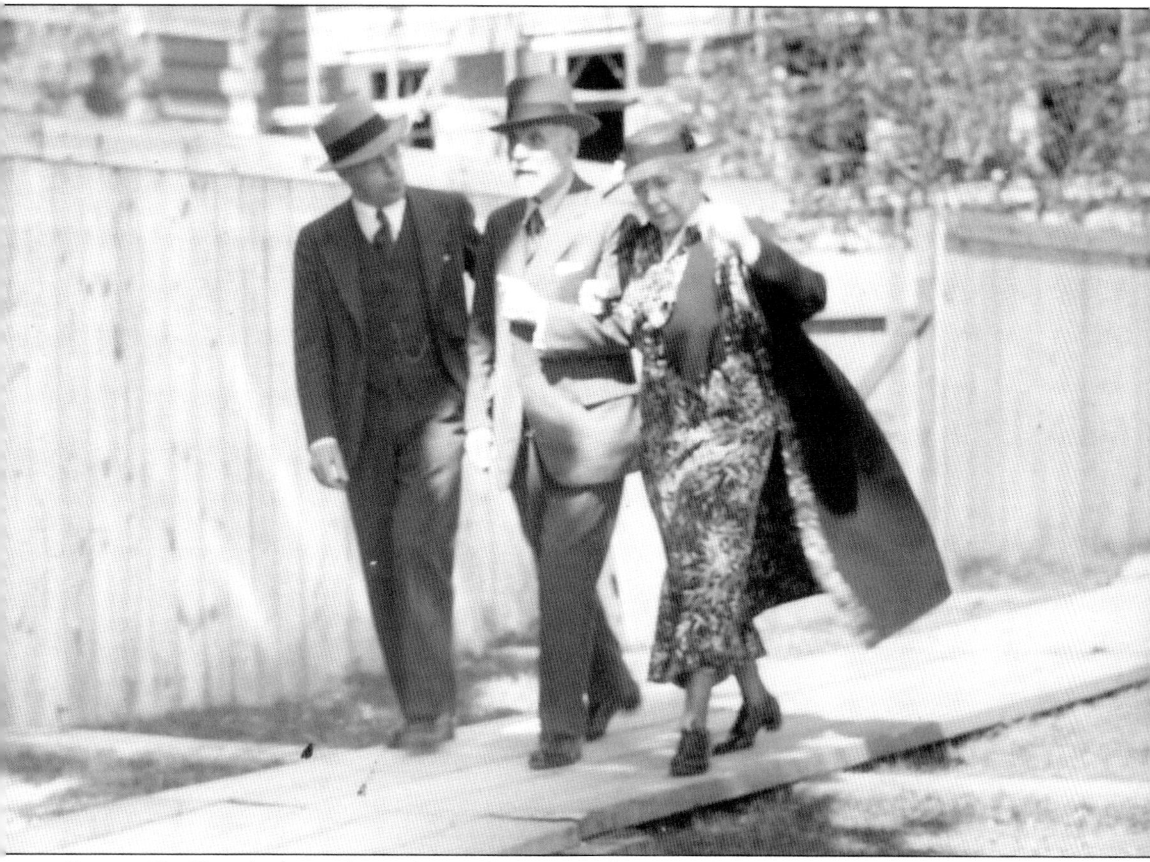

George H. Church (center) speaks to Otto K. Redgate as they walk with Laura Jones past the construction site of the new building. Jones was a significant employee of the home for 34 years. Jones signed a contract with John Sterling on May 23, 1910, to serve as matron for a $60 monthly salary. Later she became house superintendent. According to Margaret Weeks's personal recollection, Jones knew all about the laundry and its machinery. She did all the buying for the house and distributed supplies from the "soap room." She filled in for staff when sick, even operating the switchboard or the hand-operated elevators. She often worked until midnight. According to Pauline Billipp, Jones put up produce from the garden farm, extracted honey from the hives, and supervised the making of ice cream, serving it personally to residents. She selected and purchased meat at the pier for the home butcher, and she prepared the menus. Her trips away from the home were usually to visit the Littletons in Mamaroneck, where Walter Branch drove her in a surrey with a span of horses.

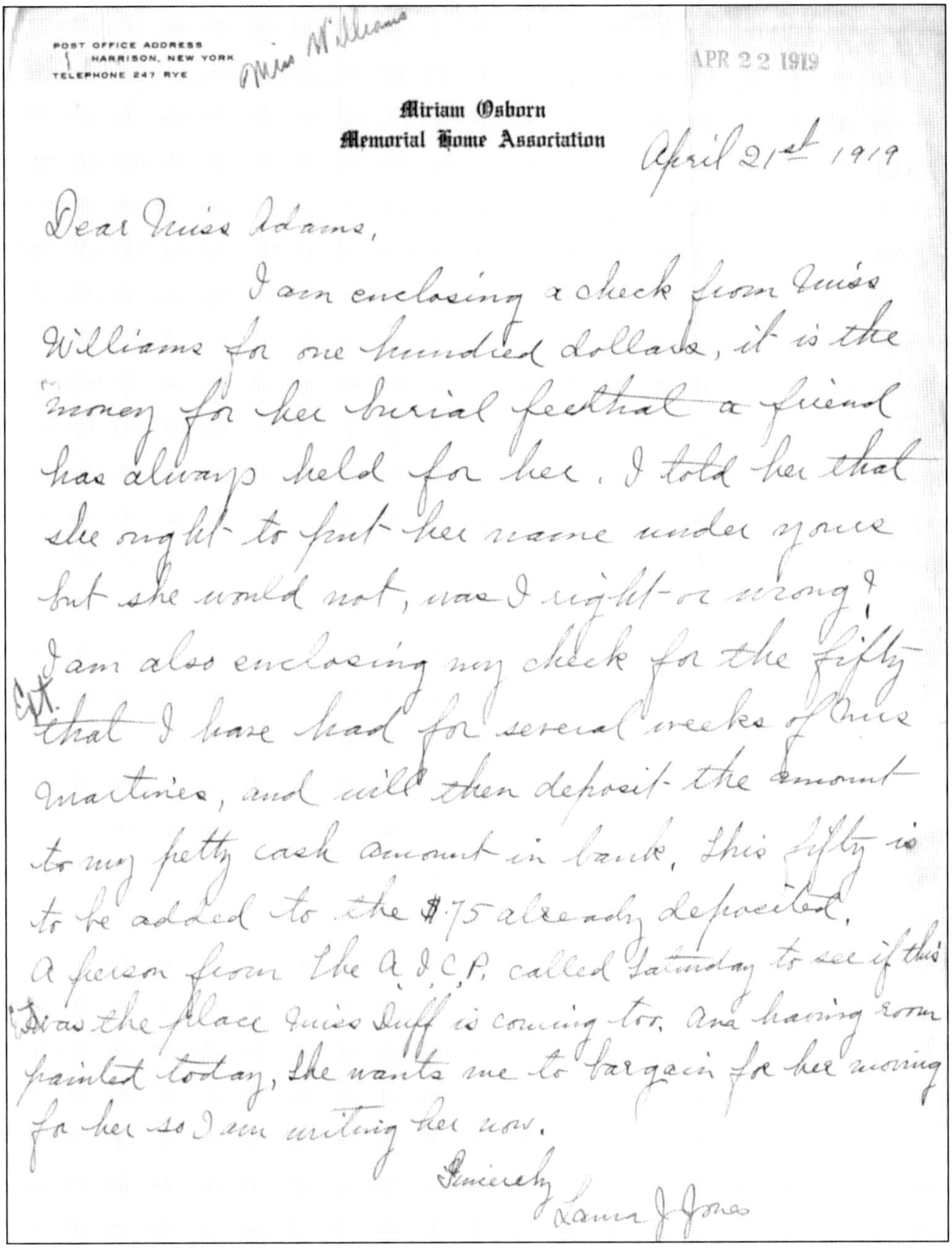

POST OFFICE ADDRESS
HARRISON, NEW YORK
TELEPHONE 247 RYE

Miss Williams

APR 22 1919

Miriam Osborn
Memorial Home Association

April 21st 1919

Dear Miss Adams,

I am enclosing a check from Miss Williams for one hundred dollars, it is the money for her burial fee that a friend has always held for her. I told her that she ought to put her name under yours but she would not, was I right or wrong? I am also enclosing my check for the fifty that I have had for several weeks of Miss Martines, and will then deposit the amount to my petty cash amount in bank, this fifty is to be added to the $75 already deposited. A person from the A.I.C.P. called Saturday to see if this was the place Miss Duff is coming to, am having room painted today, she wants me to bargain for her moving for her so I am writing her now.

Sincerely
Laura J Jones

In a letter to Helen Adams, Laura Jones sought advice on handling a financial question. Jones was the third person hired as matron in the first two years the home was open; the others were not satisfactory. In a recollection, Adams wrote that Jones was hired through civil service as a teacher of sewing at the Bedford State Reformatory for Girls where she advanced to being in charge of the "Honor Cottage." She changed the lives of many girls and was recommended to The Osborn by Mrs. Robert C. Black, a member of both boards. Adams described Jones as having a deep sense of right and wrong, justice and kindness. She lived to be 80 years old. She served the home with every fiber of her being according to Mrs. Albert W. Putnam, trustee and president of the board of lady managers.

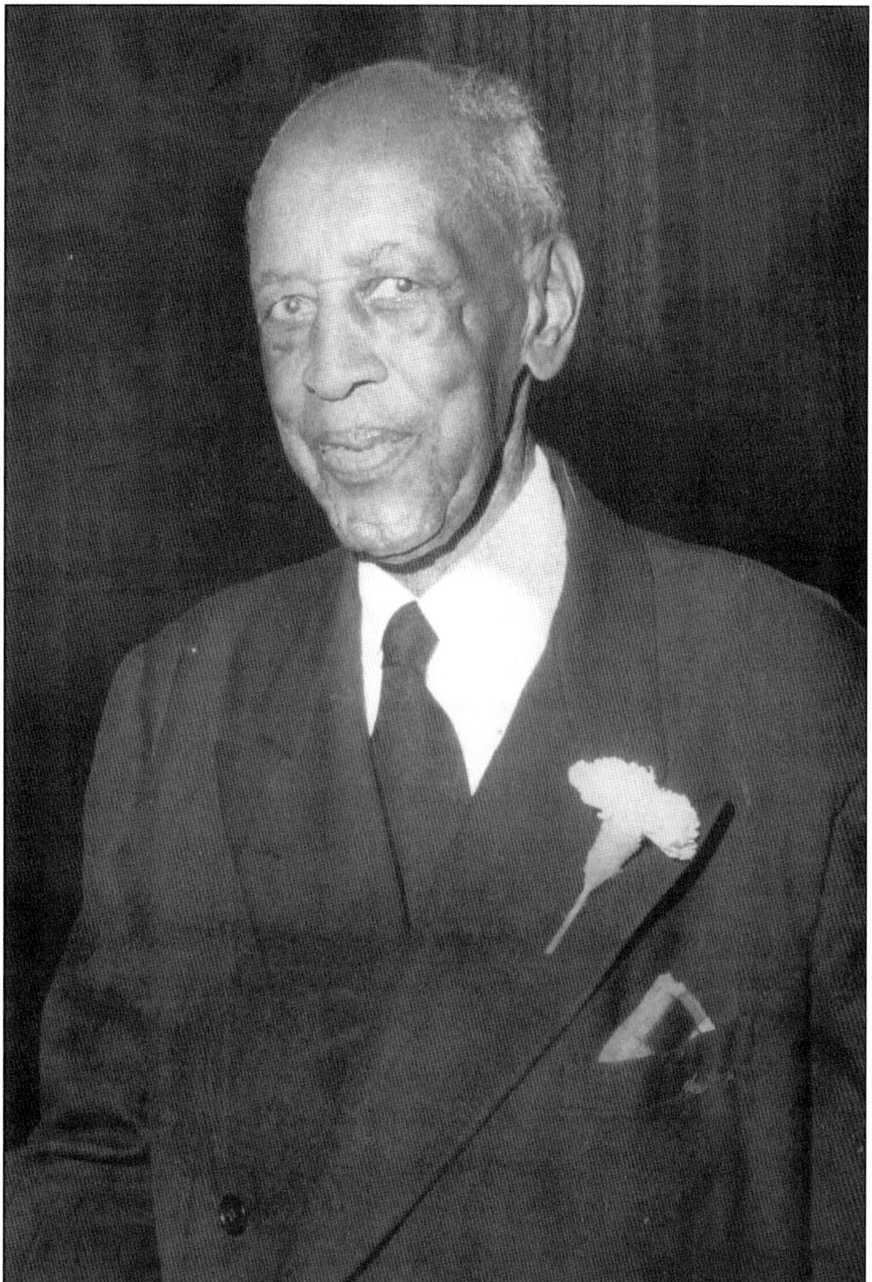

Perhaps no person was more important to resident life than Walter Branch. Quotations taken from conversations with him include this: "My message to ladies of the House is this, I was left here by my boss to take care of you all and to do things for you and to make you happy." A letter by Augusta B. Travis, who like her mother was a resident of the home, attests that he did. She wrote, "My mother was thrilled by the charm and atmosphere of the Home; it was like entering a big beautiful estate. A man was at the door in tails and tie. I now know him as my friend Walter." John Sterling hired Branch in 1904 after observing work he was doing on shingles at Tahoma with his brother, Charlie. Branch died in 1968. (Courtesy of the Journal News.)

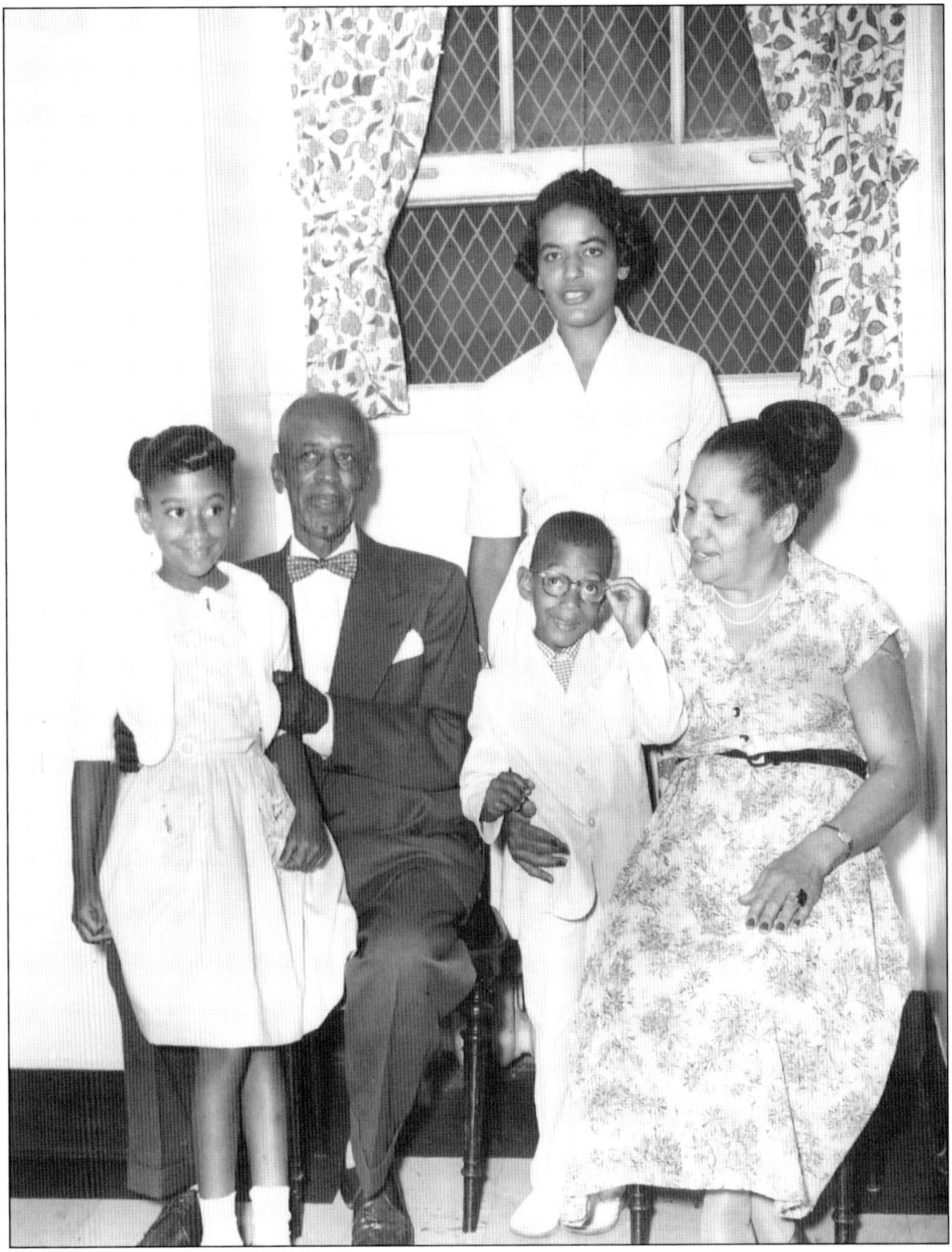

Walter Branch is pictured seated, second from left, with his second wife, Emma, a grandchild, and two great-grandchildren. John Sterling arranged an introduction of Branch to Ada, the daughter of George Wilson, Sterling's coachman. After a time of visiting at the Wilson home, Walter and Ada eloped to Mamaroneck. Some years after Ada died, Branch married her sister Emma in 1952. They continued living in the green cottage on the home grounds where Branch lived since 1906. Branch worked for The Osborn Home for 64 years and is buried in The Osborn cemetery among the residents he knew.

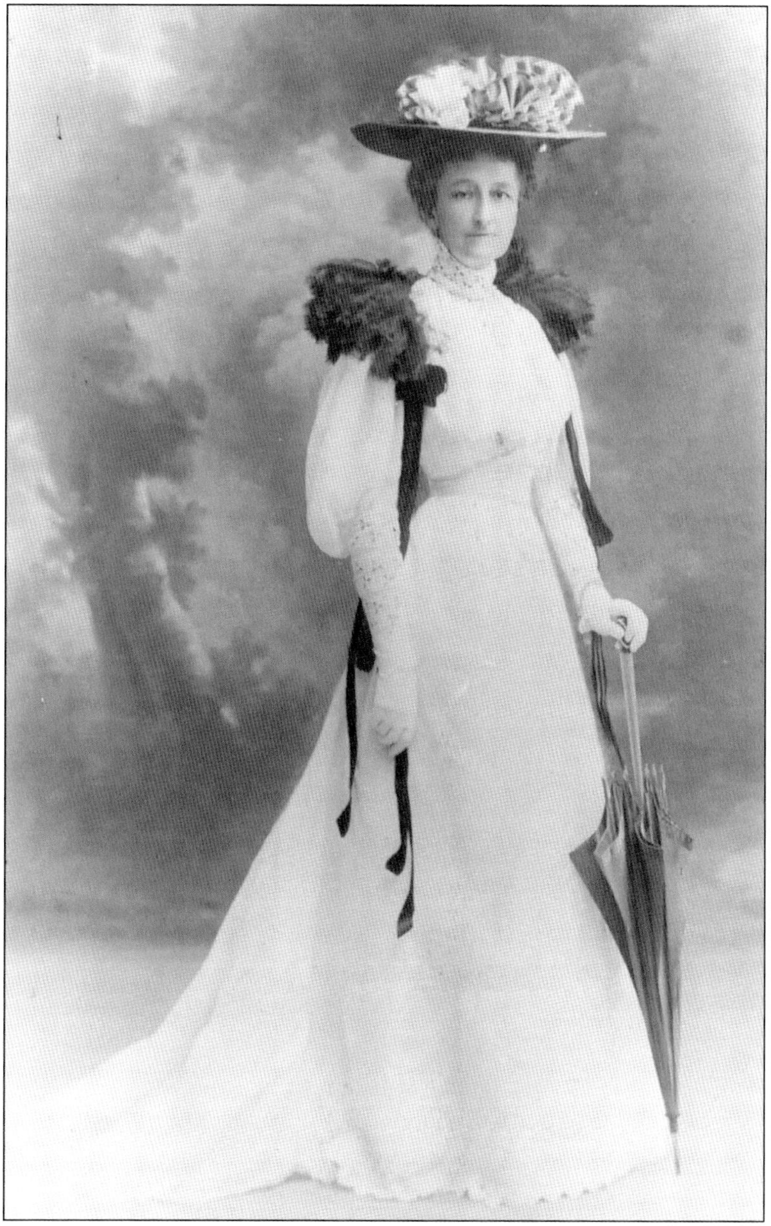

Mary "Minnie" Cadwalader Jones was the first president of the board of lady managers. The board of nine women, formed in 1907, was responsible at first for all policy decisions regarding life at the home, and it interviewed each applicant to judge suitability for admission. Olive Trowbridge served as the secretary. When the duties became too burdensome, the board delegated administrative decisions to the staff. Jones was the sister-in-law of writer Edith Wharton, whose style was influential during the Gilded Age. Jones served as part-time literary agent for Wharton. Jones held a salon that at times included Henry James and other noted writers and painters. It was Jones who sent Wharton's early stories to James. Jones was a leader in New York society and an active member of the American Society for the Prevention of Cruelty to Animals. She was author of a variety of books and articles ranging from travel to nurses' education. She served on the board of lady managers until 1929.

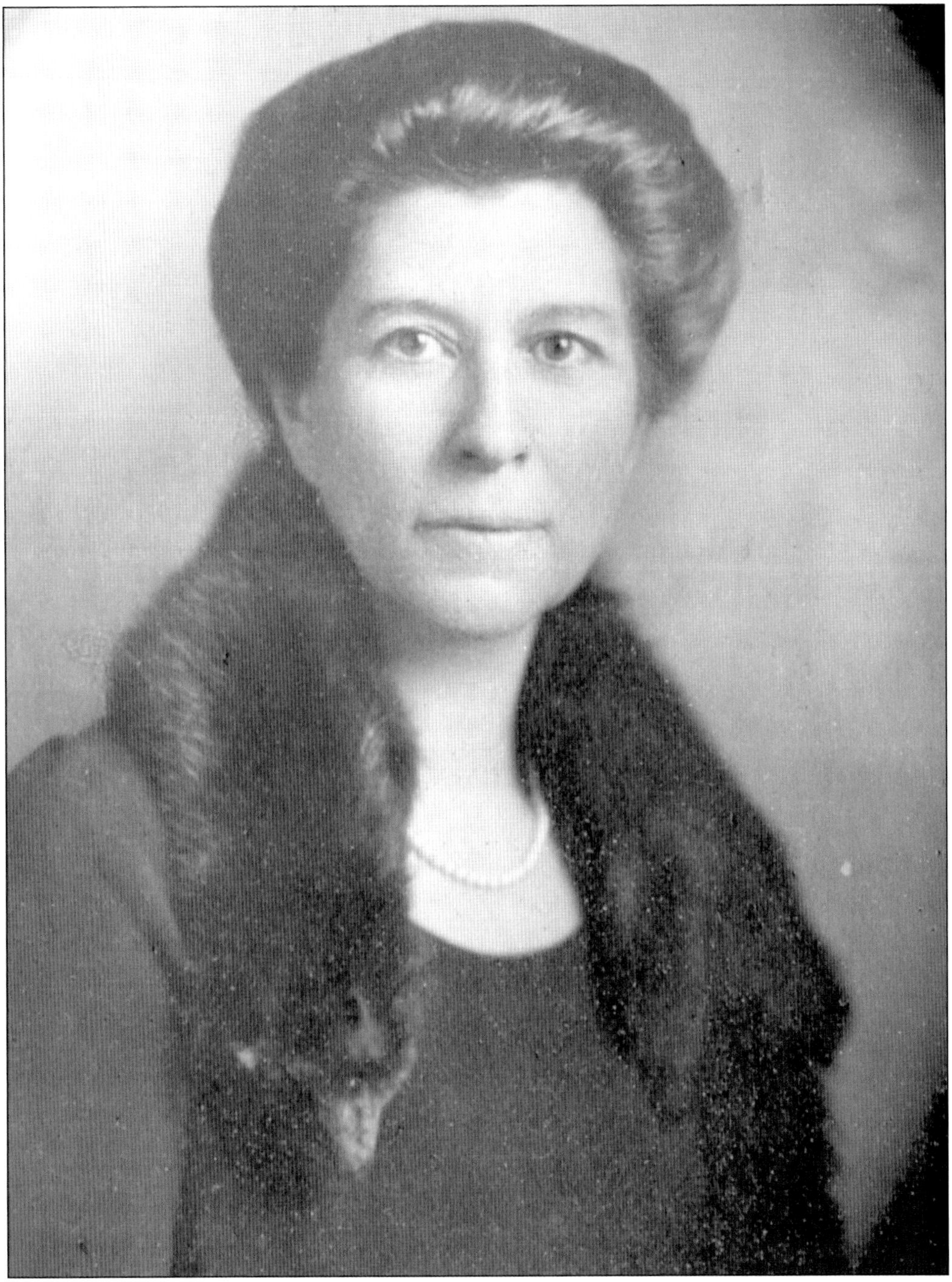

Mrs. Percy A. Rockefeller (Isabel Goodrich Stillman) was elected to the board in 1918 and became its second president when Mary Cadwalader Jones resigned in 1929. She was the daughter of First National City Bank president James Stillman. Her husband, Percy, graduated from Yale University and like John Sterling was a member of Skull and Bones. He served on the board of directors of many major corporations such as Bethlehem Steel, National City Bank of New York, New York Edison Company, and Western Union and Telegraph. He was a trustee of Sterling. A daughter, Faith Rockefeller Model, also served on the board of lady managers of The Osborn.

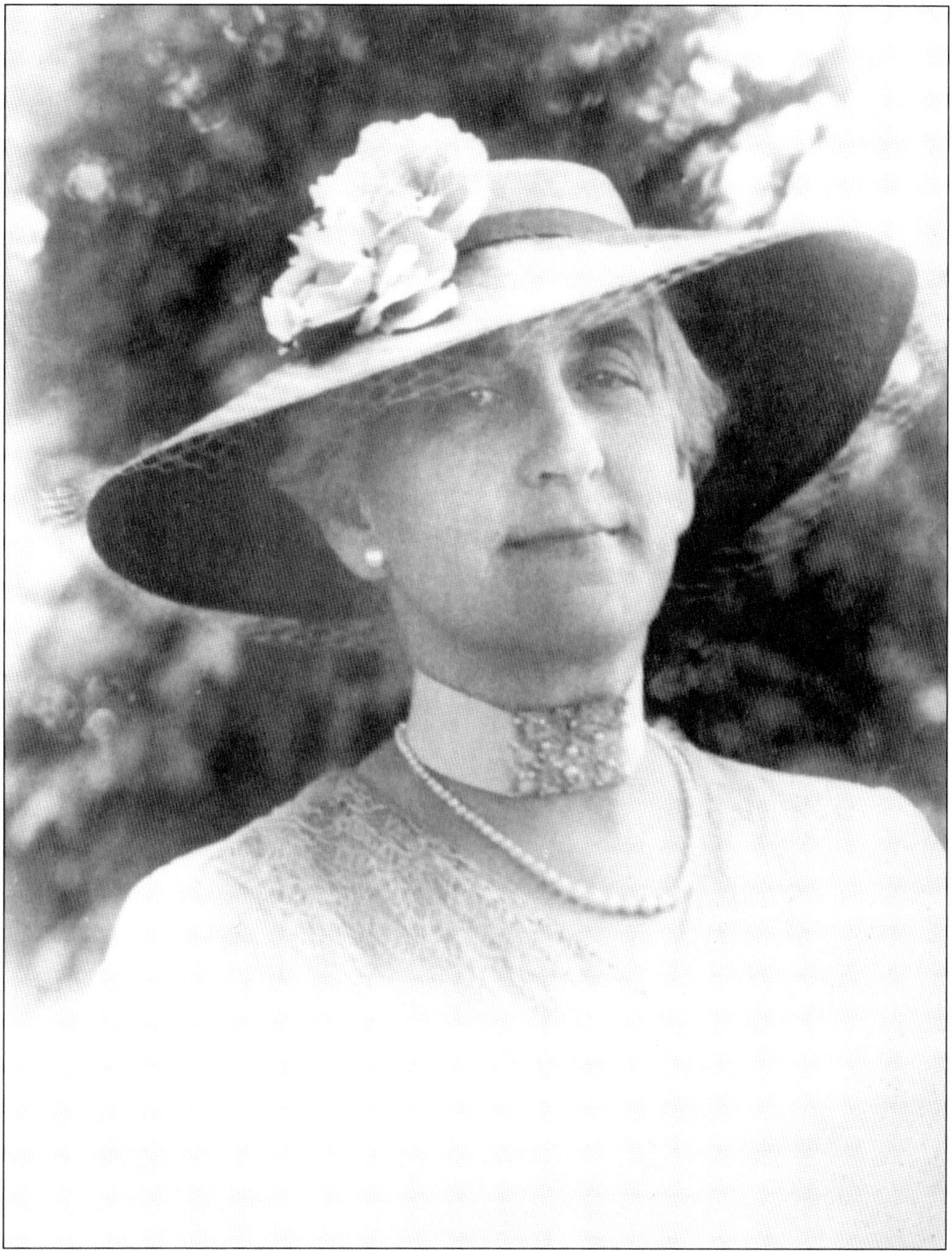

Mrs. William VanSchoonhoven Thorne was a member of the first board of lady managers and was president from 1933 to 1937, suggesting that she served the home at least 30 years. Her husband, like many of Sterling's associates, was a Yale graduate and significantly involved with many of the nation's early railroad systems. He was manager and treasurer of the Presbyterian Hospital from 1899 to 1920. It was from the families of Sterling's prominent colleagues that the women were invited to join the board of managers. Finally, on April 15, 1908, the day Miriam Osborn would have been 68 years old, the home was ready for occupancy. The board of managers was present to greet residents and visitors as they arrived.

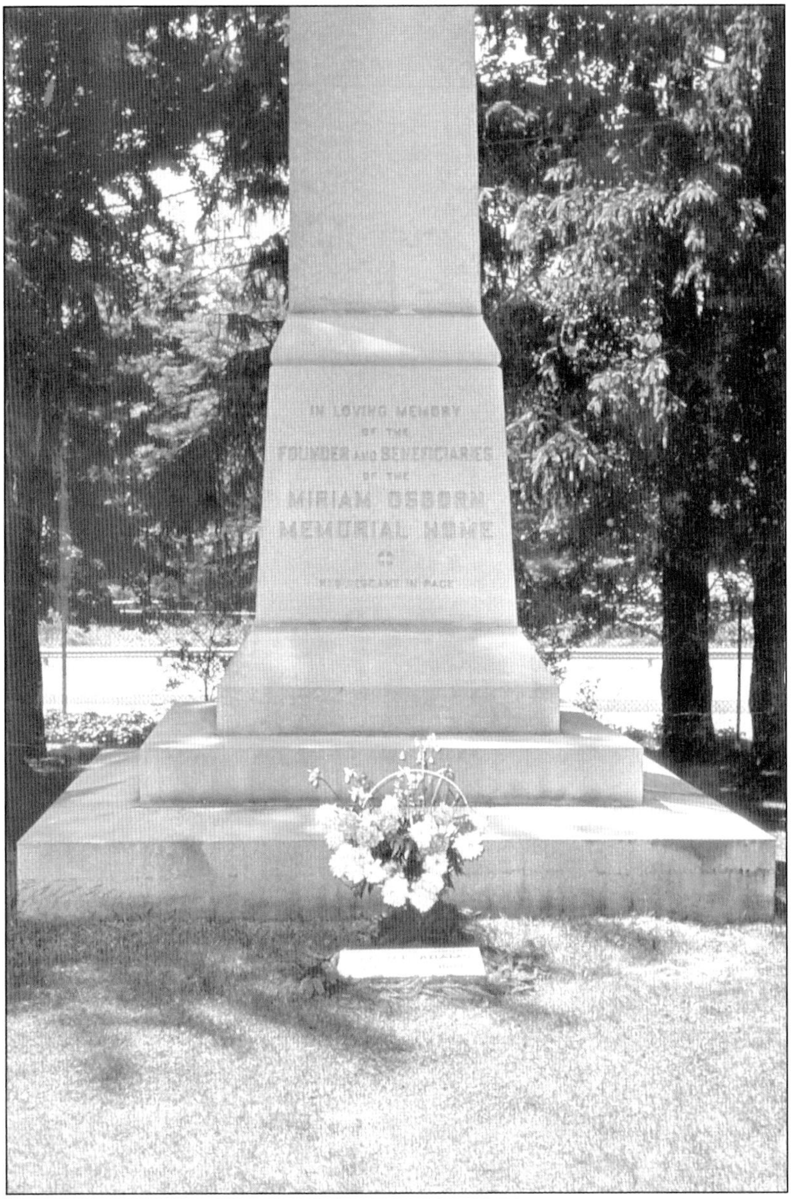

Flowers adorn the grave site of Helen Adams at the base of the monolith in The Osborn cemetery. Fred R. Diering, the superintendent of Woodlawn Cemetery, advised John Sterling about the cemetery construction. Diering directed the excavation of the land and the landscaping. Plans included a central monument. A 45.5-foot obelisk, cut of one piece of Barre granite from the Presbrey-Leland Company, slipped from the rigging while being erected and broke into several pieces. It took some time to locate the granite for another monolith and to carve it out of the rock bed. The second monument was five feet taller than the first, making it the second-tallest cemetery monument at the time in the country. Dr. Anson Phelps Stokes, secretary of Yale University, suggested the inscription, "In loving memory of the Founder and Beneficiaries of the Miriam Osborn Memorial Home." He was an Episcopal priest who later served as the resident canon at the National Cathedral in Washington, D.C. The first person buried in the new cemetery was Isabella Irwin, on January 7, 1916.

Three

The Sterling Years

At the beginning of the 20th century, the pieces of the puzzle were falling into place. Miriam Osborn's gossamer dream was poised to become a reality. The brick-and-mortar manifestation of an idea rested with the Osborn family's attorney and trustee John Sterling. It could not have been in more capable hands.

One of Sterling's pleasures in life, outside of work and the occasional fishing trip, was developing land. It was the only other diversion he truly enjoyed. Helen Adams, his longtime secretary, would accompany him on trips to his properties in Westchester and Connecticut where they would observe the work to clear land, grade roads, and renovate old farmhouses. Adams recalled asking him why they had not visited his most recent purchase in northern Westchester in Pound Ridge. Always the pragmatist, his reply was, "I know that once I see it I will begin to spend too much time and money on it." In all, Sterling amassed over 3,300 acres throughout Westchester and Connecticut.

The site selection for The Osborn Home went through many phases. Sites in Manhattan and the site Miriam Osborn had purchased, know as Mitchell Place, which adjoined the grounds of Tahoma, were considered. Finally the newly constituted board unanimously approved the site on Theall's Hill, and work commenced rapidly. Sterling selected Bruce Price, designer of the Osborn Recitation Hall at Yale University, as architect. He chose to construct the home in a Georgian type of design using Georgia pressed brick with white marble or cast stone quoins.

The Osborn Home would see completion, but not without several potentially disastrous travails, the most serious being the death of the architect in Paris in 1902. Fortunately, the necessary architectural details had been completed. Sterling thwarted one serious threat to the entire project earlier when Miriam's sisters contested her estate and waged a four-year battle only to have their claim thrown out of court. The construction of the home was completed in 1908 and stands today as a testament to the imagination, determination, and care of both John Sterling and Miriam Osborn.

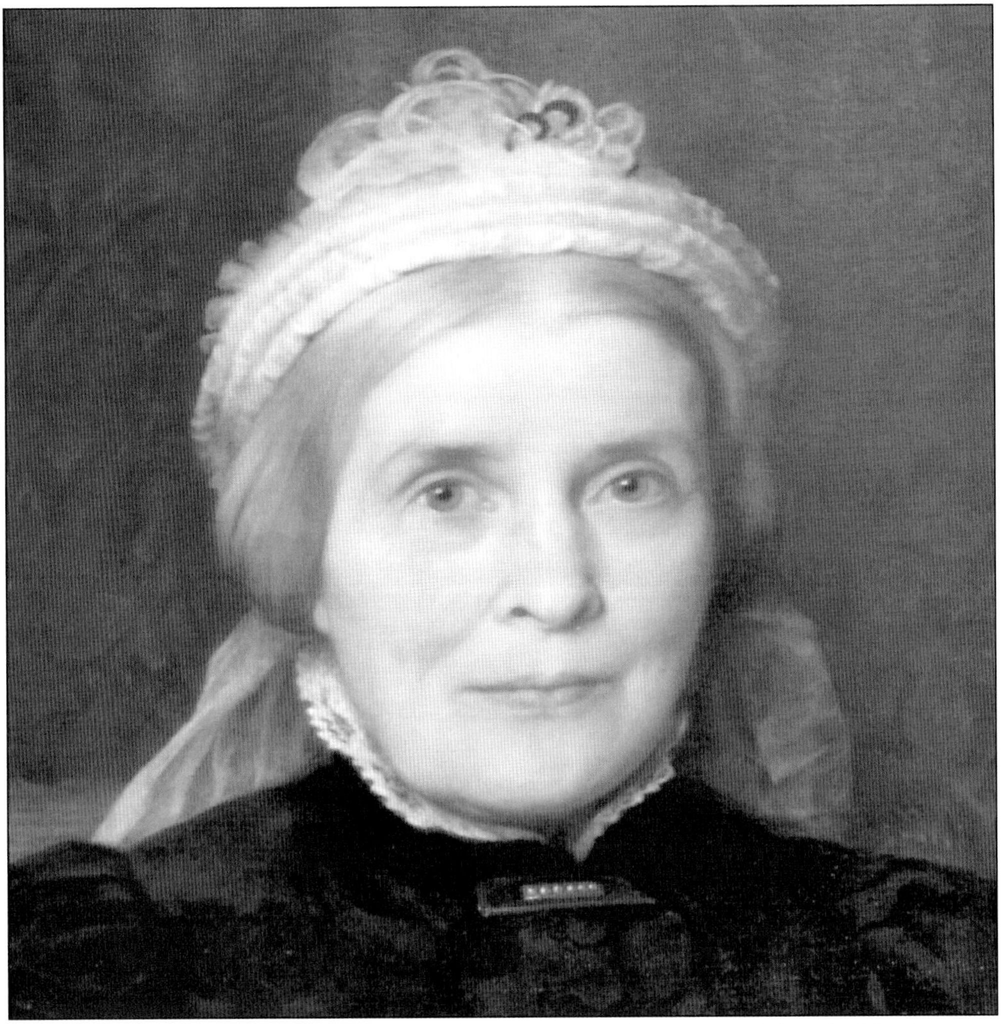

Catherine Tomlinson Plant Sterling was the epitome of the sea captain's wife. Her home in Stratford, Connecticut, was close to the harbor so she could await the return of her husband, Capt. John William Sterling, who plied the seas aboard one of the largest clipper ships of its day, the *Splendid*. Her son, John William Sterling, would achieve great things during his lifetime, most he would attribute to the upbringing he received from his mother. She was a woman of great sensitivity and caring but bred of strong New England stock; her father was a state senator and lieutenant governor of Connecticut. She was delighted John did not inherit his father's love of the sea and that he never took a sea voyage. Catherine lived a long and full life, passing away in 1905 at 89.

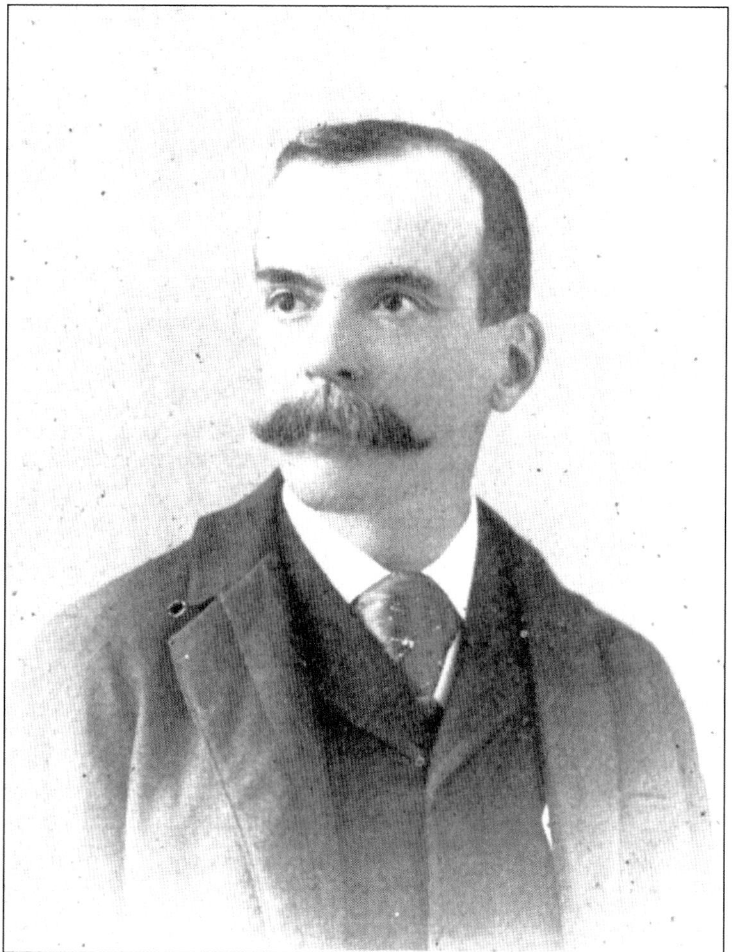

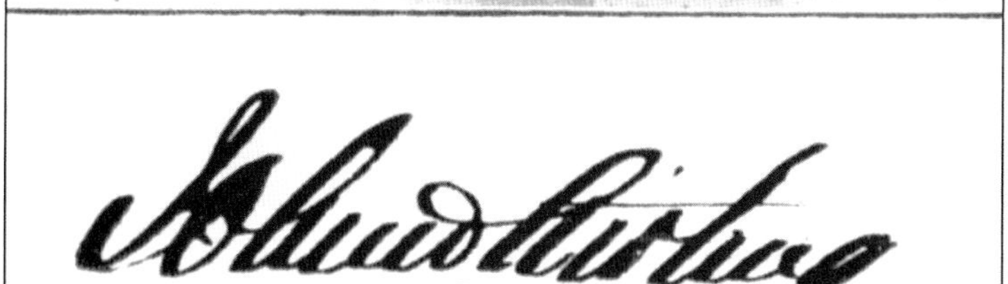

With his love of land development and his dedication to his clients, John Sterling was the perfect candidate to see through the construction of The Osborn's original buildings. A shrewd judge of character in all his business dealings, Sterling hired the best and most competent individuals in an effort to perfect Miriam Osborn's dream. For the grounds, he consulted the noted Boston landscape design family Olmstead on the parklike design he envisioned. For the supporting farms and vegetable gardens that would feed the home's early inhabitants, he sought advice from L. A. Clinton, the noted Cornell University professor. For the cemetery, he looked to the person who was then developing the layout for one of the nation's great cemeteries, Woodlawn, located in the Bronx. Today Woodlawn is known as the cemetery of the Gilded Age's elite, but its design is owed to Fred R. Diering, who assisted in the layout of The Osborn cemetery and its present location.

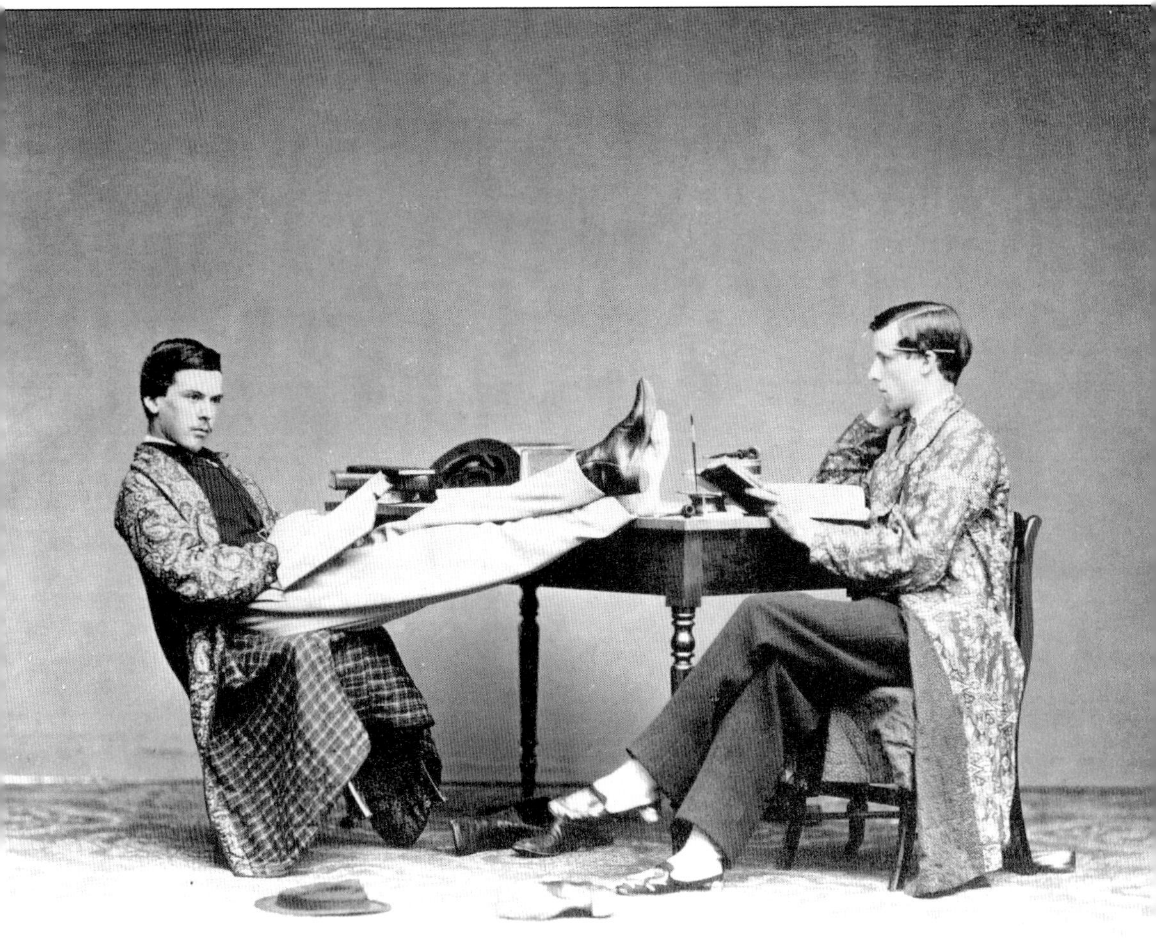

John Sterling's success at Yale University surprised all but himself. This jaunty photograph of Sterling and his roommate belies the serious nature of this active student. This personal diary quotation gives insight into the young man Sterling was and the adult he would become. "Prof. Porter has expressed himself very much pleased with my progress during the past year. Prof. McWhorter told me yesterday that Prof. Porter during the winter made the remark to him that he thought if I should go on as I had commenced life that I would arrive at equal distinction with Daniel Lord, for I had something of the same kind of talents—soundness of judgment, accuracy, reliability, indomitable perseverance and integrity. Certainly that is a very high compliment and should serve as a very great encouragement to me in my progress through life."

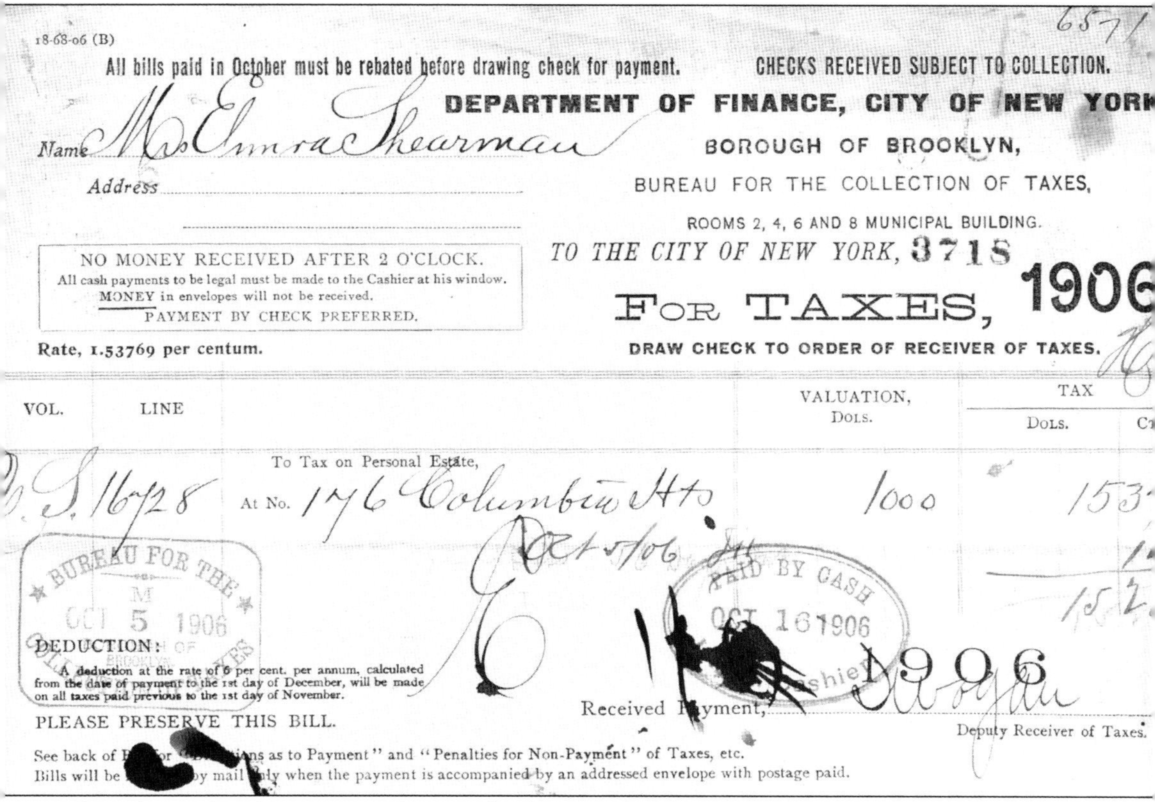

18-68-06 (B)

All bills paid in October must be rebated before drawing check for payment. CHECKS RECEIVED SUBJECT TO COLLECTION.

DEPARTMENT OF FINANCE, CITY OF NEW YORK

Name Mrs Elmira Shearman

BOROUGH OF BROOKLYN,

Address

BUREAU FOR THE COLLECTION OF TAXES,

ROOMS 2, 4, 6 AND 8 MUNICIPAL BUILDING.

NO MONEY RECEIVED AFTER 2 O'CLOCK.
All cash payments to be legal must be made to the Cashier at his window.
MONEY in envelopes will not be received.
PAYMENT BY CHECK PREFERRED.

TO THE CITY OF NEW YORK, 3718

FOR TAXES, 1906

Rate, 1.53769 per centum.

DRAW CHECK TO ORDER OF RECEIVER OF TAXES.

VOL.	LINE		VALUATION, DOLS.	TAX DOLS.
S	1628	To Tax on Personal Estate, At No. 176 Columbia Hts	1000	153

DEDUCTION:
A deduction at the rate of 6 per cent. per annum, calculated from the date of payment to the 1st day of December, will be made on all taxes paid previous to the 1st day of November.

PLEASE PRESERVE THIS BILL.

Received Payment, 1906

Deputy Receiver of Taxes.

See back of [illegible] as to Payment" and "Penalties for Non-Payment" of Taxes, etc.
Bills will be [illegible] by mail only when the payment is accompanied by an addressed envelope with postage paid.

The relationship between Sterling and Thomas Shearman was a perfect legal marriage. Shearman's ability in the courtroom was unparalleled during the Victorian age, and Sterling's ability to accomplish vast amounts of detail-oriented back office and behind-the-scenes work made them a formidable duo. As the firm grew, Sterling took on more and more of the work. Shearman chose to work from his home in Brooklyn, coming to court as the work dictated. When Shearman passed away in 1900, Sterling was named as his estate's trustee, and with his usual combination of compassion and efficiency, he saw to the estate provisions and the care of the Shearman family, doing whatever was required and visiting Shearman's wife at her Brooklyn home on a regular basis to see to her welfare.

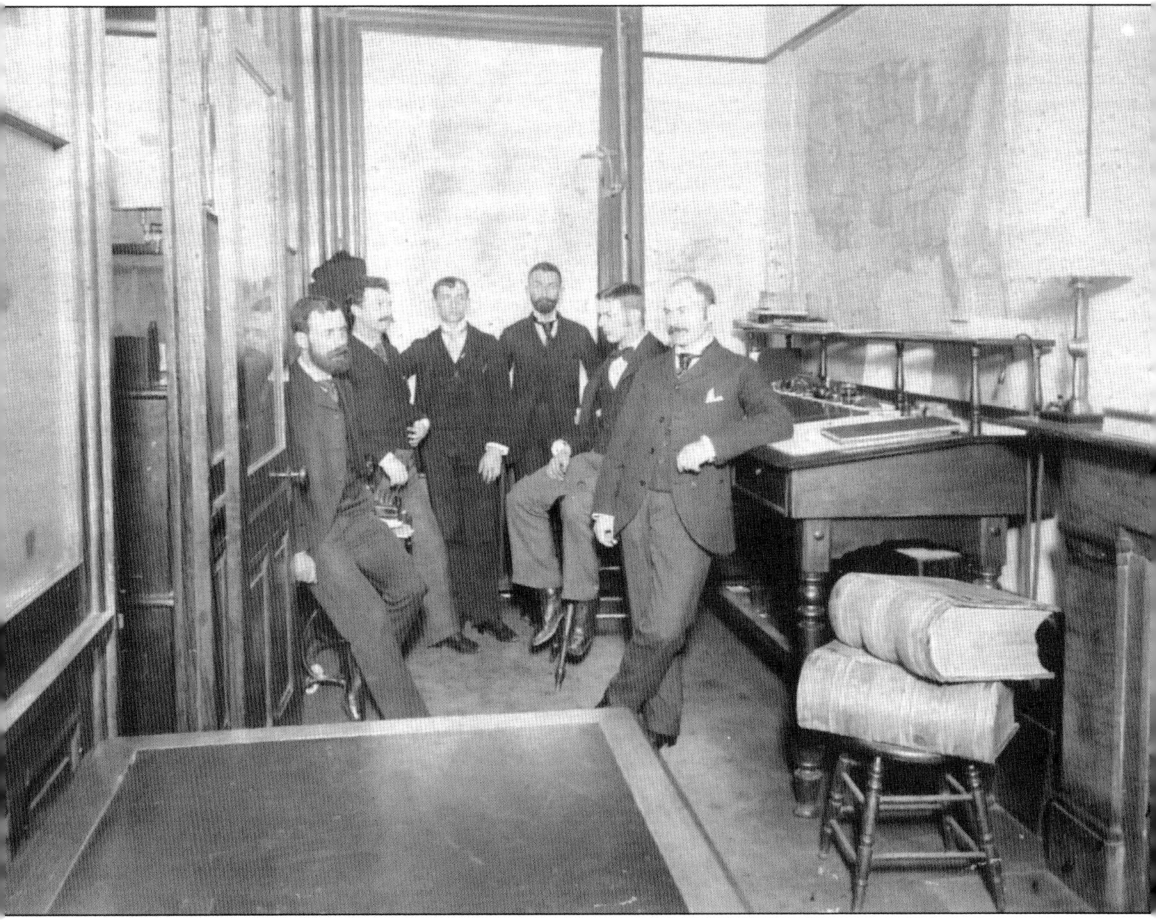

With all the difficult litigation stemming from the activities of John Sterling's clients, there was no shortage of work. Sterling engaged the services of George H. Church (whose office is pictured above) to handle many of the accounting intricacies and forensic work needed in several of their more prominent cases. One of the more interesting cases stemmed from the efforts of Jay Gould and Jim Fisk in September 1869 to corner the gold market. Known as "Black Friday," it created widespread panic. After this event, the work required by the firm, known then as Field and Shearman, the predecessor to Shearman and Sterling, was extensive. It brought great attention and business to the firm and its partners and the young Sterling. Once baptized in this crucible of the law, Sterling never looked back as he became the confidant to many of the great men who built this country and its financial and industrial institutions.

THIS AGREEMENT, made the eighth day of ~~December~~ January in the year one thousand nine hundred and ~~five~~ six by and between Christopher Campbell of the City of New York

party of the first part (hereinafter designated the Contractor), and the MIRIAM OSBORN MEMORIAL HOME ASSOCIATION, party of the second part (hereinafter designated the Owner),

WITNESSETH that the Contractor , in consideration of the agreements herein made by the Owner , agrees with the said Owner as follows :

ARTICLE I. The Contractor shall and will provide all the materials and perform all the work and comply with all conditions and provisions of this Contract and the Specifications, referred to herein, for the completion of the Miriam Osborn Memorial Home at Harrison, N. Y., as shown on the drawings and described in the specifications, prepared by Bruce Price & de Sibour, Architects, which drawings and specifications are identified by the signatures of the parties hereto, and are made hereby a part of this contract.

ART. II. It is understood and agreed by and between the parties hereto, that the work, included in this contract, is to be done under the direction of the said Architects and that their decision as to the true construction and meaning of the drawings and specifications shall be final. It is also understood and agreed by and between the parties hereto, that such additional drawings and explanations as may be necessary to detail and illustrate the work to be done are to be furnised by said Architects, and they agree to conform to and abide by the same as far as they may be consistent with the purpose and intent of the original drawings and specifications referred to in Art. I.

It is further understood and agreed by the parties hereto that any and all drawings and specifications prepared for the purposes of this contract by the said Architects are and remain their property and that all charges for the use of the same and for the services of said Architects are to be paid by the said Owner.

ART. III. No alterations shall be made in the work except upon written order of the Architects ; the amount to be paid by the Owner or allowed by the Contractor by virtue of such alterations to be stated in said order. Should the Owner and Contrator not agree as to amount to be paid or allowed, the work shall go on under the order required above, and in case of failure to agree, the determination of said amount shall be referred to arbitration, as provided for in Art. XII. of this contract.

ART. IV. The Contractor shall provide sufficient, safe and proper facilities at all times for the inspection of the work by the Architects or their authorized representatives ; shall, within twenty-four hours after receiving written notice from the Architects to that effect, proceed to remove from the grounds or buildings all materials condemned by them, whether worked or unworked, and to take down all portions of the work which the Architects shall by like written notice condemn as unsound or improper, or as in any way failing to conform to the drawings and specifications, and shall make good all work damaged or destroyed thereby.

ART. V. Should the Contractor at any time refuse or neglect to supply a sufficiency of properly skilled workmen, or of materials of the proper quality, or fail in any respect to prosecute the work with promptness and diligence, or fail in the performance of any of the agreements herein contained, such refusal, neglect or failure being certified by the Architects, the Owner shall be at liberty, after three days written notice to the Contractor, to provide any such labor or materials, and to deduct the cost thereof from any money then due or thereafter to become due to the Contractor under this contract ; and if the Architects shall certify that such refusal, neglect or failure is sufficient ground for such action, the Owner shall also be at liberty to terminate

The loss of architect Bruce Price was barely felt, with the home's drawings completed prior to his death in Paris in 1902. As always, Sterling showed his eye for detail and construction, not to mention his ability to write a thorough contract. The detail of the completed building was the result of the artistic eye of Price and keen nose for detail of Sterling. In pages of the contract between the contractor and the owner, represented by Sterling, he made very exacting notes on many aspects of the construction, from the finest details of flooring composite to the finishes on the doors and moldings at the floor base. The level of detail in this period made the buildings what they are today, structures of lasting architectural beauty.

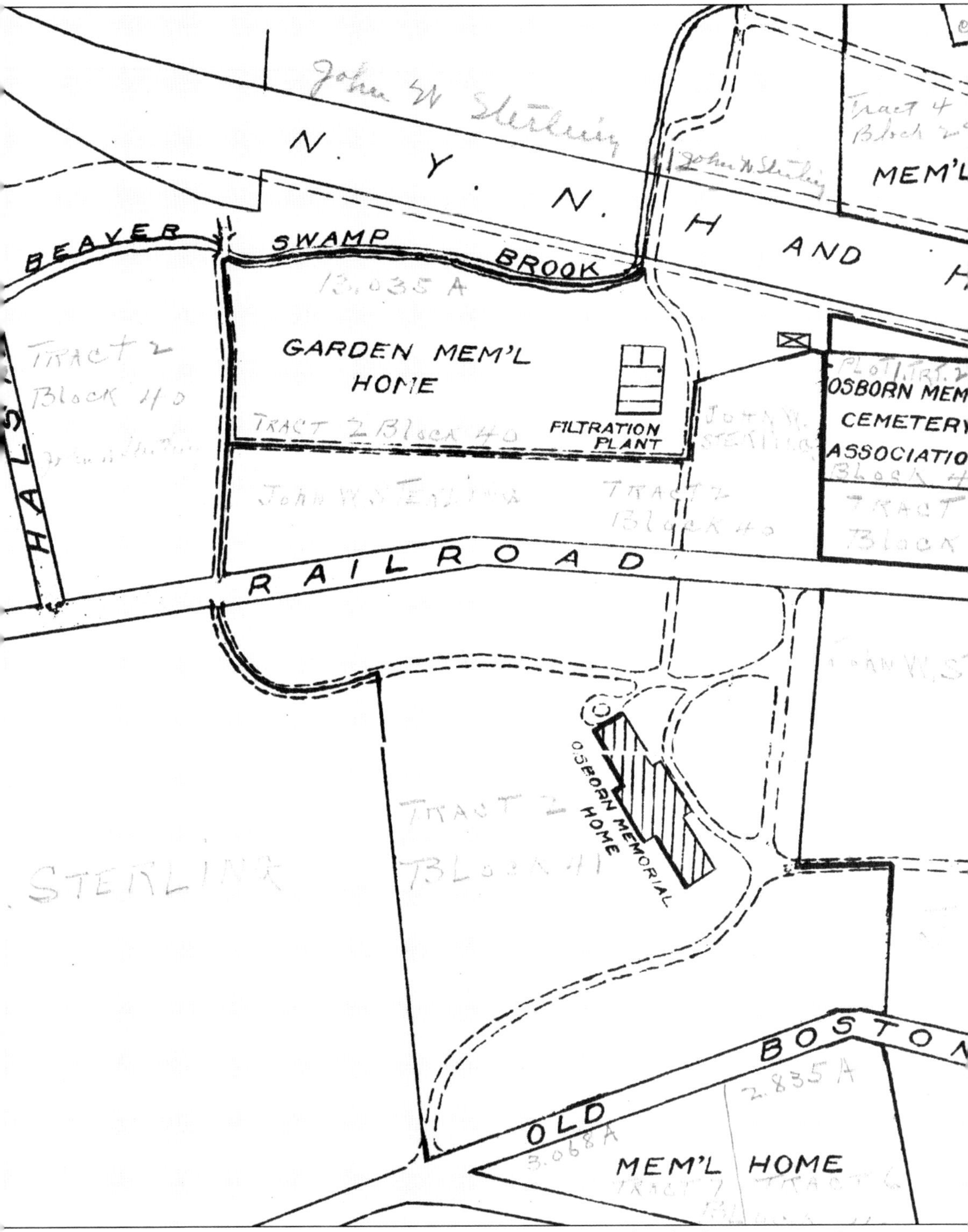

The site around Theall's Hill was believed to be very beneficial to the future "inmates" as it was close enough to the shore to afford healthful breezes but not so close as to cause undo alarm from storms or flooding. The location also had the added benefit of close proximity to both Boston

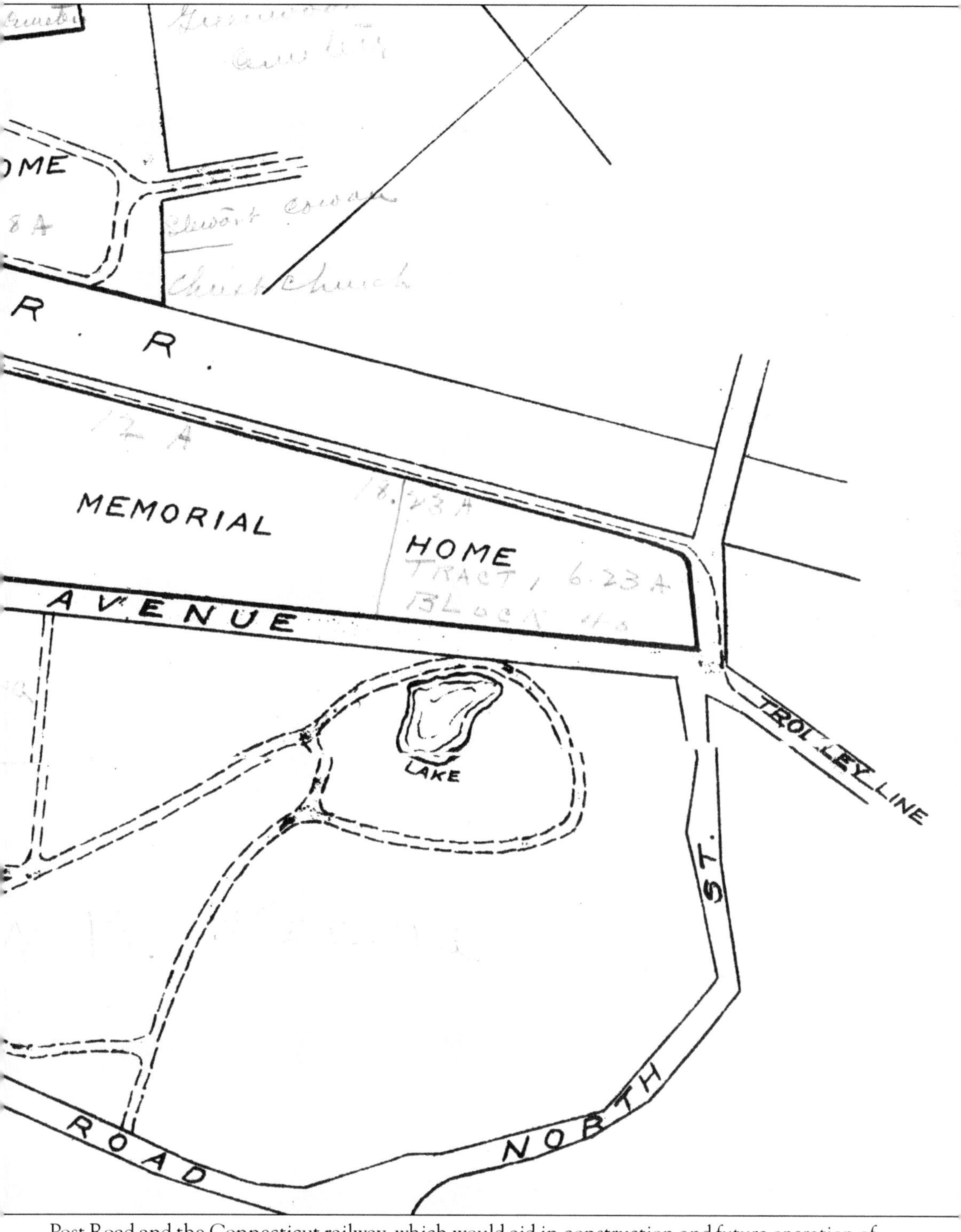

Post Road and the Connecticut railway, which would aid in construction and future operation of the home. There was adequate water from wells and an old ice pond called Mead Pond.

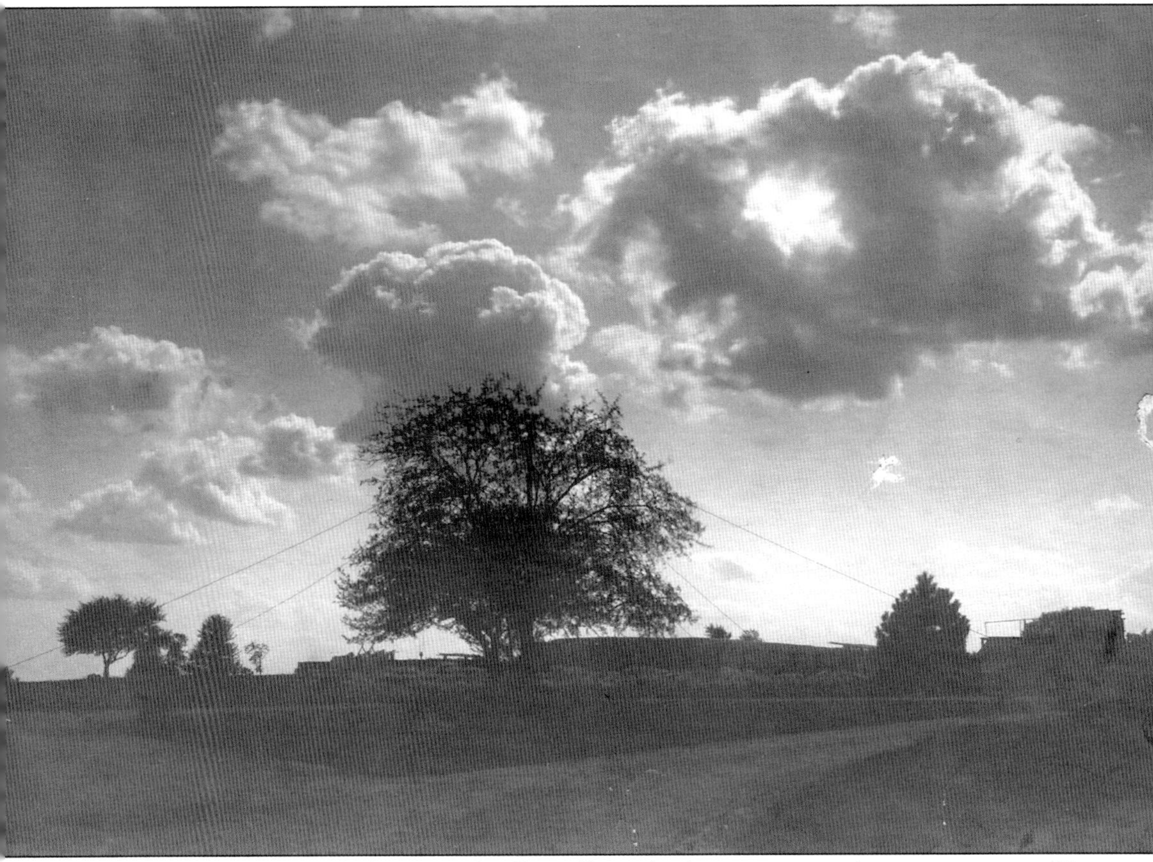

Much of the early work done on Theall's Hill involved excavation and site preparation. The trees that were worth keeping were tied off with cable to protect them during the rigors of construction. One of the more difficult aspects of the early stages was finding enough good blue stone for construction of the foundation, moat, and surrounding walls. The stone near the site was flawed. First stone was brought in from Greenwich, Connecticut, but the expense of hauling the heavy loads proved too much for the extensive job. An exhaustive search located good quality stone on the property of Joseph Park of Harrison who donated it to the home.

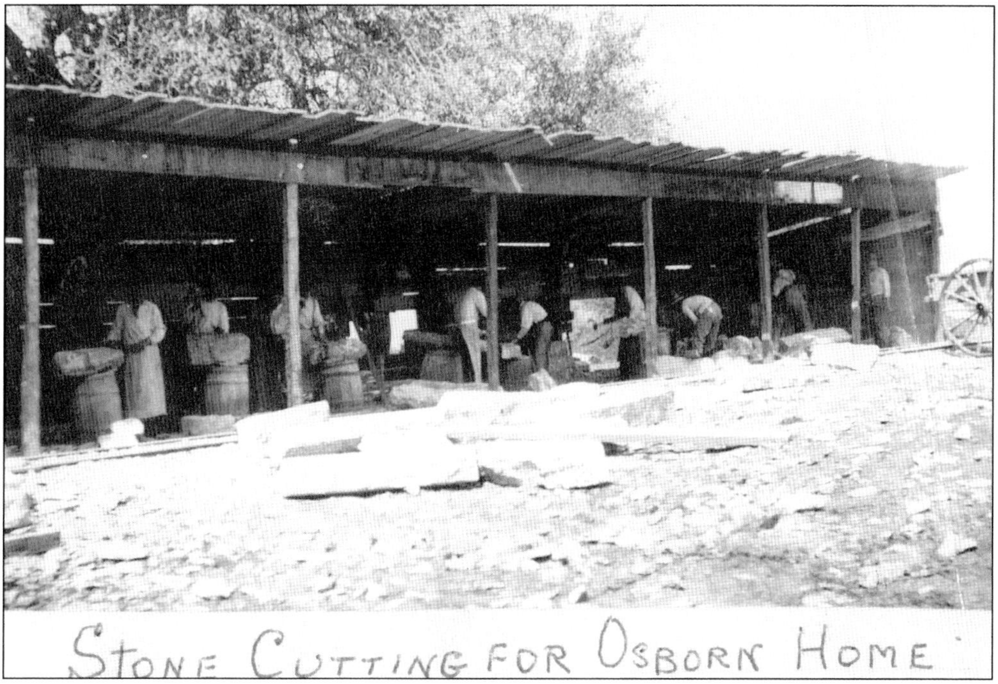

The cutting and laying of stone was as difficult as obtaining stone for the home. Weeks and Company was hired to oversee the building of The Osborn. George Mertz of Port Chester built the interior partitions, and George A. Suter and Company was in charge of heating equipment. Francis Brother and Jellette Company did the electrical work. During 1902, a great disturbance arose in the Westchester labor market, accompanied by riots. In those days, unskilled labor received between $1.25 and $1.50 per 10-hour day. The Osborn provided the extra benefit of housing for its workers and, in some cases, their families. This, however, did not prevent the disturbances in other areas from spilling over to The Osborn construction site. Any situations were handled quickly and capably by either Matthew M. Moralee, the home superintendent, or by John Sterling, behind the scenes.

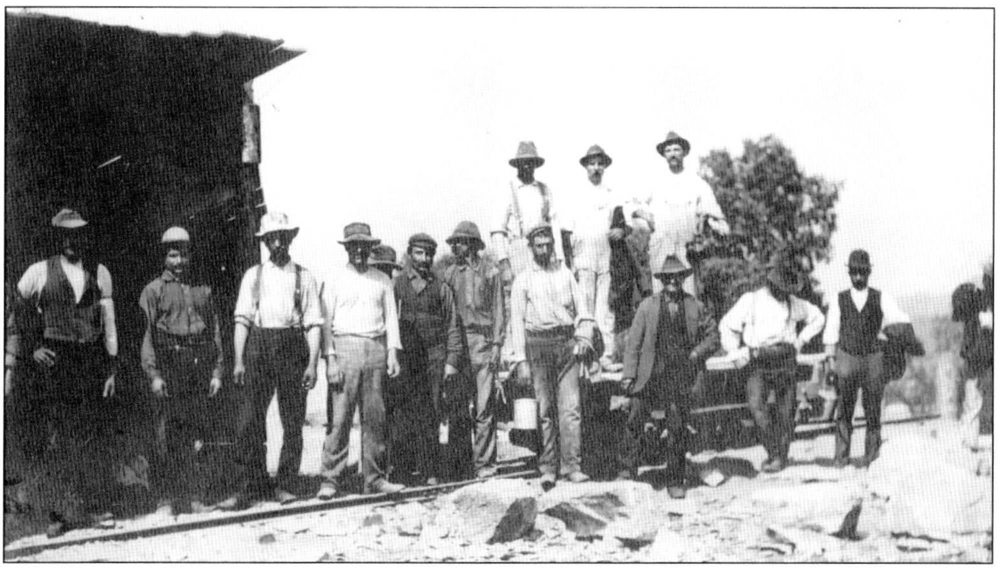

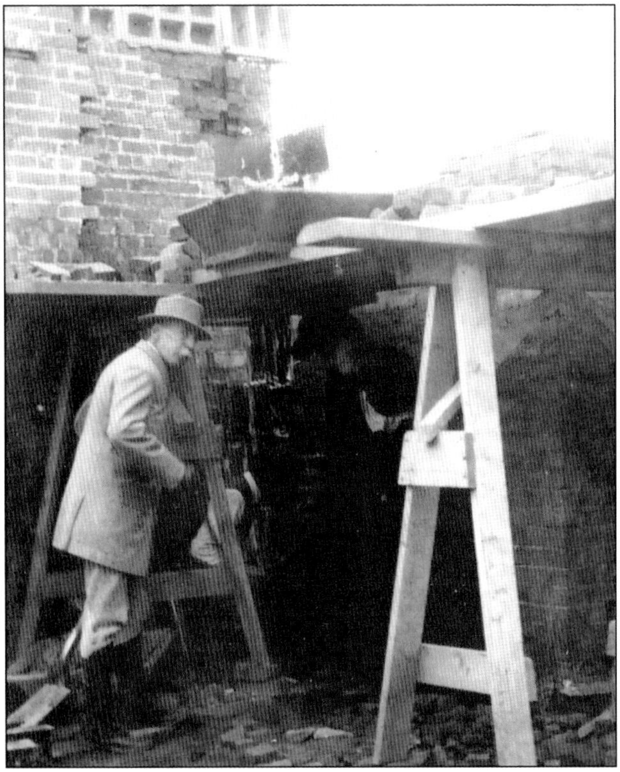

John Sterling's attention to detail was not just reserved for the details of the office. On a weekly basis, he visited the construction site to oversee the work. His love of the outdoors and horseback riding was a holdover from his vigorous childhood. At Yale University, one of his other great interests was boxing. Always an active man, he would, weather permitting, walk daily across Central Park from his Fifth Avenue home to the Sixth Avenue elevated train, arriving at his Wall Street office promptly at 8:30 a.m. He shunned most social occasions and maintained a very simple diet. His secretary and one of the great figures of The Osborn Home, Helen Adams, tells how he would eat the same lunch daily, consisting of black coffee, rich milk, French bread, and unsweetened apple puree.

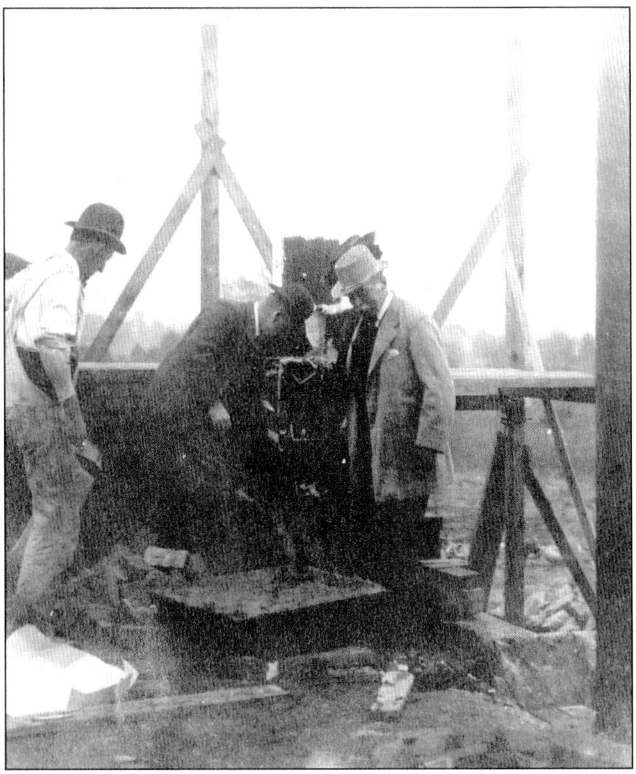

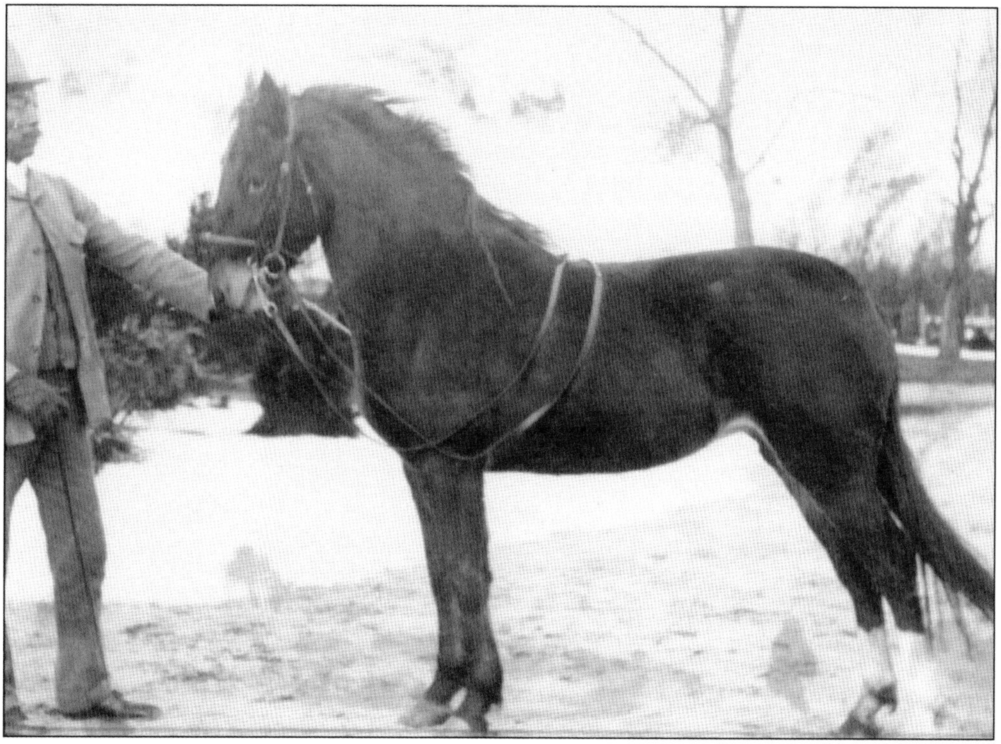

As construction moved into high gear, many of Sterling's prize horses, from his Connecticut and Harrison farms, were put to good use. Pictured above is Cordy, one of his prize draft horses, with George, a stableman. Other horses were Olive, his prize saddle horse, and draft horse Nancy. Sterling took pleasure in naming horses after family members. Cordy was named for his sister Cordelia and Olive for Miriam's niece and Sterling's ward. Although the mechanized age had begun in the previous century, machines performed little work at the home. Horses pulled heavy loads, and men did heavy lifting, utilizing block and tackle and pulleys. The Osborn's detail is a tribute to the skill and craftsmanship of the builders of the era. The blue stone foundation and moat are in excellent shape after 100 years.

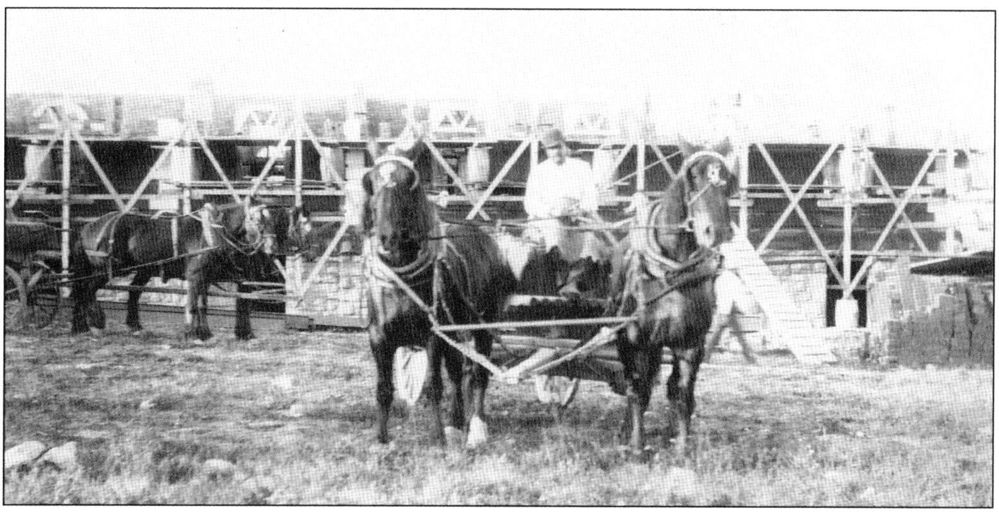

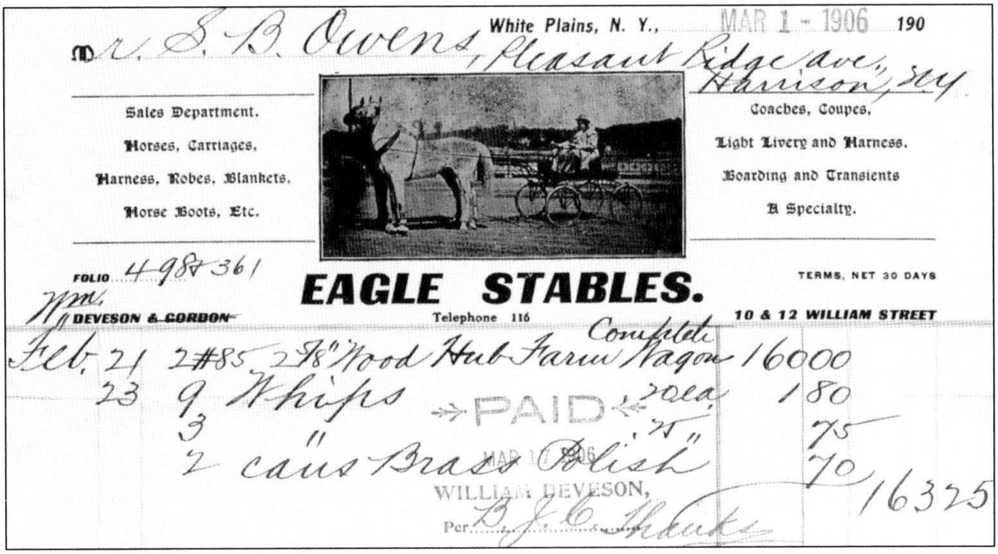

Mr. S. B. Owens, Pleasant Ridge ave., Harrison, N.Y.
White Plains, N. Y., MAR 1 - 1906 190

Sales Department.
Horses, Carriages,
Harness, Robes, Blankets,
Horse Boots, Etc.

Coaches, Coupes,
Light Livery and Harness.
Boarding and Transients
A Specialty.

FOLIO 498 361
EAGLE STABLES.
TERMS, NET 30 DAYS
Wm. DEVESON & ~~GORDON~~
Telephone 116
10 & 12 WILLIAM STREET

Feb. 21	2 #85 2 7/8" Wood Hub Farm Wagon Complete	160 00	
23	9 Whips 20 ea	1 80	
	3 " 25 "	75	
	2 cans Brass Polish	70	163 25

PAID MAR 1 1906
WILLIAM DEVESON,
Per B. J. C.

The supplies for work are displayed in these bills of sale for one wagon, 12 whips, and two cans of brass polish. What is most interesting is the cost of the whips and wagon; the whips were a mere 20¢ and 25¢ apiece, and the total cost for a complete farm-style wagon was $160. The invoice for the manure has a wonderful drawing of the docks and barges located at East 64th Street and the river in Manhattan. Obviously good use was made of the waste product of the primary means of travel by most New Yorkers of that time. One could scarcely imagine such an enterprise existing today; however, with environmental movement so strong it is certainly worth a brief and nostalgic thought.

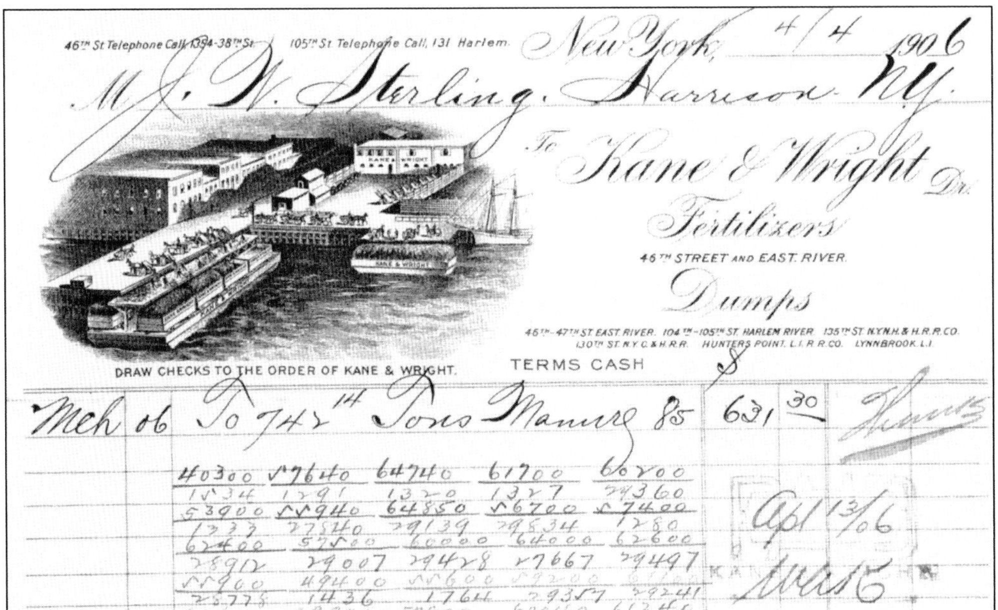

46TH St Telephone Call 1394-38TH St. 105TH St Telephone Call, 131 Harlem.
New York, 4/4 1906
M J. W. Sterling. Harrison N.Y.
To Kane & Wright Dr.
Fertilizers
46TH STREET AND EAST RIVER.
Dumps
46TH-47TH ST EAST RIVER. 104TH-105TH ST. HARLEM RIVER. 135TH ST. N.Y.N.H.& H.R.R.CO.
130TH ST. N.Y.C.&H.R.R. HUNTERS POINT. L.I. R.R.CO. LYNNBROOK L.I.
DRAW CHECKS TO THE ORDER OF KANE & WRIGHT.
TERMS CASH

Mch 06	To 742 14 Tons Manure 85	631 30

Apl 13/06

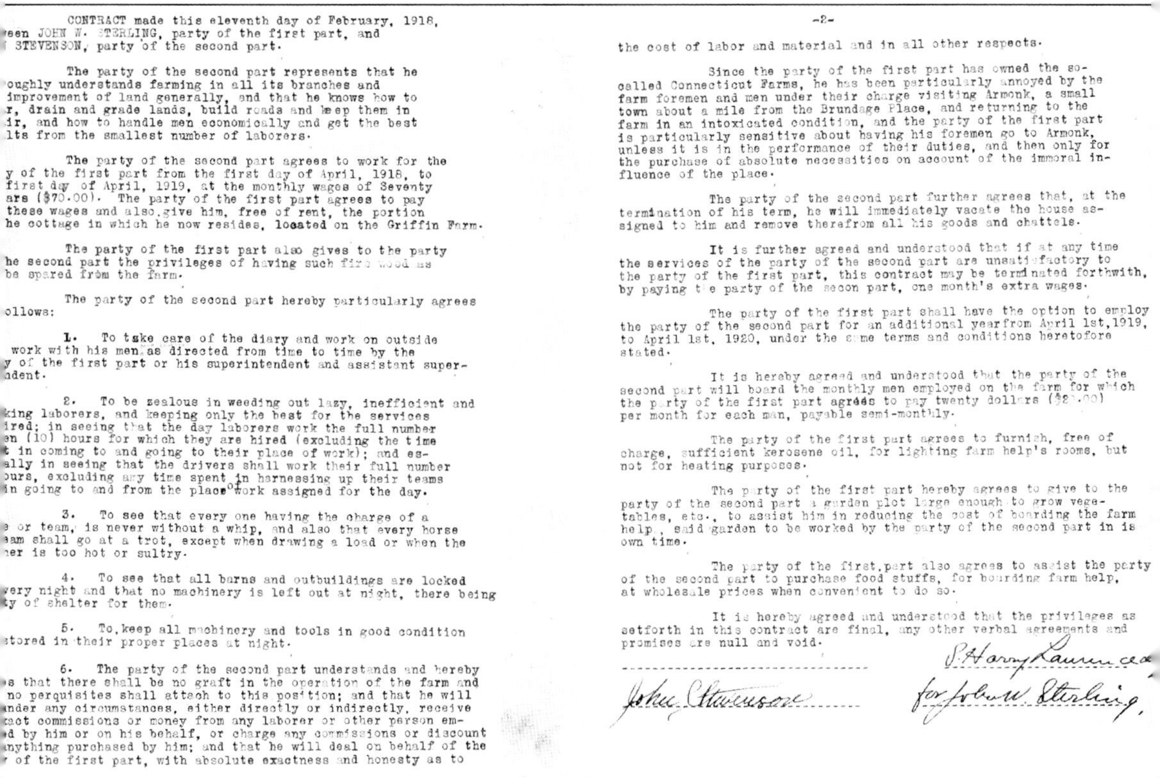

CONTRACT made this eleventh day of February, 1918,
een JOHN W. STERLING, party of the first part, and
STEVENSON, party of the second part.

The party of the second part represents that he
oughly understands farming in all its branches and
improvement of land generally, and that he knows how to
r, drain and grade lands, build roads and keep them in
ir, and how to handle men economically and get the best
lts from the smallest number of laborers.

The party of the second part agrees to work for the
y of the first part from the first day of April, 1918, to
first day of April, 1919, at the monthly wages of Seventy
ars ($70.00). The party of the first part agrees to pay
these wages and also give him, free of rent, the portion
he cottage in which he now resides, located on the Griffin Farm.

The party of the first part also gives to the party
he second part the privileges of having such fire wood as
be spared from the farm.

The party of the second part hereby particularly agrees
ollows:

1. To take care of the diary and work on outside
work with his men as directed from time to time by the
y of the first part or his superintendent and assistant super-
ndent.

2. To be zealous in weeding out lazy, inefficient and
king laborers, and keeping only the best for the services
ired; in seeing that the day laborers work the full number
en (10) hours for which they are hired (excluding the time
t in coming to and going to their place of work); and es-
ally in seeing that the drivers shall work their full number
ours, excluding any time spent in harnessing up their teams
in going to and from the place of work assigned for the day.

3. To see that every one having the charge of a
e or team, is never without a whip, and also that every horse
eam shall go at a trot, except when drawing a load or when the
her is too hot or sultry.

4. To see that all barns and outbuildings are locked
very night and that no machinery is left out at night, there being
ty of shelter for them.

5. To keep all machinery and tools in good condition
stored in their proper places at night.

6. The party of the second part understands and hereby
s that there shall be no graft in the operation of the farm and
no perquisites shall attach to this position; and that he will
under any circumstances, either directly or indirectly, receive
act commissions or money from any laborer or other person em-
d by him or on his behalf, or charge any commissions or discount
anything purchased by him; and that he will deal on behalf of the
of the first part, with absolute exactness and honesty as to

-2-

the cost of labor and material and in all other respects.

Since the party of the first part has owned the so-called Connecticut Farms, he has been particularly annoyed by the farm foremen and men under their charge visiting Armonk, a small town about a mile from the Brundage Place, and returning to the farm in an intoxicated condition, and the party of the first part is particularly sensitive about having his foremen go to Armonk, unless it is in the performance of their duties, and then only for the purchase of absolute necessities on account of the immoral influence of the place.

The party of the second part further agrees that, at the termination of his term, he will immediately vacate the house assigned to him and remove therefrom all his goods and chattels.

It is further agreed and understood that if at any time the services of the party of the second part are unsatisfactory to the party of the first part, this contract may be terminated forthwith, by paying the party of the secon part, one month's extra wages.

The party of the first part shall have the option to employ the party of the second part for an additional yearfrom April 1st,1919, to April 1st, 1920, under the same terms and conditions heretofore stated.

It is hereby agreed and understood that the party of the second part will board the monthly men employed on the farm for which the party of the first part agrees to pay twenty dollars ($20.00) per month for each man, payable semi-monthly.

The party of the first part agrees to furnish, free of charge, sufficient kerosene oil, for lighting farm help's rooms, but not for heating purposes.

The party of the first part hereby agrees to give to the party of the second part a garden plot large enough to grow vegetables, etc., to assist him in reducing the cost of boarding the farm help, said garden to be worked by the party of the second part in is own time.

The party of the first part also agrees to assist the party of the second part to purchase food stuffs, for boarding farm help, at wholesale prices when convenient to do so.

It is hereby agreed and understood that the privileges as setforth in this contract are final, any other verbal agreements and promises are null and void.

John Stevenson — S. Harry Lawrence for John W. Sterling

This contract between John Sterling and John Stevenson, who was being hired as a farm manager for one of Sterling's Harrison properties, is interesting since it further demonstrates Sterling's shrewd head for business and his no-nonsense approach to work. His forthrightness was certainly an important part of what made him so successful in all his business dealings. Combined with his attention to detail, it is obvious why he was able to amass the fortune he did. His work ethic was most certainly passed down to his colleagues and staff, and by this contract, he expected no less from the day laborers working on his Westchester and Connecticut properties. The term "stern but fair taskmaster" most assuredly applies to him. It cannot be denied, he did have a softer side, which he reserved for the women in his life, many of whom it was his responsibility to look after.

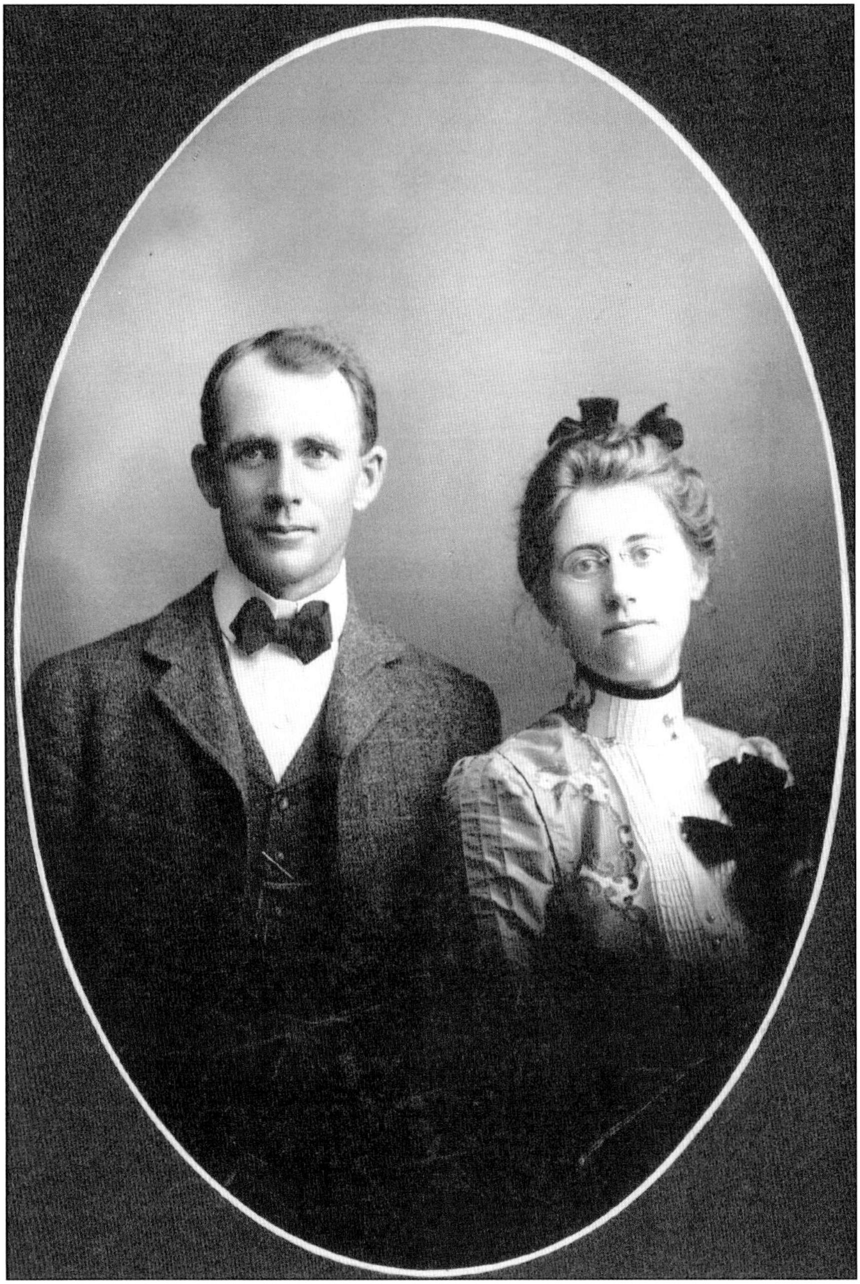

The contractor Wheeler and Company chose Max Carter as the construction manager for the building of the home. It is safe to say that it chose well. It was Carter's job to follow to the letter the design created by architect Bruce Price, and he did. Because the project lasted almost four years, Carter brought his wife, Ida, to the Harrison site, and she remained with him throughout the construction process. This was characteristic for projects of the day. Travel to and from distant work sites could take days, and having one's family nearby improved the output and level of work. The Osborn offered housing to some of the laborers and their families in an effort to be supportive and competitive in the labor market. This practice continues today with staff homes on the property and apartments for line staff in the lodge.

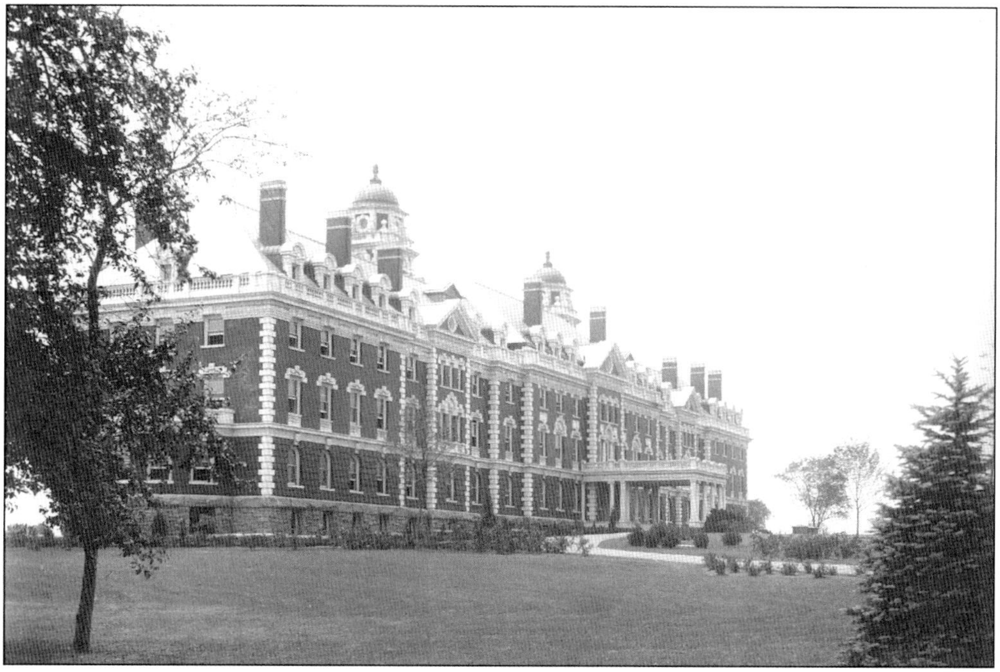

The Osborn building is a grand sight viewed from the north lawn or in the picture below from the south lawn. Although in 1908, sitting atop what appears to be a very regal Theall's Hill, it appeared very different from today's home; one cannot help but marvel at the gleaming marble pediments and the stark beauty of its Georgian-themed towers. Certainly this was the building that architect Bruce Price envisioned on this site. Although wings of comparable architectural beauty were added at later dates, the original Osborn building more than captures the dream of Miriam Osborn for a lovely home for genteel women to live out their days in comfort and safety surrounded by verdant grounds. Had she lived to see the home's completion, she would have been impressed with the building that bears her name.

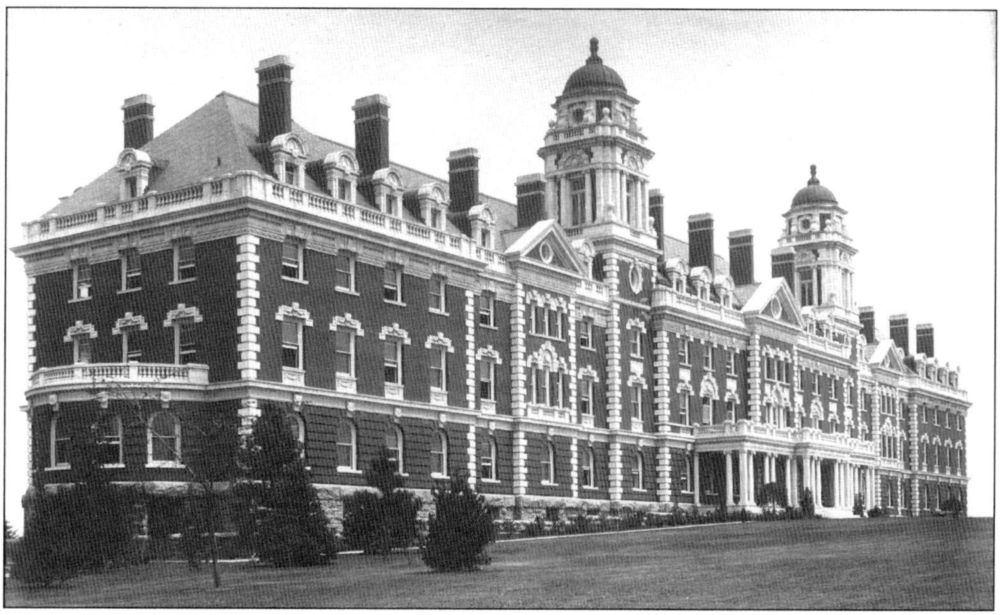

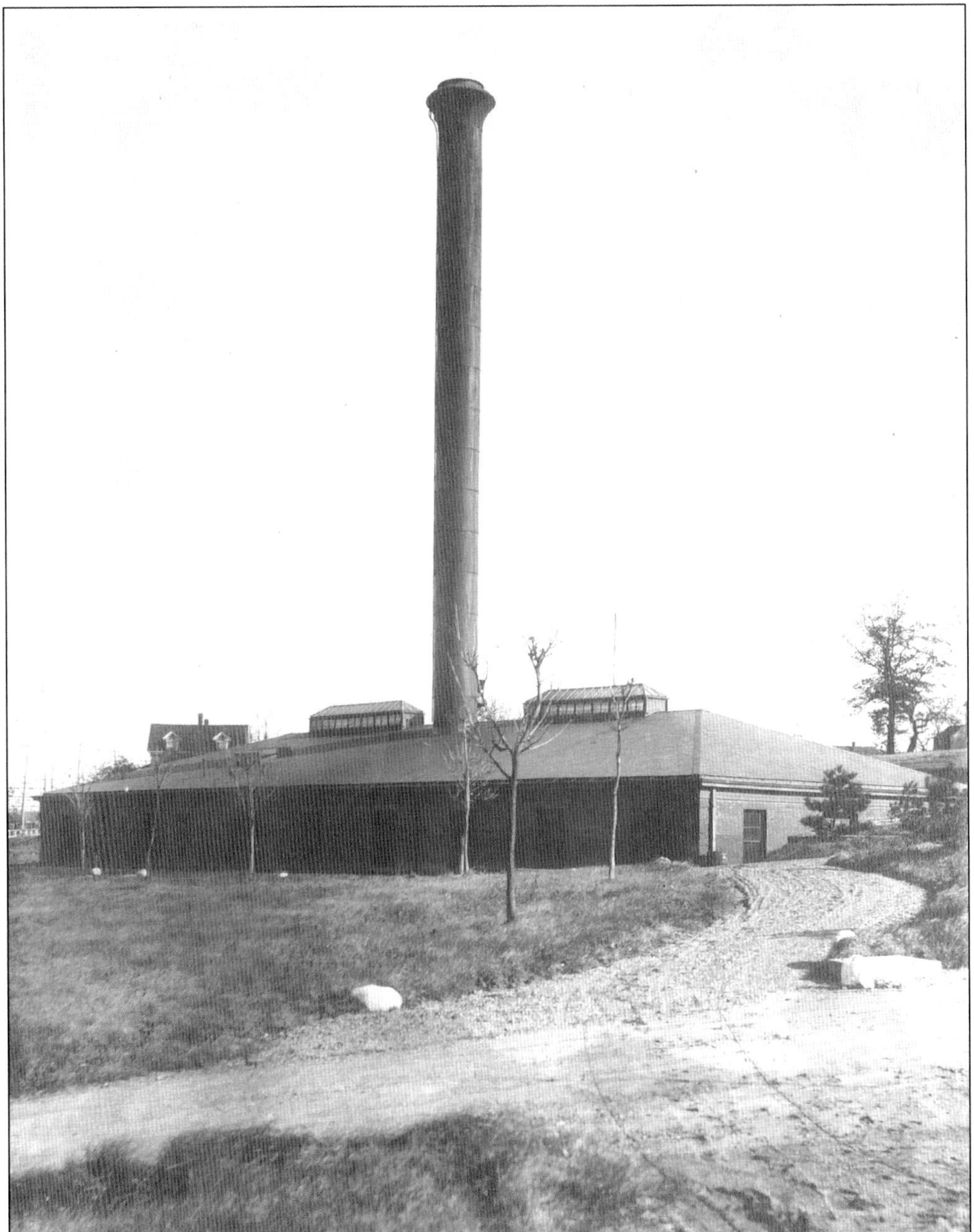

The construction of the powerhouse at the base of Theall's Hill was an advancement that John Sterling felt necessary to supply heat and electricity to the home and to keep it self-sufficient. This was the final construction project that Sterling would oversee; he passed away on July 5, 1918, while on his annual fishing trip to Canada with some of his closest friends. This annual trip was his only time away from the duties of his work at the home. In building the powerhouse, he constructed a tunnel, 16.5 feet below the surface of the ground, that ran all the way to the basement of the home. There was one small problem with the tunnel for future generations, however. The tunnel is not in a straight line but rather a sloping curve that requires all the piping to be cut to lengths necessary to make the bend in the line.

Four

The Growth Years

Prior to John Sterling's death, the wheels had been set in motion for The Osborn to expand beyond its current size. The need for an institution of its kind was realized fully once it opened its doors, so that by the 1920s the need was outstripping the supply of available accommodations. It had also become apparent to those running the facility that there was an increased need for greater nursing care than had previously been realized. Although Sterling had been toying with the idea of expansion, the creation and follow-through work fell to those whom he had chosen as board members and employees. His choices could not have been better: Helen Adams, his longtime secretary; George B. Cortelyou, board member, friend, and business associate; and John A. and Chauncey B. Garver, board members and colleagues.

Although he was gone, Sterling's presence was felt keenly in all the work that would be done from 1920 to 1940. He left the funds to endow two additional wings, one in the name of his late mother, Catherine Sterling, and the other in the name of his closest business associates and friends, Donald Alexander Smith and George Stephen. Sterling had handled much of the financing for these men as they constructed the Canadian transcontinental railway. He also applied the money left to him, $100,000 from Miriam Osborn through a holographic codicil in her will, to the building of a dining wing equipped with a new state-of-the-art kitchen.

Over the years, countless employees who played parts both large and small in the care of its residents have displayed the selfless service to The Osborn and its vision and mission, handed down from its founder, Miriam Osborn. Too numerous to mention in any chapter, it is important to note that all who have served here did their best in caring for both the residents and the home itself. It suffices to say that The Osborn would not be celebrating this milestone of 100 years without all of these individuals.

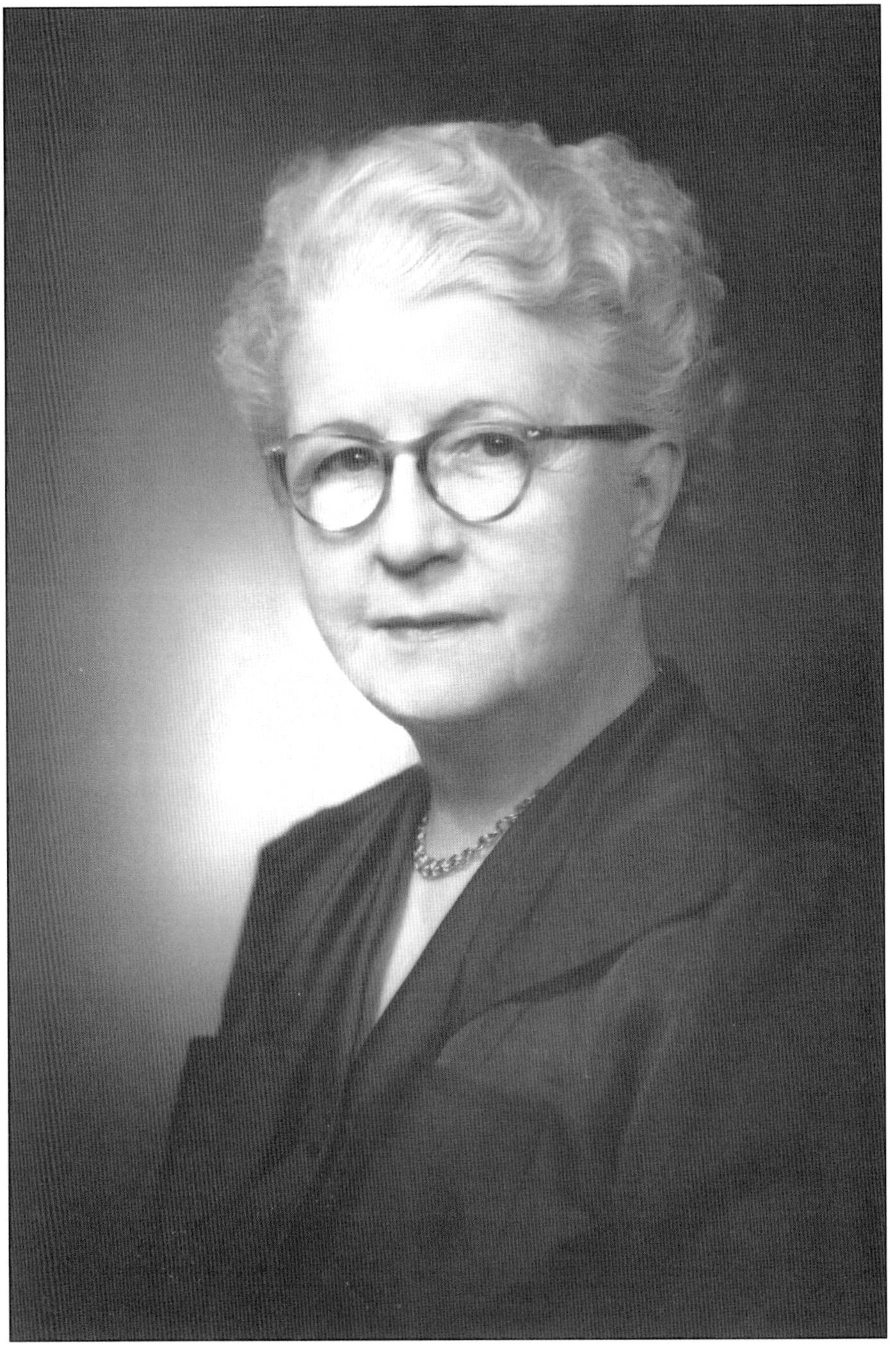

One of the true guiding angels of The Osborn Home was Helen Adams. Her association with The Osborn spans more than half a century; it is hard to say if it was luck or divine providence that she came to work for John Sterling, but it goes without saying that had she not, much of what The Osborn is about today and what is known about its history would not exist. Adams possessed a sharp mind and keen sense of purpose. She joined the accounting firm of George H. Church working primarily for the Shearman and Sterling account in 1904. At about the same time, Sterling lost his longtime personal secretary and was in need of a replacement.

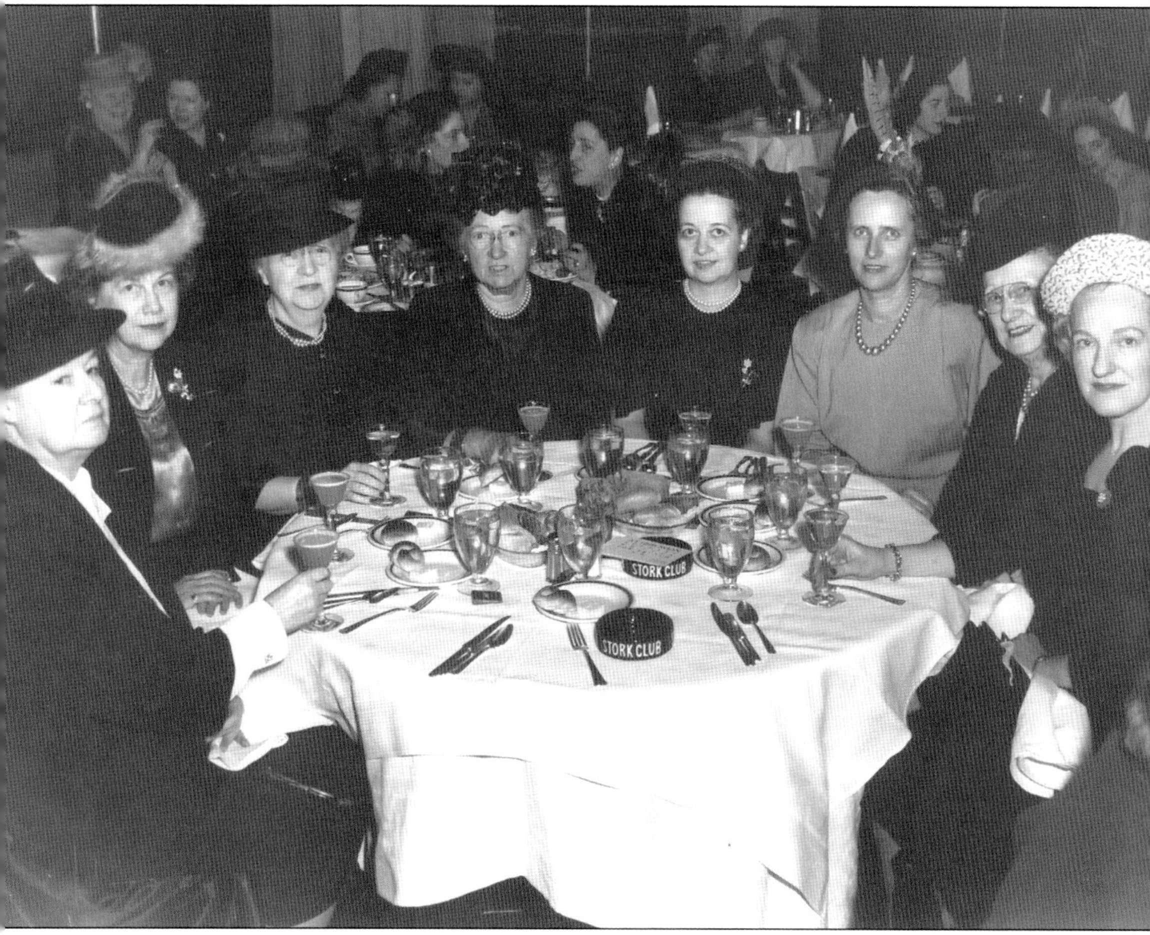

Adams's work for Sterling was related to the home and its construction and management. She served at varying times as the secretary and treasurer on the board of trustees as well as being elected a full board member in 1937. Adams also had increasing responsibilities with the operations of The Osborn. Eventually she was executive superintendent of the home. Her long service ended in May 1947. Seen here with other members of the staff and members of the board of lady managers, she is celebrating her retirement at the Stork Club in New York. Adams is seated third from the left. Although she had retired, her association with the home did not end there. She went on to become a member of The Osborn's resident family and lived out her years there. Much of what is known about the home's first 50 years is due to Adams's efforts to document them.

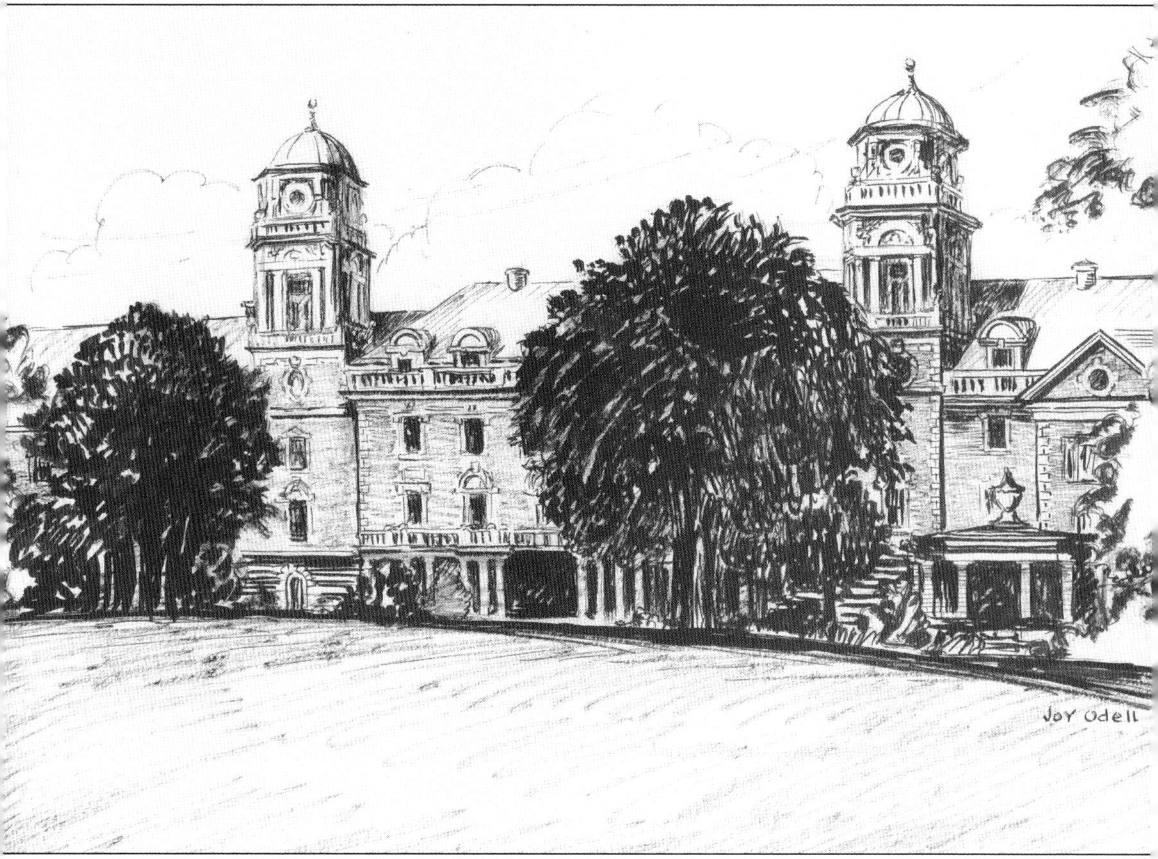

Helen Adams never sought credit for her accomplishments. At the time of her retirement, for which this drawing was created, she had overseen the design and construction of both the Strathcona and Sterling wings at The Osborn. She had also experienced two wars, as well as the difficulties of the 1929 stock market crash and subsequent depression, and their effects upon the home. Through all this, she guided the home and its residents and staff while expanding The Osborn to twice its original size as well as ushering a new era of state-of-the-art nursing care. Much of the credit for the planning and the design of the infirmary wing belongs to Adams, who recognized the need to offer ever-increasing levels of skilled nursing care to the home's residents as they aged. This was a very new phenomenon. In the 1920s, eldercare was in its infancy.

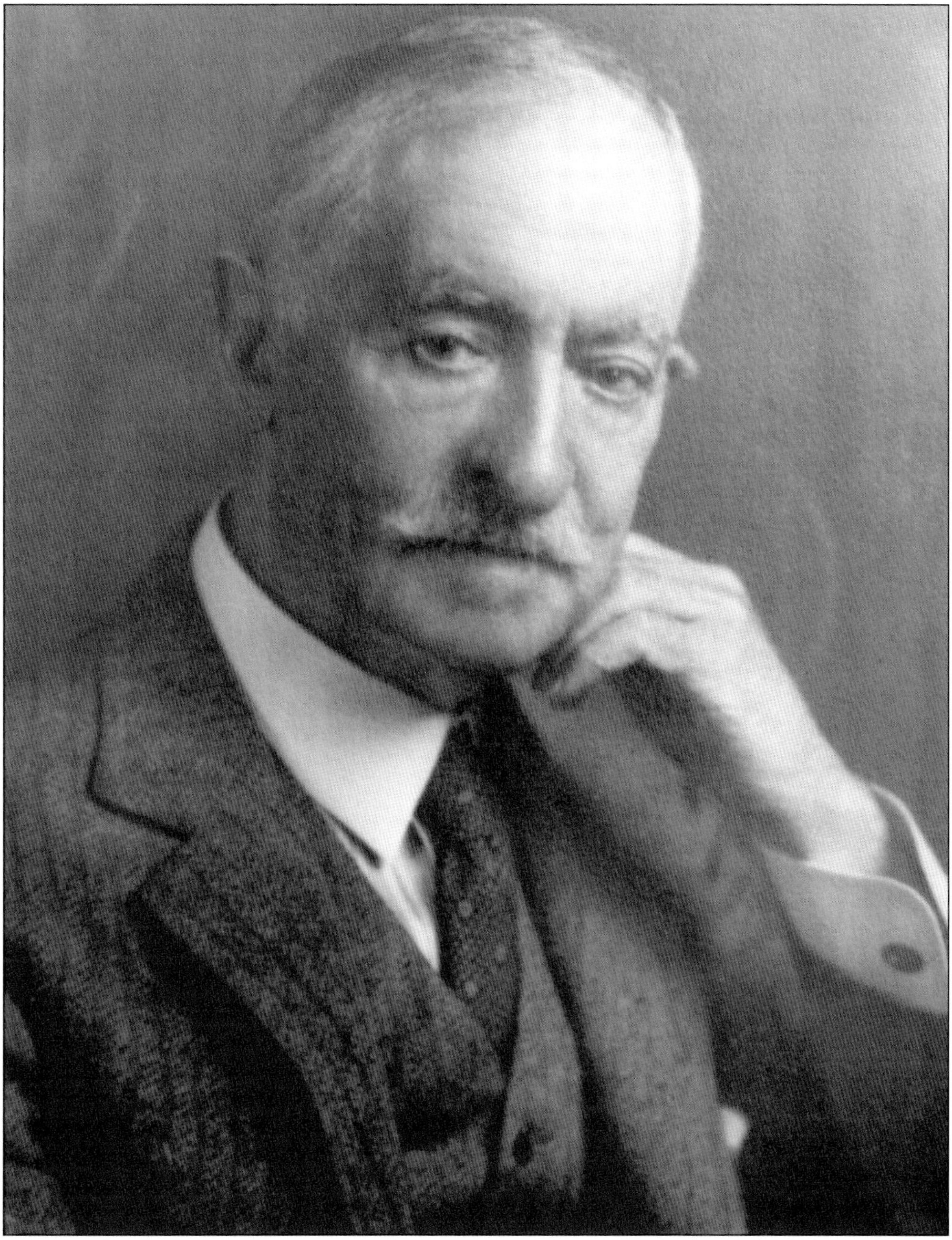

Helen Adams was not alone in her efforts to ensure the legacy of The Osborn after John Sterling's passing. A pivotal figure in the home's growth and continued existence was John A. Garver. Garver was a colleague of Sterling at the firm of Shearman and Sterling; he joined the firm as an associate in 1879 and five years later became a full member of the firm. It was his job initially to assist Thomas Shearman in court litigations, and after Shearman's passing, he became the chief litigator for the firm. Garver served many years on the board and was its vice president from 1925 to 1936. Many of the financial wizards of the day sought his sound judgment and council, and his talents led to the success of the home during a difficult period.

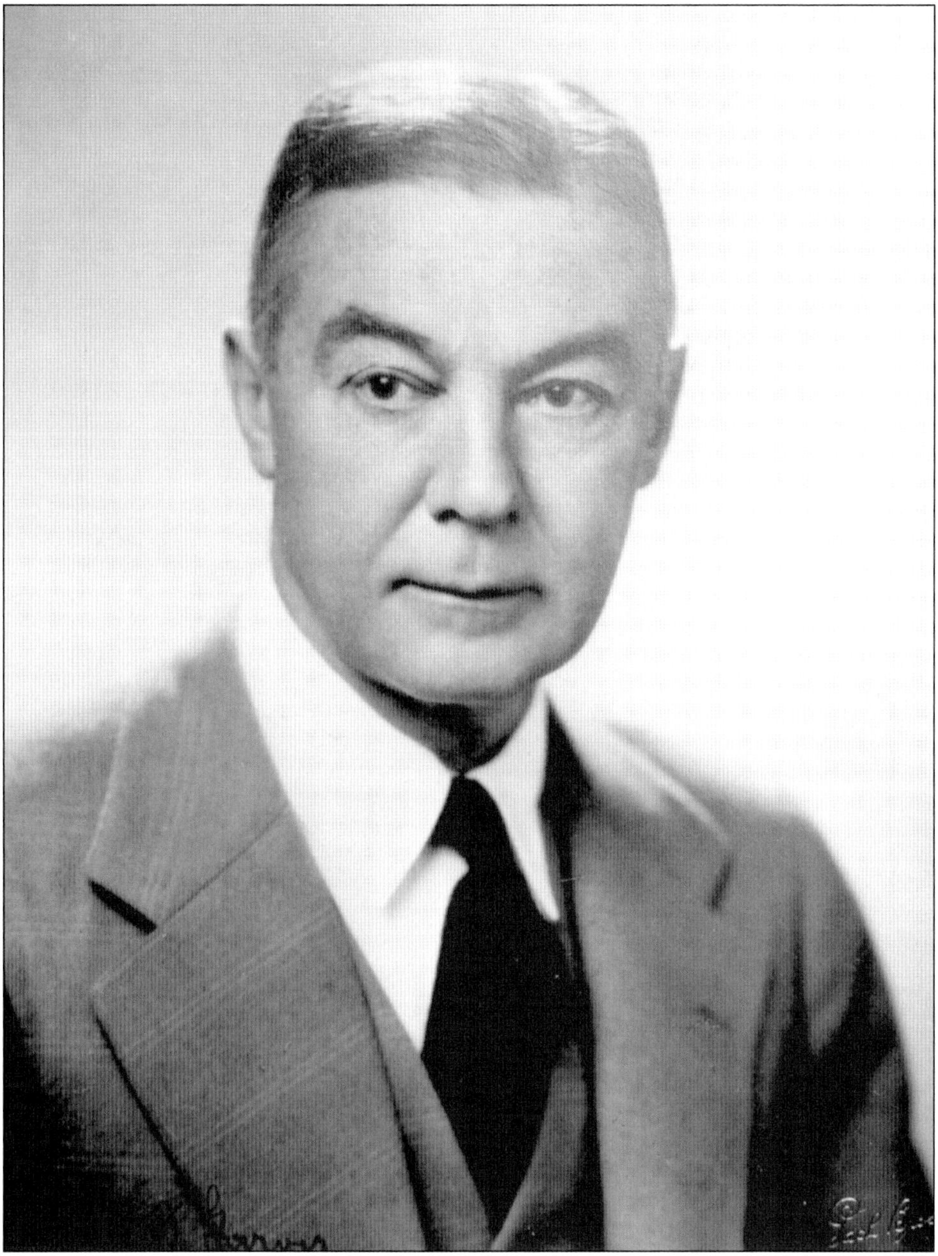

Following in his father's footsteps, Chauncey B. Garver went into law with the firm of Shearman and Sterling. Along with his distinguished law career, he also provided inestimable service to The Osborn, initially in assisting the home in its legal needs through the firm and ultimately as a board member at The Osborn. He culminated his many years of service as the board's president from 1940 to 1965. As the senior partner at Shearman and Sterling, Garver had the opportunity to alter the name of the firm to reflect his contributions and involvement, and as his father before him, he chose to maintain the firm's name as it had been. This reflects the humility of both men as well as their respect for John Sterling and Thomas Shearman. The length of Garver's service to the home spanned 35 years, and his involvement in all aspects of The Osborn is etched in its history.

George B. Cortelyou was a board member and president of the board from 1920 to 1940. Cortelyou served three successive U.S. presidents: William McKinley and Grover Cleveland as their personal secretaries, a position of great importance at the time, and Theodore Roosevelt as his personal secretary and eventually in his cabinet as the secretary of the treasury. It was in his role as secretary that he showed his proficiency when he calmed the markets after the "Panic of '07." He safely guided Roosevelt's ambitious fiscal policies to success and in doing so achieved great esteem from both Wall Street and government officials. As president of the board of The Osborn, he oversaw the doubling of the size of the home, and he built a solid foundation that would see The Osborn through its first 50 years. (Below, courtesy of Charles Penrose.)

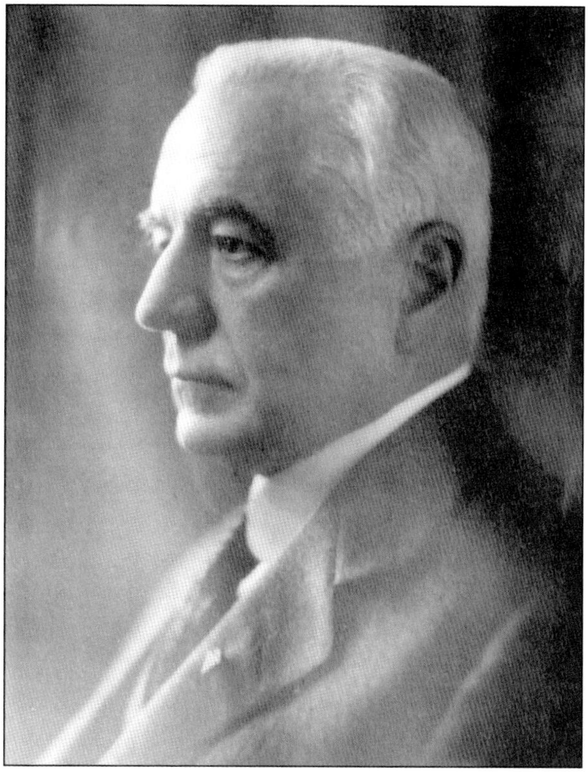

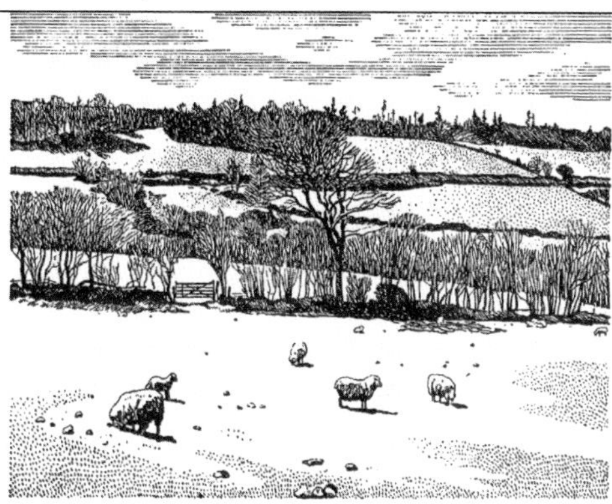

"The greatest asset of any nation is the spirit of its people, and the greatest danger that can menace any nation is the breakdown of that spirit—the will to win and the courage to work."

—George B. Cortelyou

George B. Cortelyou Dies at 78; Secretary to Three Presidents

Consolidated Gas Ex-Head Thrice Named to Cabinet by Theodore Roosevelt

Special to the Herald Tribune

HALESITE, L. I., Oct. 23.—George Bruce Cortelyou, who held three Cabinet posts under President Theodore Roosevelt and was president of the Consolidated Gas Company of New York from 1909 to 1935, died of a heart attack early today at his home here. He was seventy-eight years old. Mr. Cortelyou suffered a slight heart attack last week. He was found dead in bed at 6 a. m. today.

Surviving are his wife, the former Miss Lily Morris Hinds, whom he married on Sept. 15, 1888; three sons, William W., Peter C. and George B. Cortelyou jr., and a daughter, Mrs. Jacob F. Wintz. Funeral services will be held at 2:30 p. m. Friday in St. John's Protestant Episcopal Church, Huntington, L. I.

Mr. Cortelyou had served in a personal secretarial capacity to three Presidents. He was a stenographer and executive clerk to Grover Cleveland in his second administration and assistant secretary and secretary to President McKinley and President Theodore Roosevelt.

President Roosevelt created the Department of Commerce and Labor, in 1903 and on Feb. 16 appointed Mr. Cortelyou secretary of the department, a new Cabinet post. He held the place until July 1, 1904.

When Mr. Roosevelt was renominated by the Republicans in 1904, Mr. Cortelyou resigned from the Cabinet to become chairman of the Republican National Committee, succeeding Mark Hanna, to manage the campaign. He held the post for three years.

After Mr. Roosevelt's re-election Mr. Cortelyou was appointed Postmaster General and remained in that place until March 4, 1907, when he was appointed Secretary of the Treasury. He held that office until March 8, 1909, just after the inauguration of President Taft. Then he was chosen president of the Consolidated Gas Company.

Showed Ability in Crises

As secretary to President McKinley, Mr. Cortelyou was standing by the President at Buffalo when he was shot on Sept. 16, 1901. His handling of arrangements for the President's care when others lost their heads and the able way in which he shouldered responsibilities in the eight days before the President died, brought widespread attention. A few years later, during another national crisis, his ability again came to the fore. He was Secretary of the Treasury during the panic of 1907, and his careful engineering brought the country through without disaster.

A descendant of an old and well-to-do family, Mr. Cortelyou was born in New York on July 26, 1862, the son of Peter C. and Rose Seary Cortelyou. He attended the Hempstead Institute, Hempstead, L. I., and the State Normal School at Westfield, Mass. He studied music, intending to become a teacher and taught for a while in positions obtained for him by Professor Ephraim Hinds, principal of the Hempstead Institute, whose daughter he later married.

While he was teaching, he studied stenography and became so proficient that he decided to make it his profession. He defeated thirty candidates in a competitive examination for a stenographer's job in the office of the Federal Appraiser in New York. In 1885 he entered a partnership with James E. Munson, originator of the Munson system, as general law and verbatim reporter, but after four years re-entered the government service as confidential secretary to the postoffice inspector in charge of New York, and subsequently went to Washington, where he became successively private secretary to the Fourth Assistant Postmaster General, acting chief clerk and Acting Fourth Assistant Postmaster General.

When Grover Cleveland was re-elected in 1892, Mr. Cortelyou prepared to leave Washington with the other Republicans, but Robert A. Maxwell, the new Fourth Assistant Postmaster General, asked him to remain and presently recommended him to the President, who wanted a stenographer. He got the place. It was the turning point in his career.

He remained attached to the White House staff for eleven years, when he was appointed to the Cabinet. As secretary to President McKinley he was regarded as virtually a Cabinet member and did much of the office work during the war with Spain. He also found time to acquire a law degree at Georgetown University in 1895.

Mentioned for Presidency

When he resigned from the Cabinet in 1909 to become president of the Consolidated Gas Company, he had been offered many other positions, among them the presidencies of the Union Trust Company and the Knickerbocker Trust Company. His name had even been mentioned for the Republican nomination for President until Mr. Taft's evident popularity brought Mr. Cortelyou's retirement from the field.

As president of the Consolidated Gas Company he saw that concern expand in size from total assets of $332,324,856 in 1909 to more than $1,300,000,000 in 1934. In 1927 the largest stock financing ever undertaken by a gass or electric company was transacted by the Consolidated under Mr. Cortelyou's guidance.

While he was president of the company, the Edison building, with its graceful tower and artistic lights, was built at Fourteenth Street and Irving Place, on the site of the old Academy of Music. His love for music, which in the early days had made him seek a musical career, was still active at this time, and he arranged for the last performance in the historic building. Despite his widespread interests and heavy duties he found time to keep up with his music all his life and was an accomplished amateur pianist.

Mr. Cortelyou was spokesman for a nation-wide group of public utilities interests representing investments of $17,500,000,000 in fighting government ownership of the industry. He was a bitter opponent of government operation of public utilities, believing it unfair to shut off private enterprise, and at the same time doubting the efficiency of the political machinery of government in conducting a business of that kind.

He resigned from the Consolidated Gas Company in 1935. He was a director of the New York Life Insurance Company and of D. Appleton-Century Company, honorary president of the McKinley National Memorial Association, president of the Miriam Osborn Memorial Home Association and a member of the Merchants' Association of New York, the Metropolitan Museum of Art, the Holland Society and the Navy League. He became chairman of the board of sponsors of the Greater New York Safety Council last year.

Mr. Cortelyou was the only man to become president of both the American Gas Association and the National Electric Light Association.

On hearing of Mr. Cortelyou's death yesterday, Floyd L. Carlisle, chairman of the board of the Consolidated Edison Company, said that he was a "valuable and valued public servant, no less in the field of American business than in the distinguished public offices which he filled so ably."

George B. Cortelyou died on October 23, 1940. The following is a quote from the dedication speech made by Cortelyou at the laying of the cornerstone for the Strathcona wing of The Osborn: "May this Home with its further facilities of this beautiful new building with whatever may be added to this structure or equipment in the future, endure through the years, responsive always to its beneficent purpose—a memorial of the firm foundations that rest upon such abiding friendships."

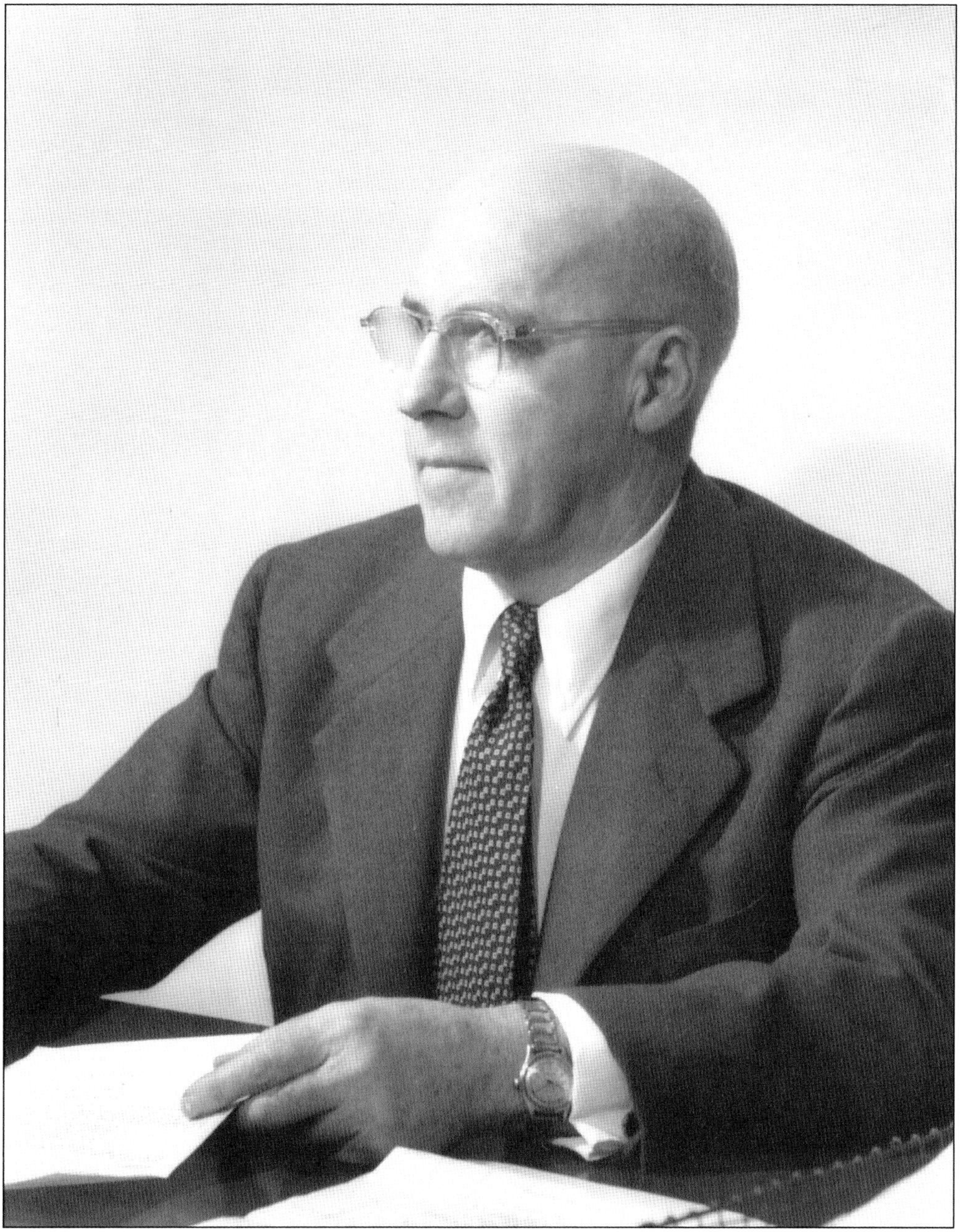

During the early years of growth in the 1930s, Otto K. Redgate was the one man relied upon to make certain that the construction of the new wings went as planned. He was hired in 1929 from Pasadena, California, where he was the plant superintendent for the Institute of Technology. There he held the license of a master plumber. All his skills were needed in the coming years as the board and Helen Adams planned significant growth as a result of the estate left by John Sterling and the plan to upgrade the existing building, bringing it up to standards of the day. Redgate's steadfast approach to his responsibilities never overshadowed his concern for the residents, making certain they were disturbed as little as possible by the tumult going on around them.

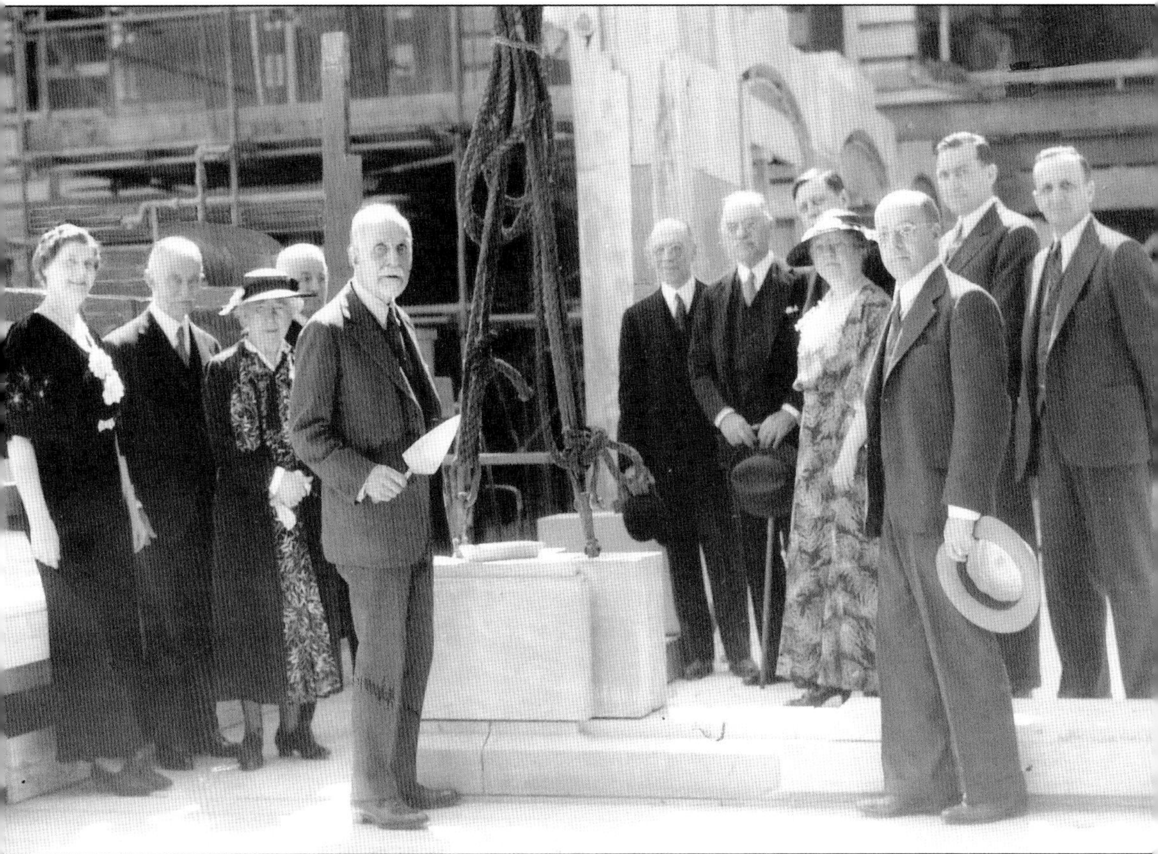

In this group photograph, many of the people who have been previously mentioned come together for the laying of the cornerstone of the Sterling wing. George H. Church, the longtime treasurer for the board of trustees of The Osborn, is handling the trowel. Two of the ladies present are Helen Adams (behind Church) and Laura Jones, the home's superintendent (right). Their attendance along with John A. Garver, George B. Cortelyou, James Gamble Rogers (architect), Otto K. Redgate, and R. Eugene Curry makes for a who's who of the early years of The Osborn. Each of these individuals had the spirit to do good works and carry on the mission of Miriam Osborn and John Sterling.

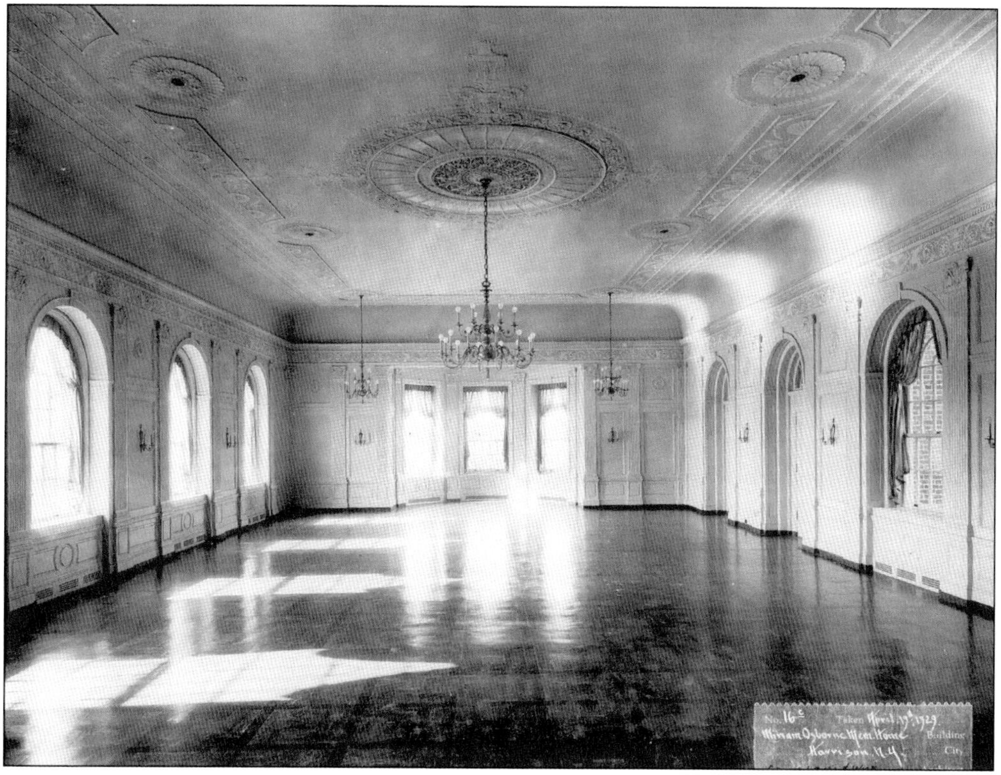

Prior to the construction of the Strathcona wing, it was decided that there was a pressing need to increase the scope of the dining program. If the population was going to expand, it would need a dining pavilion larger than currently existed. Sterling set forth in his will that the monies left to him by Miriam Osborn in the codicil of her will go to some special purpose of the home. The board felt this was the perfect purpose for this money. The ceilings that were designed with beautiful Wedgwood relief plaster and ornate dental crown molding provide an aura of elegance befitting The Osborn and its residents.

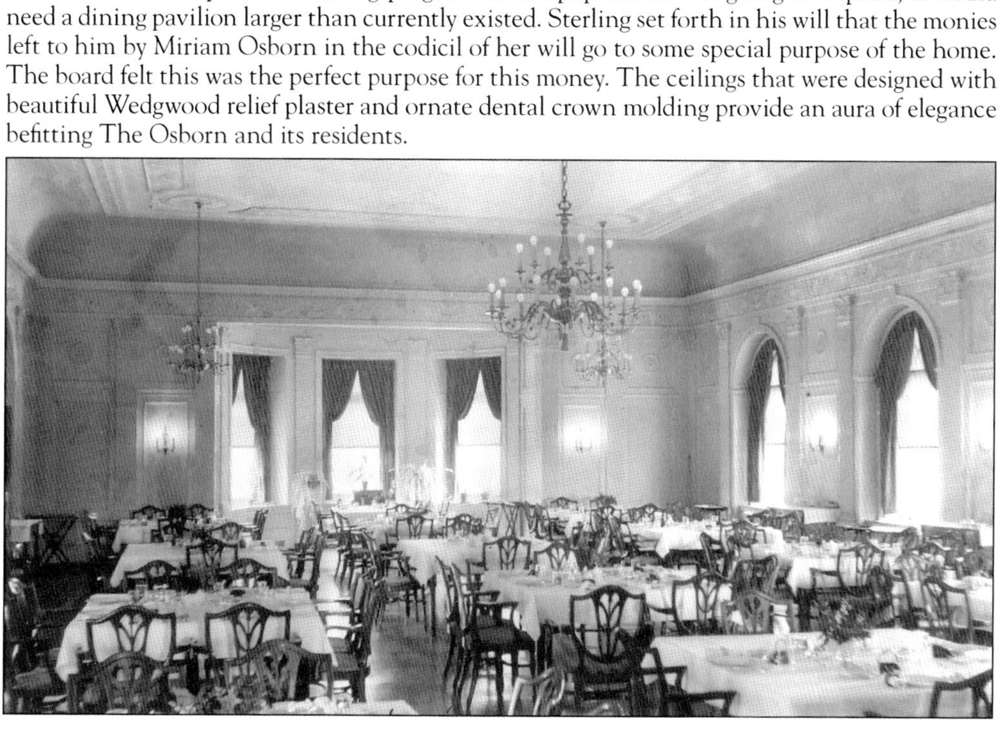

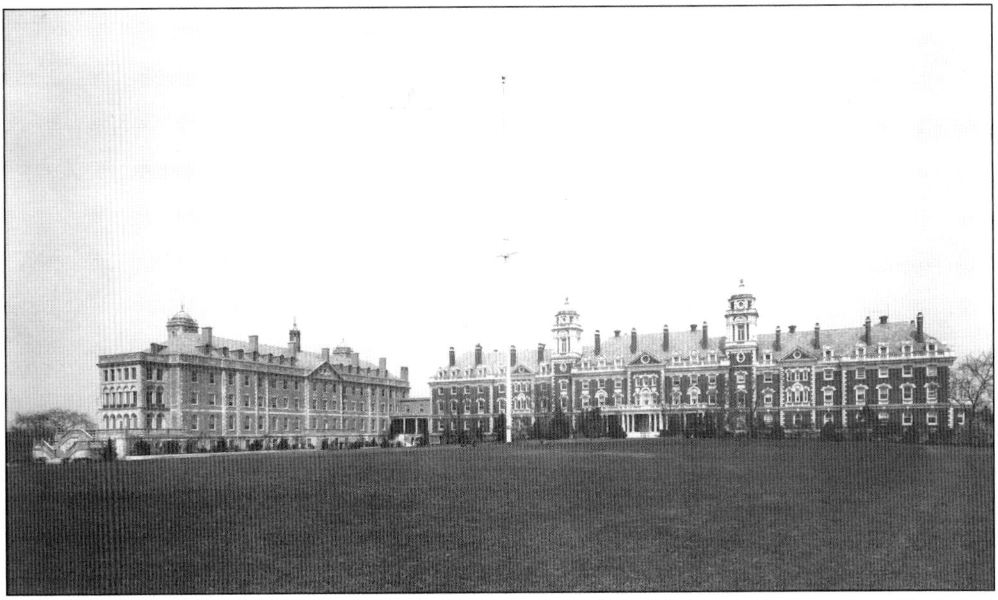

After John Sterling began devising plans for additional buildings on the campus, he engaged the firm McKim, Mead and White to supply plans for this proposal. The ideas he received ranged from a nine-story tower to outbuildings connected by tunnels or covered breezeways. None was deemed possible, and plans were temporarily shelved. After Sterling's estate was probated and the monies for additional buildings were available, the board decided it was time for the expansion. Helen Adams, then thoroughly involved in the home's operations, felt the need for an infirmary wing outweighed all other considerations. After much thought, the firm of Crow, Lewis and Wick was chosen to design the new Mount Stephen-Strathcona Infirmary wing. It contained 64 individual patient rooms, hospital-style support services, and three bright sunporches. Additional staff housing was included on the ground floor.

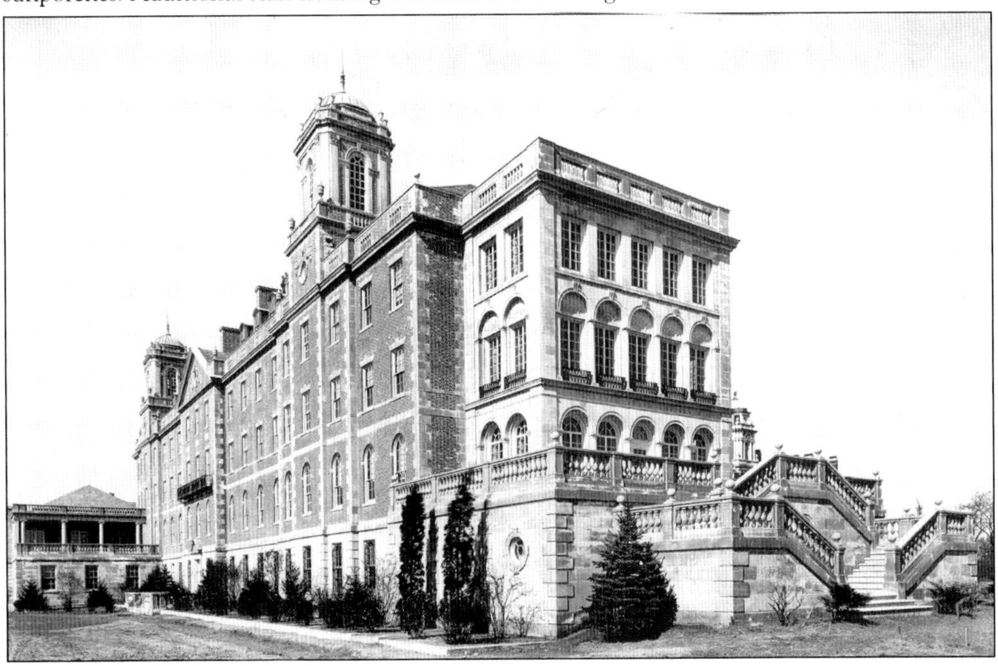

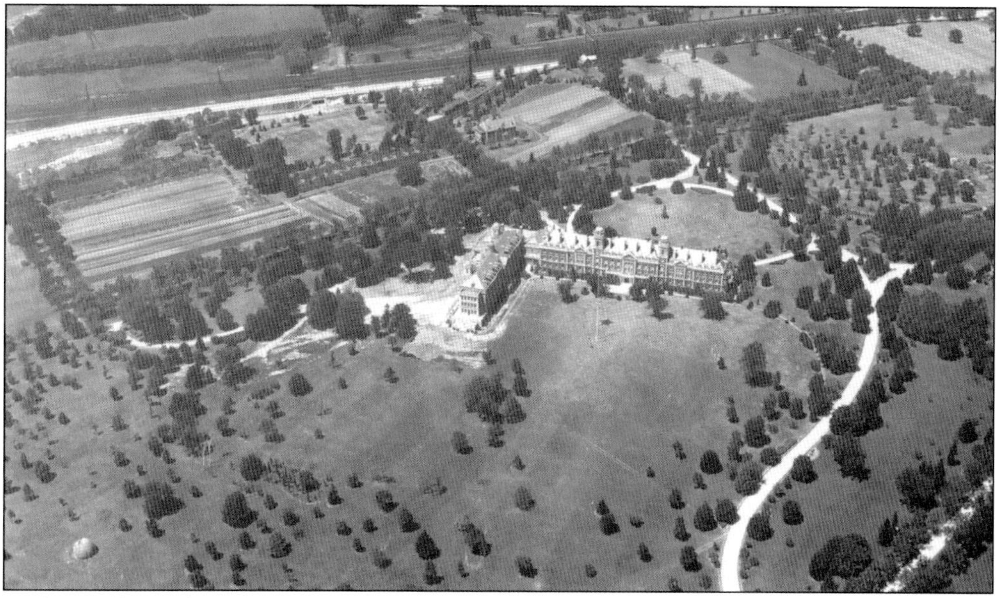

In his will, Sterling left instructions that one of the additional buildings, to be called Strathcona, was to be dedicated to his lifelong friends George Stephen (Lord Mount Stephen) and Donald Alexander Smith (Lord Strathcona) and to each of their wives, and to Smith's mother. The long and productive friendship and business relationship between these men was a result of Sterling handling much of the legal work and capital-raising endeavors in the United States for the construction of the transcontinental Canadian railway. Buoyed by their success at having completed the construction of the Strathcona wing and dining pavilions in 1929, Helen Adams and the board of trustees now turned their attentions to completing Sterling's second bequeathal, the wing to be named for his mother, Catherine Tomlinson Plant Sterling, as seen below.

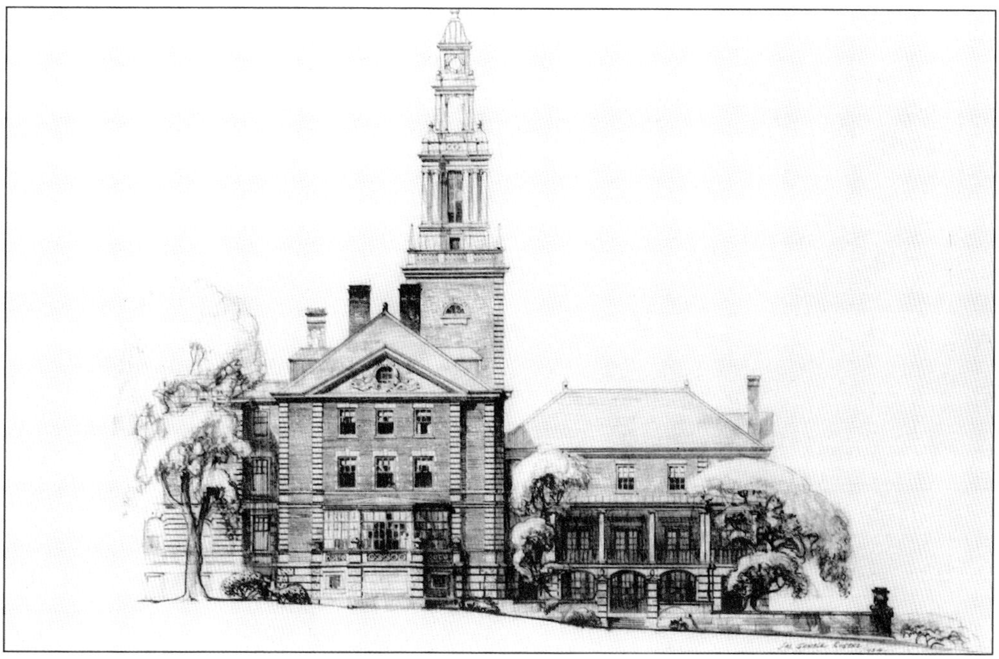

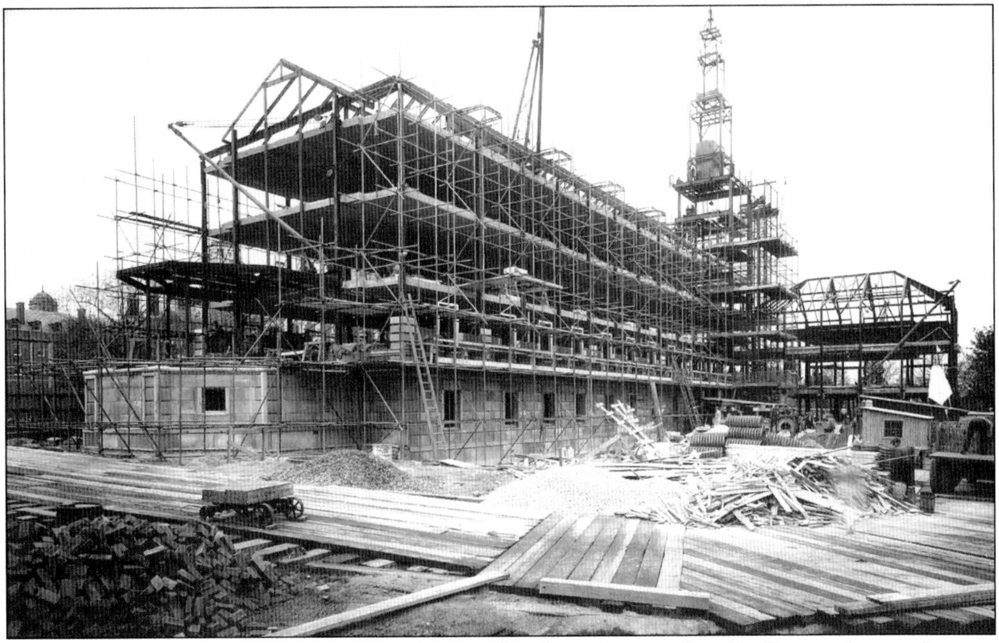

The Sterling Building was designed by the noted architect James Gamble Rogers. In its selection process, the board chose very wisely. Had John Sterling lived long enough to select the design for the wing to bear his mother's name, it most probably would have looked as it does in the rendering by the architect James Gamble Rogers. Rogers, unlike the main building's architect, Bruce Price, had a significant fine arts background, graduating from Yale University and the École des Beaux-Arts in Paris in 1899. His style can best be described as neoclassical revival. For the Sterling wing, he envisioned a Colonial church and spire with the solarium serving as an attached chapel. The building was planned for 60 new residents and provisions were made for an auditorium and lounge for entertaining.

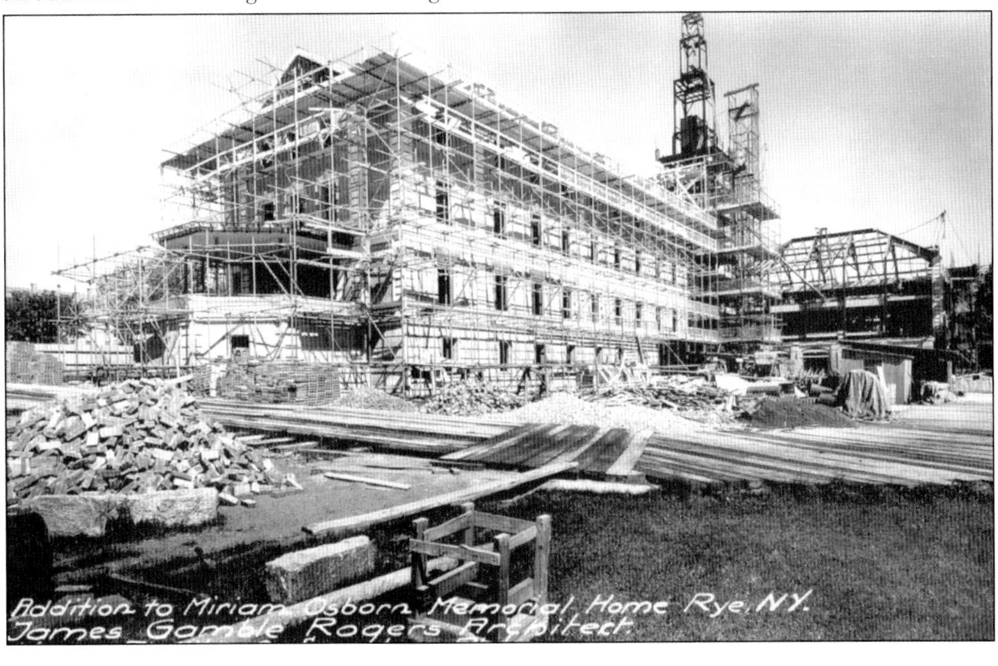

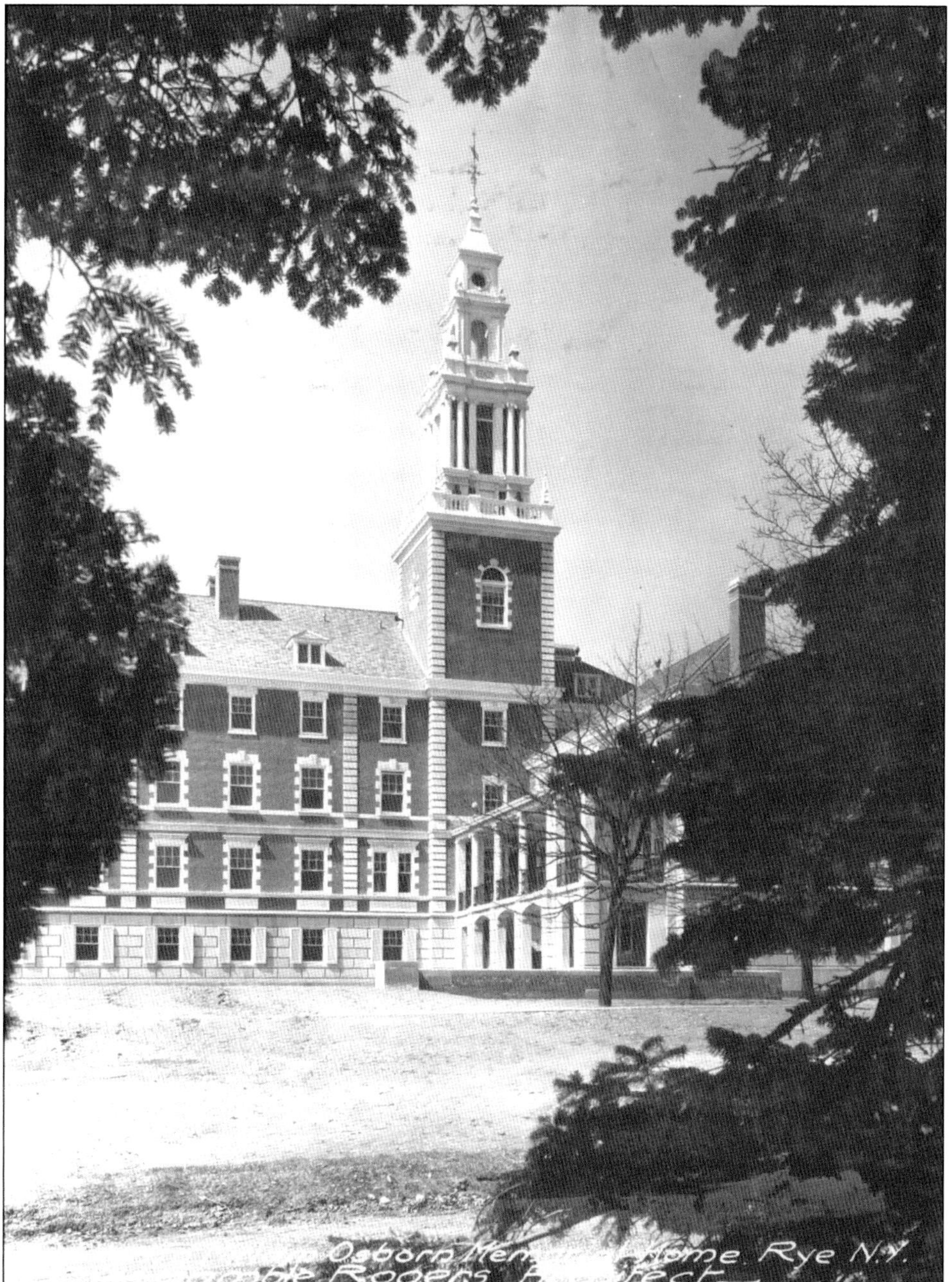

The spire of the Sterling wing, the work of the architect James Gamble Rogers, has stood as a beacon on Rye's highest point for 70 years. The Sterling wing was dedicated to Sterling's mother, Catherine, on May 18, 1938, with a total cost of construction and furnishings to that point of $709,797. All felt this was money well spent, and with all the new spaces for entertainment, in the words of Helen Adams, "the family became quite gay." Also, 23 staff rooms were added in the lodge building across Theall Road. This continued The Osborn's tradition of offering its employees the best in possible accommodations as an added benefit to their employment at the home.

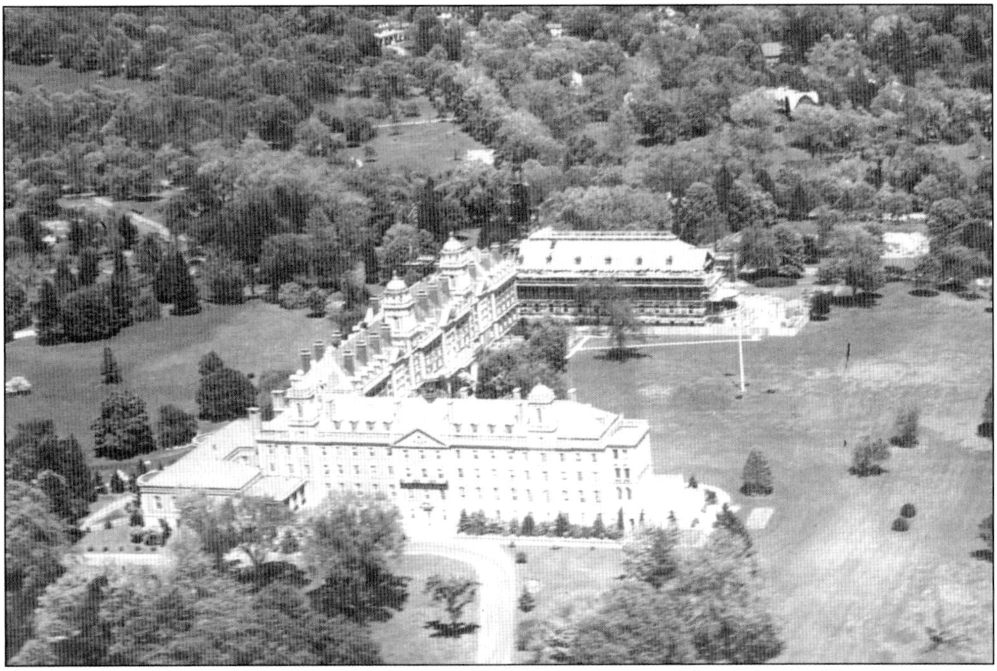

The buildings and grounds of today have a different appearance from these photographs. The 21 chimneys on the original building were removed because they leaked into the roof. Similar chimneys, which were built on the Strathcona wing for ornamental purposes, leaked from the time the building opened and were removed. The only chimneys that remain today exist on the Sterling wing. In the aerial photograph, in the upper left-hand corner, there is a road heading northeast. This road constitutes the main entrance to the home at the time. This too is no longer in existence. Much has changed since these buildings were completed, yet much has stayed the same, not the least of which is Miriam Osborn's original vision of "a home for genteel women in difficult circumstances."

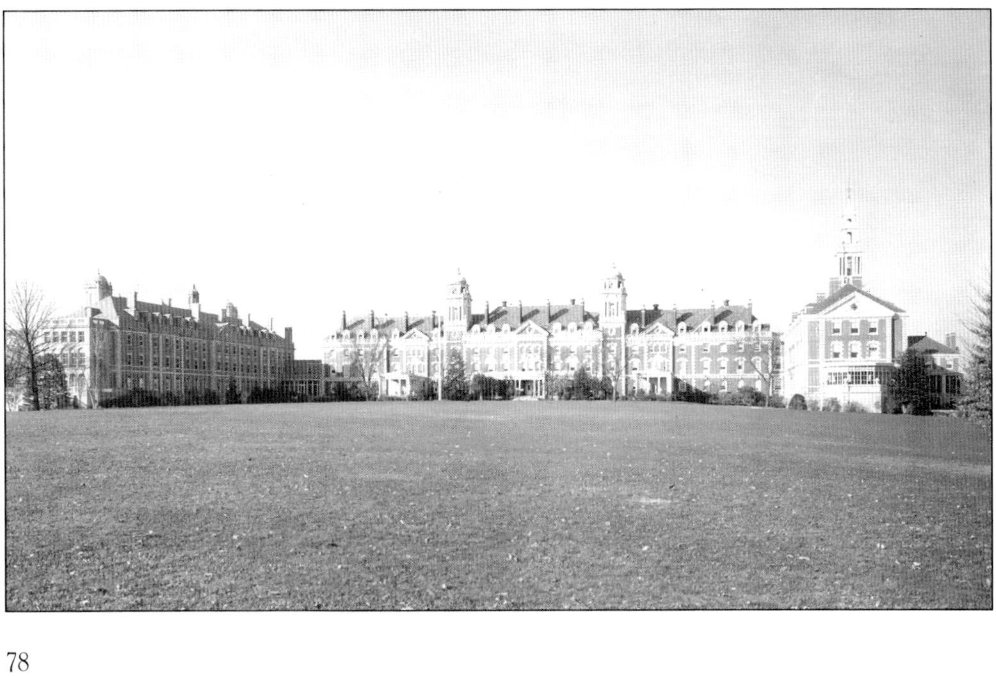

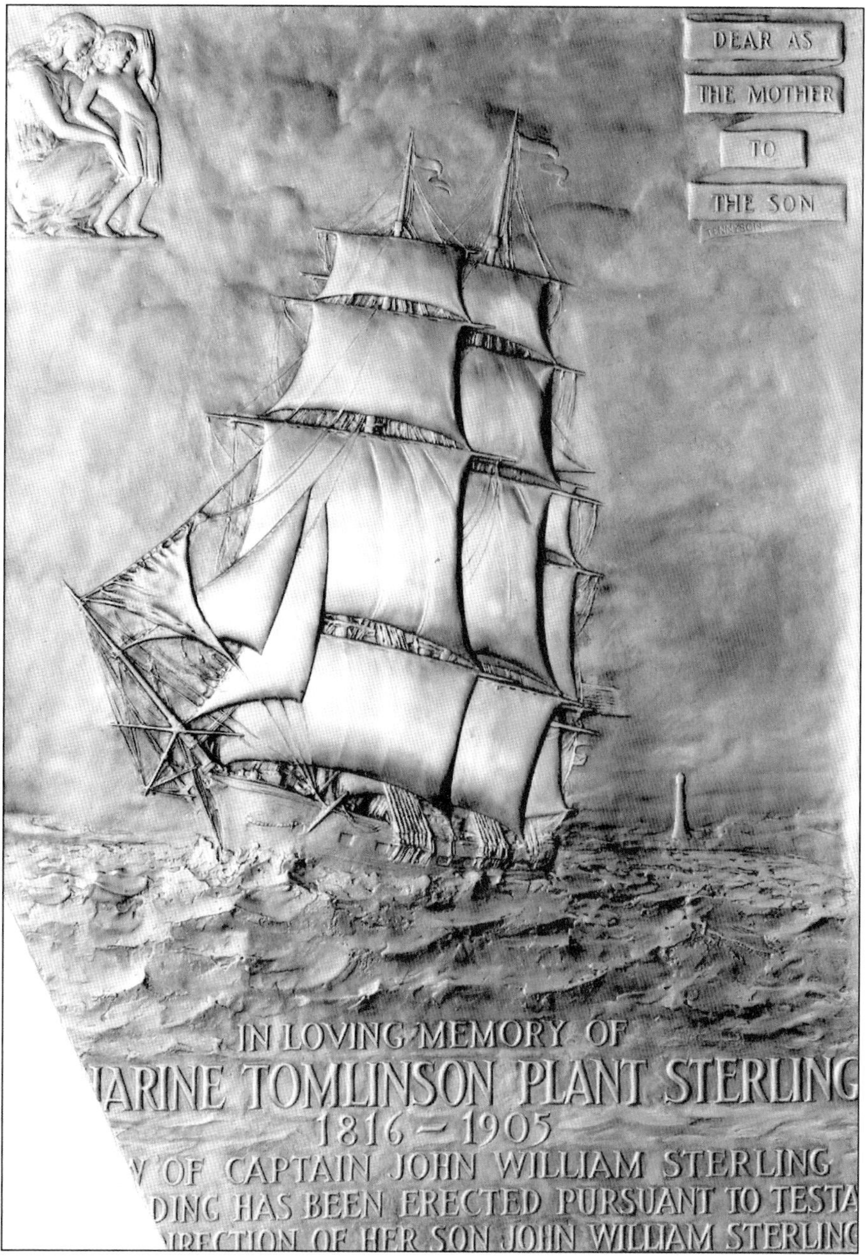

This plaque proudly hangs in the lounge of the Sterling wing just outside the auditorium. It commemorates John Sterling's wish to have the wing named and dedicated to his mother, to whom he was very close. Portraits of Catherine and John Sterling also hang in the lounge, creating the feel of a family home, which The Osborn has always maintained. The plaque was commissioned by architect James Gamble Rogers and created by the sculptor Rene P. Chambellan, who counts among his many works the sculpture of Atlas holding the world on his shoulders that was commissioned for Rockefeller Center. How John Sterling felt about his mother can be summed up best by his niece, who spoke at the dedication ceremony and said of Catherine Sterling, "One could always trust grandmother to understand. She asked so little, she gave so much."

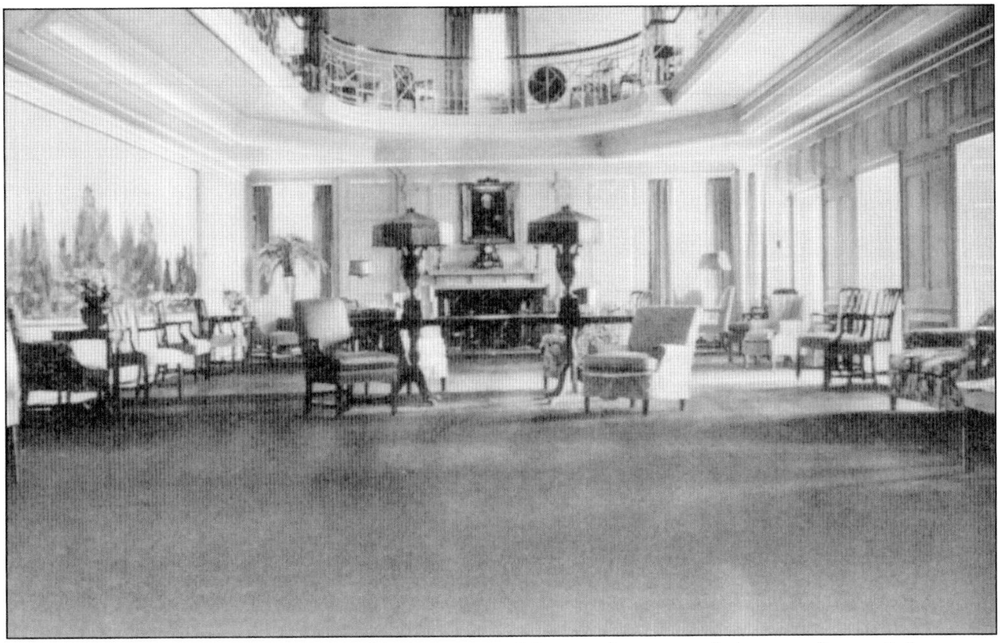

The interest shown by James Gamble Rogers and his application of the neoclassical design to the exterior also carried over to the interiors with barrel-vaulted ceilings, interior balconies, and a sweeping grand staircase to the mezzanine level. Rogers was assisted ably by Rene Chastel of J. H. Thorpe and Company of New York, whom James Gamble Rogers regarded as an expert in interior design in the matter of colors and fabrics. Although the furnishings have changed many times over the years, the public spaces retain the style and grace that Rogers had intended as a reflection of the woman for whom the building is named.

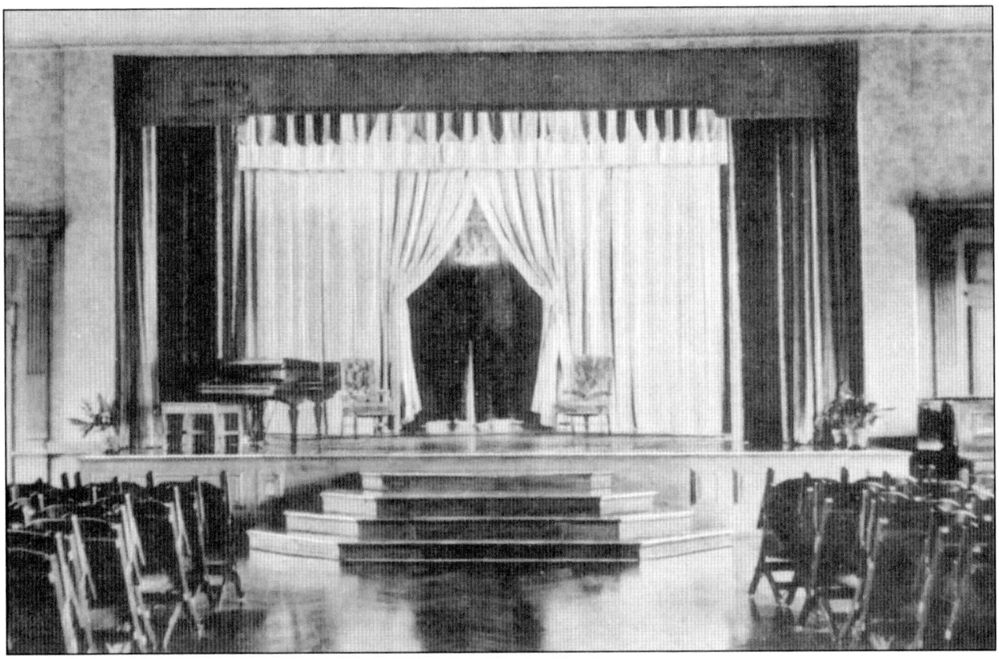

Managers understood that the happiness of the residents was only ensured by the quality and happiness of the line staff. Staff satisfaction was the hallmark of the two men who served as director, each for many years, R. Eugene Curry (right), following Helen Adams from 1948 to 1970, and Harold O. Mawhiney (left) from 1970 to 1988. Many parties were held on the grounds for the sole benefit of the people who work here. In the 1950s Christmas party photograph below, the hallways are literally alive with dancing and celebration. Although The Osborn has outgrown its ability to celebrate in this fashion, today many of the same traditions continue, with annual picnics to Rye's Playland Park and a return to the staff Christmas party on campus. Included in The Osborn's current mission is the goal to maintain staff satisfaction.

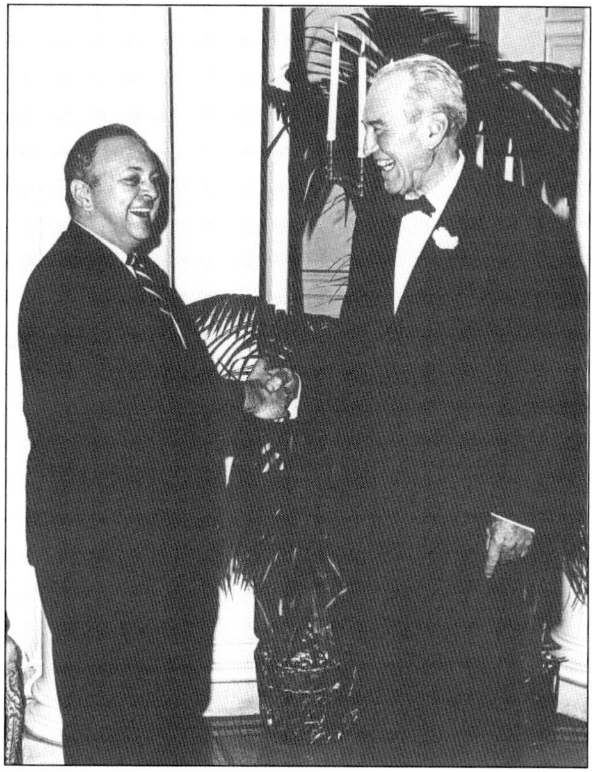

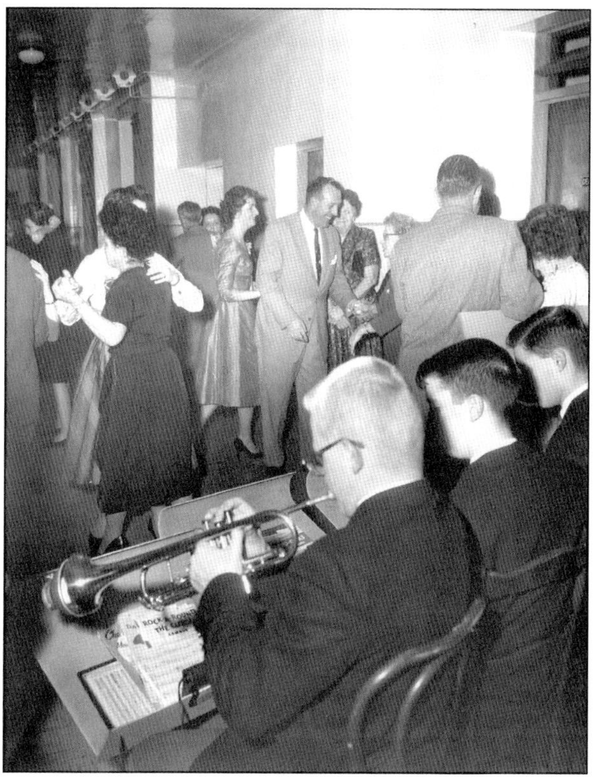

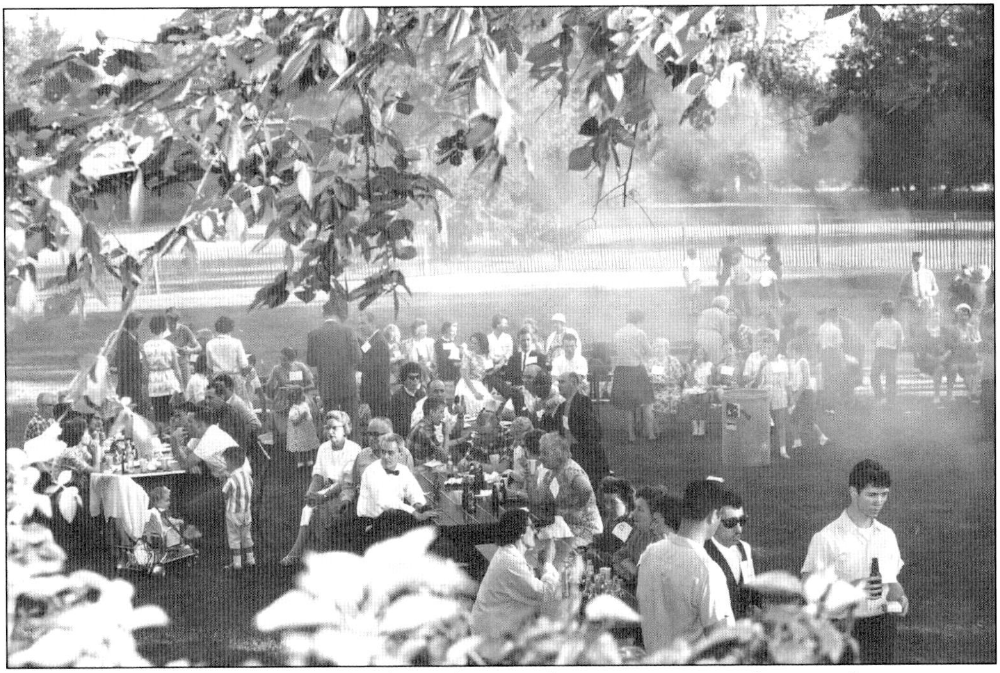

The south lawn of The Osborn has been the site of numerous events, from resident parties to the lawn concerts of today. The bucolic setting on which John Sterling erected a scaffolding more than a century ago in order to plan the building and grounds was a stroke of genius. It is hard to believe today that the lawn on which staff softball games were held and resident croquet is played was nothing more than a farmer's field at one time. Through the vision and determination of one man, so much happiness has come to so many. Residents who have looked out each morning and seen glorious sunrises and staff members who have had the opportunity to walk the pathways for exercise and relaxation owe a debt of gratitude to Sterling and all those who followed his lead.

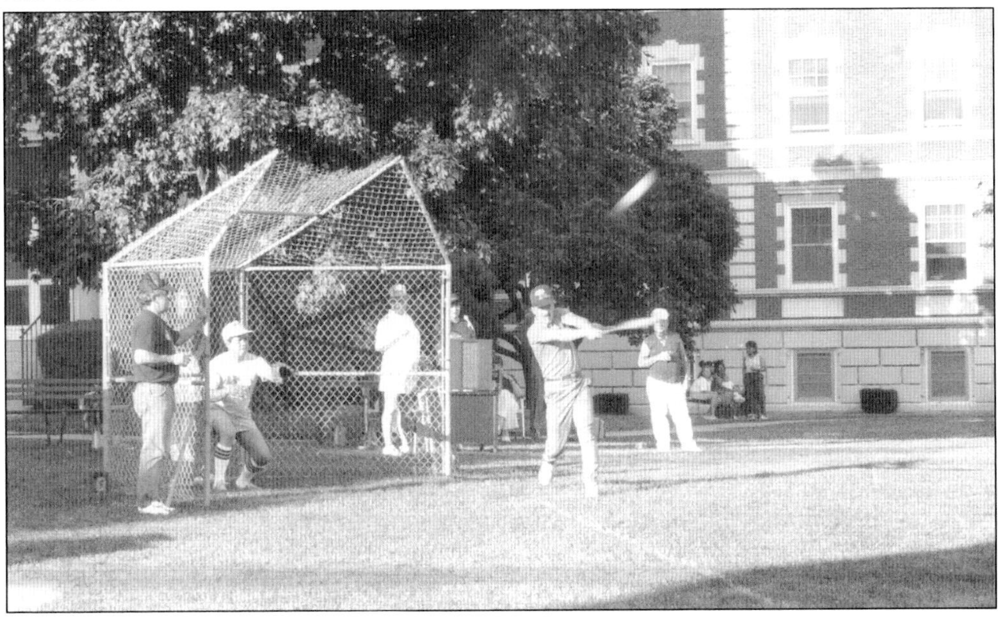

Five

Life at The Osborn

Imagine 100 years ago, 1908. Mother's Day was observed for the first time. Women competed in the Olympics for the first time, yet did not have the right to vote. The first person died in an airplane, flown by Orville Wright, and the Ford Model T was introduced. Since 1908, life at The Osborn has been lived in keeping with the times. When the home opened, each beneficiary had her own room, but the rooms lacked running water. The home generated its own electricity until December 18, 1926, when the Westchester Lighting Company installed new wiring to deliver alternating current. The home operated a dairy until August 1930 when the herd tested positive for tuberculosis. The home sold the site of the dairy in 1941. In time, new buildings were added, technology brought conveniences, and knowledge of disease and disability improved the care residents received. There were two world wars and a financial panic during its first 50 years. Yet from April 15, 1908, when the first 12 residents arrived until today, there has been an unwavering dedication to the well-being of those who call The Osborn home.

About 1927, Helen Adams and Laura Jones represented The Osborn at the new Welfare Council of New York City. They learned there were only 78 homes for the aged within 50 miles of New York City while the number of aged invalids was increasing. They shared information with colleagues hoping to improve the conditions for this population. By sharing information, they discovered caring for an individual at The Osborn cost more than at other institutions. To explain the greater costs, they offered that they needed cars in the country, the grounds were large, and they gave better care and food to their residents. Adams wrote in her papers, "The Osborn Home felt bound to give its ladies the comfortable living they needed for contentment in line with their previous standards of living, so long as we had the means to do it. Under all these conditions, it seemed that comparisons were useless." Commitment to quality services remains the hallmark of The Osborn.

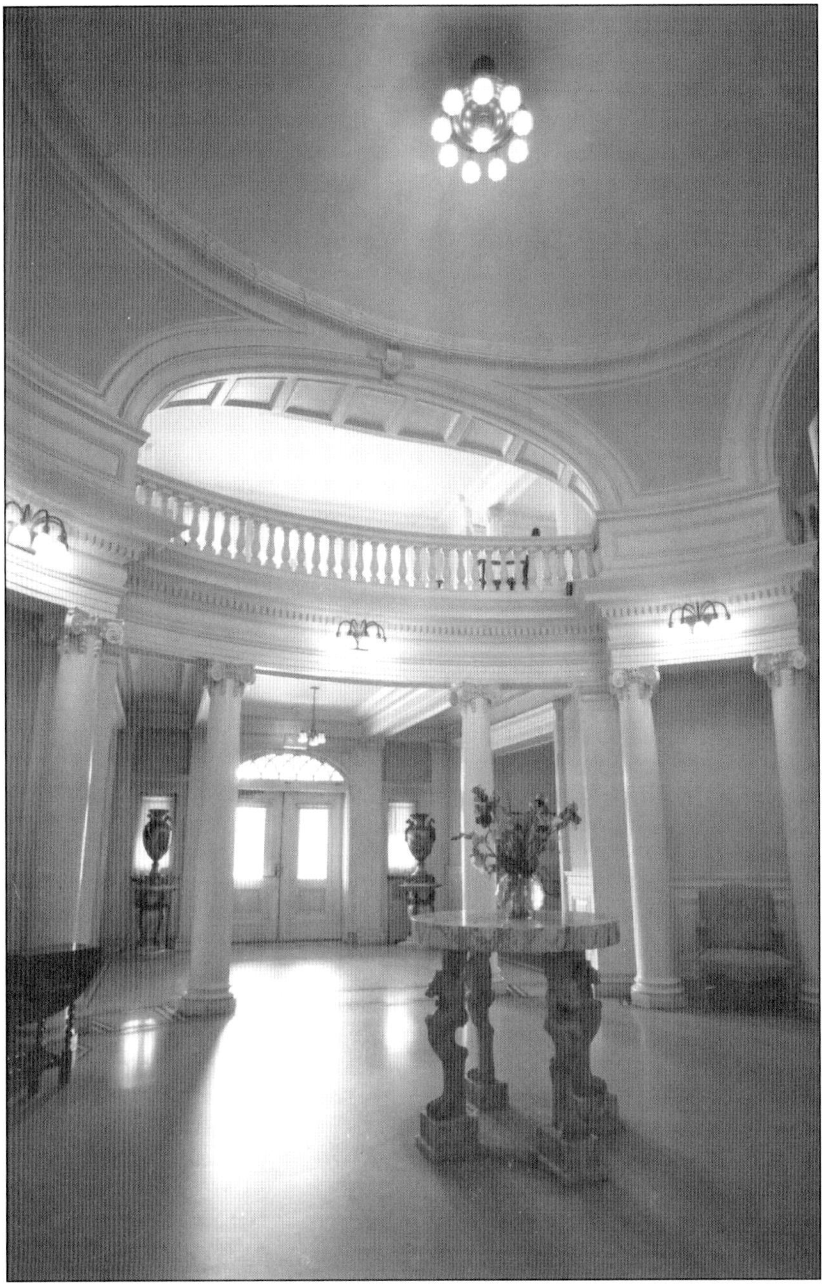

The rotunda of The Osborn building is the portal through which residents have passed for 100 years. The marble table, a Roman antique reproduction, was dressed with flowers on opening day. Herbert R. Stone, the dean of New York interior decorators, supplied the furniture, draperies, and carpet. Two large blue and gold Sevres vases, flanking the door, belonged to Miriam Osborn and were returned to the home for the opening from Howell Osborn's estate, along with paintings and statuary. Four members of the clergy officiated at the service in the auditorium. There was a luncheon afterward in the dining room. Rosamund Greig, the first matron to serve the residents, left in February 1909, and Edith V. D. Smith replaced her but was replaced within a year by Laura Jones in 1910. By 1922, there were 79 residents.

February 5, 1932

Dear Miss Jones:

I find in Miss Williams' file a copy of a letter from Mr. Sterling in which he says: "I trust you will get to Harrison on Monday without fail, as the Managers expect to have the opening exercises the next day." Monday was April 20, 1908. The opening reception was held on April 21, 1908.

Yours sincerely,

Hca.

Miss Laura J. Jones.

A letter from Helen Adams to Laura Jones, years after the opening, settles the matter of the official opening day. The opening was disputed because the first residents entered the home on April 11, 1908, and some documents revealed the anniversary of Miriam Osborn's birth, April 15, 1908, as the opening day. This letter refers to documentation from John Sterling that opening ceremonies were held on April 21, 1908.

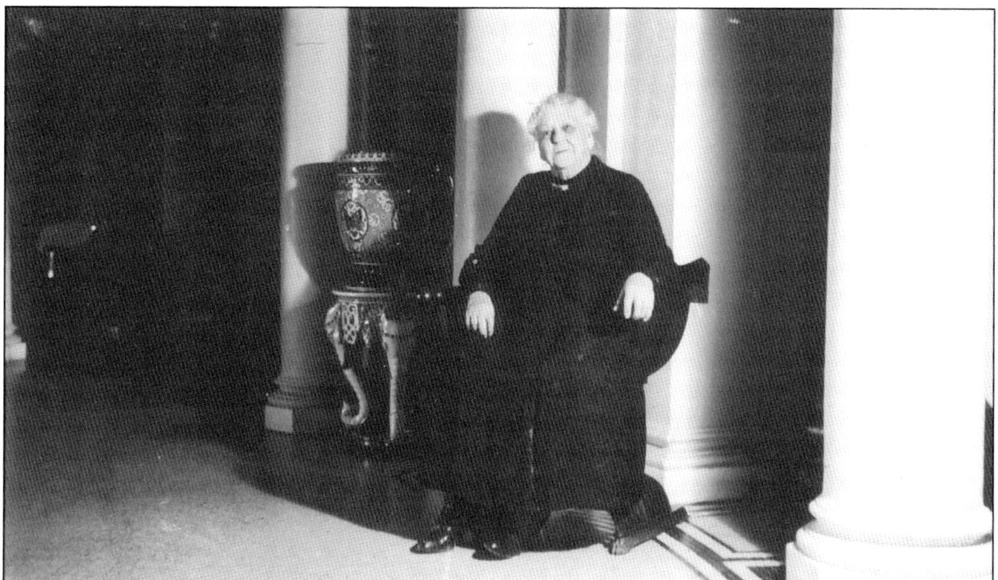

A Mrs. Stratton, one of the original 12 residents, is pictured at the age of 94 seated in the rotunda near the main entrance.

Application for Admission

TO THE

MIRIAM OSBORN MEMORIAL HOME

FOR

Aged Gentlewomen in Needy Circumstances,

RYE, NEW YORK.

Applicants were required to be a resident of New York or Westchester and pay $500 as an admission fee that later was applied toward burial expenses. The first six months were a probationary period after which the applicant was admitted for life, except if the person could not be cared for in the home, in which case the resident would be transferred to an asylum or suitable hospital.

APPLICANTS.

1. The applicant must be a resident of the County of New York or of Westchester, and have lived at least ten years in one or both of the said Counties.

2. She must be a *gentlewoman* in needy circumstances, of good education and pleasant manners, at least sixty-five years of age, of sound mind and in good average health, and must present undoubted testimonials of high character and good disposition.

3. She must be examined by the Executive Committee of the Board of Lady Managers and by a physician approved by the Board of Trustees or its Executive Committee. If approved by them, and her testimonials as to character and disposition are satisfactory, she will be placed on the Waiting List. An Applicant, whose name shall have been on the Waiting List for six months, must be re-examined by such physician.

4. She will be selected according to the position of her name on the Waiting List, except that nominees for endowed rooms shall take precedence.

5. She must before admission furnish a list of all property, both real and personal, belonging to her or to which she shall be hereafter entitled, and agree to execute an Assignment thereof in the form annexed to the Application Blank.

6. She must pay an admission fee of $500 to the Treasurer of the Board of Trustees. No admission fee will be required from Beneficiaries admitted to endowed rooms, but compliance with all other requirements will be enforced.

7. The Entrance Permit will be forfeited, if not presented within thirty days.

8. When admitted, she will be received on probation for six months and, if then approved, will be admitted for life, subject to the sufficiency of the means and accommodations of the Association.

9. She, when admitted to the Home, must sign an Agreement to take charge of the room assigned to her and keep it at all times in a neat and tidy manner, to render all the service she can for the good of the Home and the comfort of those more helpless than herself, and to comply with all the By-Laws, Rules and Regulations of the Board of Trustees and of the Board of Lady Managers, as they do now exist or shall hereafter be made or as they shall hereafter be amended.

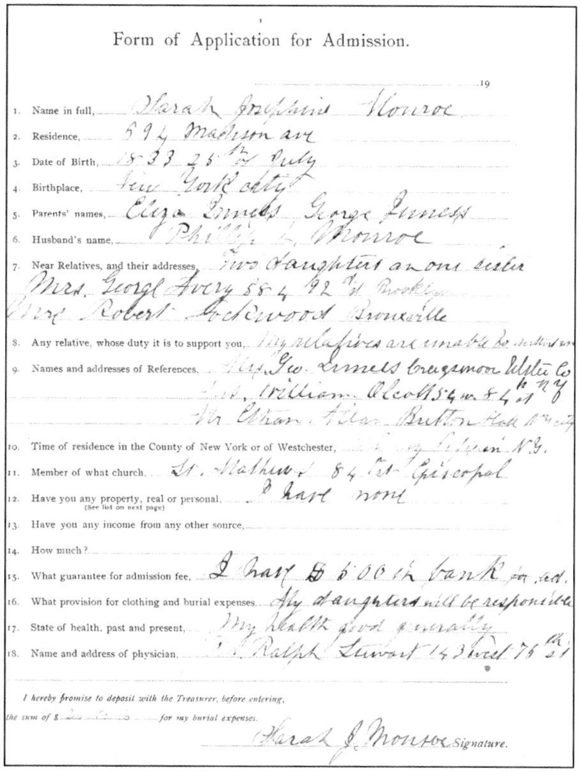

Form of Application for Admission.

.....19

1. Name in full, Sarah Josephine Monroe
2. Residence, 594 Madison ave
3. Date of Birth, 1833 25th of July
4. Birthplace, New York city
5. Parents' names, Eliza Inness George Inness
6. Husband's name, Phillip L. Monroe
7. Near Relatives, and their addresses, two daughters and one sister Mrs. George Avery 584 92nd st Brooklyn Mrs Robert Lockwood Bronxville
8. Any relative, whose duty it is to support you, [illegible]
9. Names and addresses of References, Mrs. Geo. Inness Cragsmoor Ulster Co Mrs. William Olcott 54 w. 84th st N Y Mr [illegible] Button Hall N.Y. city
10. Time of residence in the County of New York or of Westchester, [illegible] N.Y.
11. Member of what church, St. Mathews 84 St Episcopal
12. Have you any property, real or personal, (See list on next page) I have none
13. Have you any income from any other source,
14. How much?
15. What guarantee for admission fee, I have $ 6.00 in bank [illegible]
16. What provision for clothing and burial expenses, My daughters will be responsible
17. State of health, past and present, My health good generally
18. Name and address of physician, Dr. Ralph Stewart 143 West 76 st

I hereby promise to deposit with the Treasurer, before entering, the sum of $ ..... for my burial expenses.

Sarah J. Monroe *Signature.*

Sarah Monroe, one of the first 12 residents, entered the home on April 20, 1908, at the age of 74. She died on July 29, 1912, and was interred at Mount Hope Cemetery in Hastings. A note in her file dated July 9, 1912, indicates that before her death she was "crippled with rheumatis and confined to bed for three years, helpless and under the care of nurses."

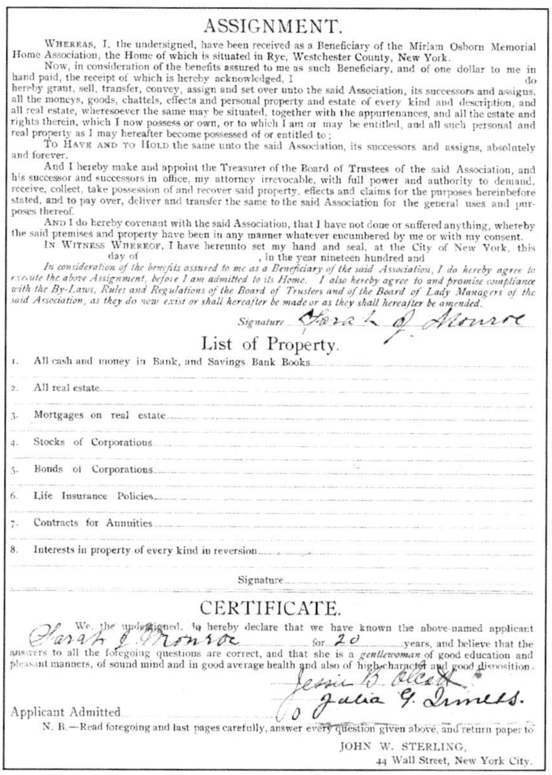

ASSIGNMENT.

WHEREAS, I, the undersigned, have been received as a Beneficiary of the Miriam Osborn Memorial Home Association, the Home of which is situated in Rye, Westchester County, New York.

Now, in consideration of the benefits assured to me as such Beneficiary, and of one dollar to me in hand paid, the receipt of which is hereby acknowledged, I do hereby grant, sell, transfer, convey, assign and set over unto the said Association, its successors and assigns, all the moneys, goods, chattels, effects and personal property and estate of every kind and description, and all real estate, wheresoever the same may be situated, together with the appurtenances, and all the estate and rights therein, which I now possess or own, or to which I am or may be entitled, and all such personal and real property as I may hereafter become possessed of or entitled to;

TO HAVE AND TO HOLD the same unto the said Association, its successors and assigns, absolutely and forever.

And I hereby make and appoint the Treasurer of the Board of Trustees of the said Association, and his successor and successors in office, my attorney irrevocable, with full power and authority to demand, receive, collect, take possession of and recover said property, effects and claims for the purposes hereinbefore stated, and to pay over, deliver and transfer the same to the said Association for the general uses and purposes thereof.

AND I do hereby covenant with the said Association, that I have not done or suffered anything, whereby the said premises and property have been in any manner whatever encumbered by me or with my consent.

IN WITNESS WHEREOF, I have hereunto set my hand and seal, at the City of New York, this day of , in the year nineteen hundred and

In consideration of the benefits assured to me as a Beneficiary of the said Association, I do hereby agree to execute the above Assignment, before I am admitted to its Home. I also hereby agree to and promise compliance with the By-Laws, Rules and Regulations of the Board of Trustees and of the Board of Lady Managers of the said Association, as they do now exist or shall hereafter be made or as they shall hereafter be amended.

Signature Sarah J. Monroe

List of Property.

1. All cash and money in Bank, and Savings Bank Books
2. All real estate
3. Mortgages on real estate
4. Stocks of Corporations
5. Bonds of Corporations
6. Life Insurance Policies
7. Contracts for Annuities
8. Interests in property of every kind in reversion

Signature

CERTIFICATE.

We, the undersigned, do hereby declare that we have known the above-named applicant Sarah J. Monroe for 20 years, and believe that the answers to all the foregoing questions are correct, and that she is a *gentlewoman* of good education and pleasant manners, of sound mind and in good average health and also of high character and good disposition.

Jessie B. Olcott
Julia G. Inness

Applicant Admitted

N. B.—Read foregoing and last pages carefully, answer every question given above, and return paper to

JOHN W. STERLING,
44 Wall Street, New York City.

Miriam Osborn Memorial Home Association

HARRISON, NEW YORK.

Feb-11 1908

Dear Madam:

Referring to your Application to become a Beneficiary of this Association, I beg to request that you attend before the Executive Committee of the Board of Lady Managers on Feb. 14 *, 190 , at* 11 *o'clock* a. *M., at* ~~*the residence of Mr. John W. Sterling, 912 Fifth Avenue (first house above 72nd Street)*~~ 3 West 47th, *in order that your eligibility may be passed upon.*

Yours very truly,

Olive E. Trowbridge
~~*Chairman of Executive Committee.*~~ Secretary

To Mrs. S. J. Monroe

The board of lady managers approved all admissions to the home. This invitation to Sarah Monroe to appear before its executive committee is dated February 11, 1908.

OFFICE HOURS
NINE TO TEN THIRTY A.M.
FIVE TO SIX P.M.

TELEPHONE 2447 COLUMBUS

17th Feby 1908

WILLIAM A. VALENTINE, M.D.
115 WEST 74TH STREET
NEW YORK

Dear Miss Trowbridge

I have examined Mrs S. A. Munroe and find her a suitable candidate for the Home. Her present debility will, I think, disappear under treatment.

Respectfully

Wm A. Valentine

Dr. William Valentine assured Olive Trowbridge that Monroe was a suitable candidate for the home. He believed her disability would improve.

LAW OFFICES,
SHEARMAN & STERLING,
44 WALL STREET,
NEW YORK.

JOHN W. STERLING
JOHN A. GARVER,
JAMES M. BECK.

CABLE ADDRESS
"NUMLATUS."

July 25, 1906.

Dear Madam:

Yours of the 23rd inst. is at hand, and it will give me pleasure to file your application for admission to the Memorial Home. You come within the limitations, so far as age is concerned. So far as I can see, you should be a very acceptable candidate. I am not quite sure whether your temporary non-residence would be a bar to your admission but will take pleasure in doing what I can to have this obviated, if the Lady Managers should in other respects think your application as worthy as I do. They have not yet been selected and probably will not be until next winter, as the building cannot be opened for inmates before next spring.

Yours very truly,

John W. Sterling.

Miss Alice Williams.

In his July 25, 1906, letter, John Sterling judges Alice Williams as a suitable candidate, noting the board of managers will not be selected to approve "inmates" until the winter. She was a cousin of Helen Adams, and yet her admission was in question because she lived in New Jersey for a time. Additionally, an applicant had to be a "gentlewoman" with references to prove it.

Extract from Miss Jones' report to Lady Managers, February 16, 1932

Miss Alice Williams became very ill, helpless and restless before she passed away on February third, in her ninety-fourth year. She was the last of the first twelve to enter the Home when it was opened, and lived here twenty-three years, 9 months and 14 days.

Miss Williams funeral service was conducted by the Rev. Mr. MacNaught and she was buried in the Home Cemetery. None of her relatives, cousins, who were children of the late Dudley Buck, were able to come and her only niece is in Switzerland.

Alice Williams had entrance permit No. 3 and entered the home on April 20, 1908, the day before its official opening. She died on February 3, 1932, at age 94 and was the last survivor of the original 12 residents. She was a resident of the home for over 23 years, as reported by Laura Jones to the board of managers.

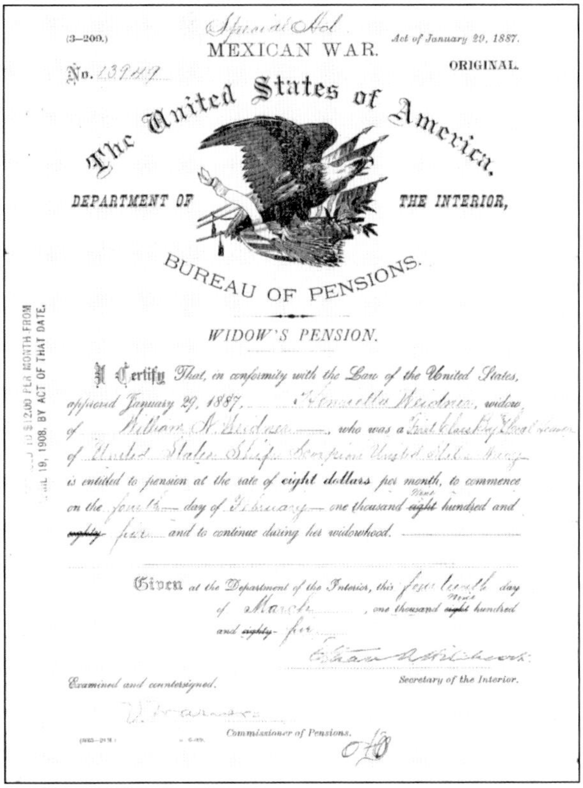
(3-209.) Special Act Act of January 29, 1887.

MEXICAN WAR.

ORIGINAL.

No. 13949

The United States of America,

DEPARTMENT OF THE INTERIOR,

BUREAU OF PENSIONS.

WIDOW'S PENSION.

I Certify That, in conformity with the Law of the United States, approved January 29, 1887, Henrietta Weidner, widow of William H. Weidner, who was a First Class Boy [illegible] of United States Ship Scorpion United States Navy is entitled to pension at the rate of eight dollars per month, to commence on the fourth day of February one thousand eight hundred and eighty five and to continue during her widowhood.

Given at the Department of the Interior, this fourteenth day of March, one thousand eight hundred and eighty-five.

[illegible]
Secretary of the Interior.

Examined and countersigned.

[illegible]
Commissioner of Pensions.

...ED TO $12.00 PER MONTH FROM ...IL 19, 1908, BY ACT OF THAT DATE.

Henrietta Weidner entered the home as one of the original 12 residents on April 20, 1908. Her husband was a veteran of the Mexican War, and as his survivor, at the time of her admission, she received a pension of $12 a month that she was required to submit to the home. The pension was increased to $30 in 1920. Residents were required to surrender property and funds in return for lifetime care. Weidner lived at The Osborn for 20 years, spending her last three years in the infirmary. Note the treatments and medications listed for her on the infirmary record. Turpentine had a variety of uses. Residents were required to be in good health on admission, but care in the infirmary was available for those with temporary health problems or long-term health needs.

NAME WEINDER, MRS. HENRIETTA

DATE	DIAGNOSIS	MEDICATIONS	REMARKS
7/12/14		A.B.& S.Tablets 2 at bedtime High Colonic irrigation Apply ice bag to abd. Codeine Sulph.gr.1/4 every 4 hrs.	Operated on at the United Hospital. Drs. LeRoy Wylie and Charles Walker, surgeons
7/13/14	Gangrenous appendix		Returned Home
8/15/14		R.& S. Mixt. drams 1 with Nux Vomica M.10, 3 times a day PC Zinc Sulph. Tr.Lavender used with packing gauze for wound daily	
8/21/14	Hernia, inoperable	S.S.Enima with drams 1 of turpentine	
9/14/14		R.& S.Mixt. with Vomica when necessary	
10/5/14		Calomel Series gr.1/4 followed in 6 hrs. with Rochelle salts, drams 2 in half glass of water Codeine Sulph. gr.1/4 at bedtime	
10/2/15	General Arterio Sclerosis Myocardial degeneration Contributory senility	Turpentine Stupes to right shoulder then apply Analgesique and cover with warm flannel	Following operation, patient under care of Doctor and foregoing medications repeated at intervals. Chronic Cystitis treated with bladder irrigation and series of urotropin at different times between the years 1914 and 1927. September 9, 1927, Adenitis developed with malignant changes. Consulation with Drs. Wang and Peterson. Confirmed diagnosis. No treatment ordered. Patient had been permanently in Infirmary from April 15, 1925 until she died March 9, 1928. Buried in Greenwood Cemetery, Brooklyn, N.Y

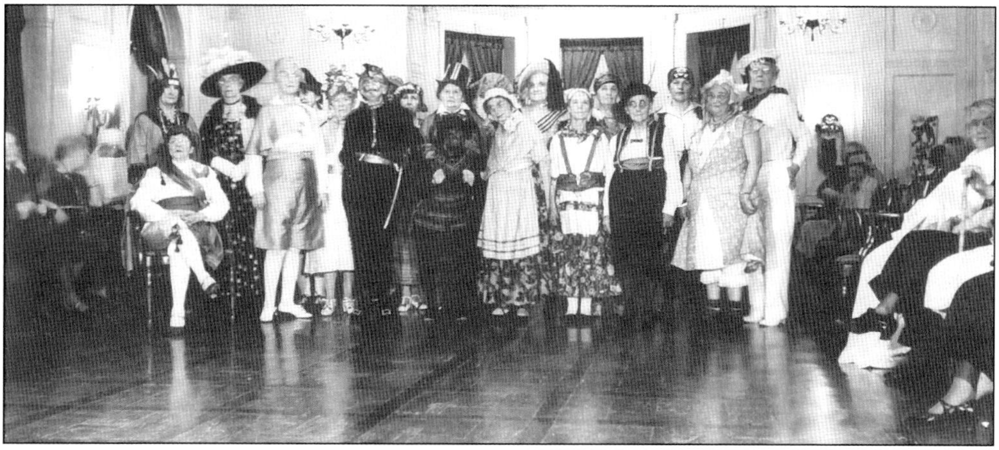

In this 1930s photograph, residents are dressed in Halloween costumes. Life in the home included elaborate celebrations in which everyone participated. Staff frequently used the term "family" to describe the cohesiveness of the group.

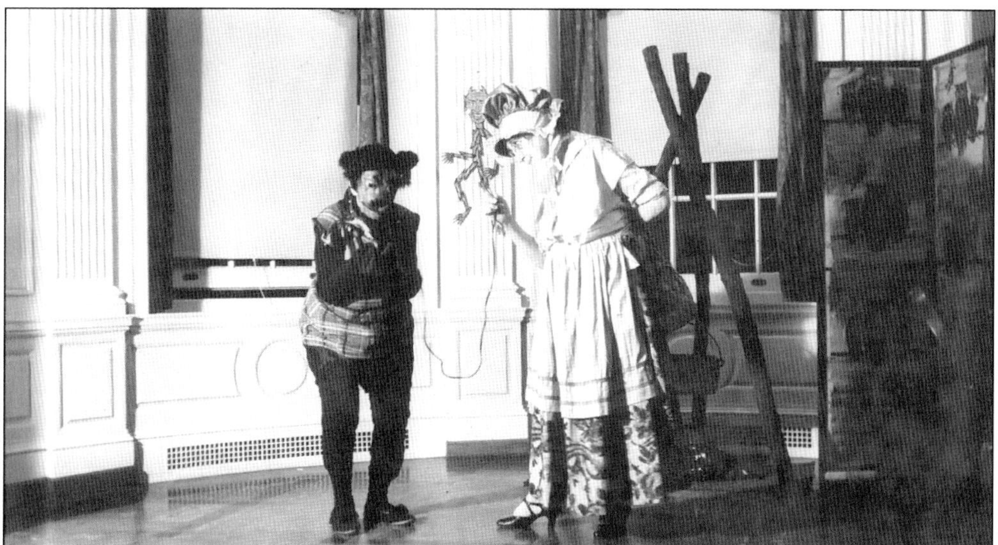

Two residents are dressed as Old Mother Hubbard and her dog for a Halloween celebration in 1937.

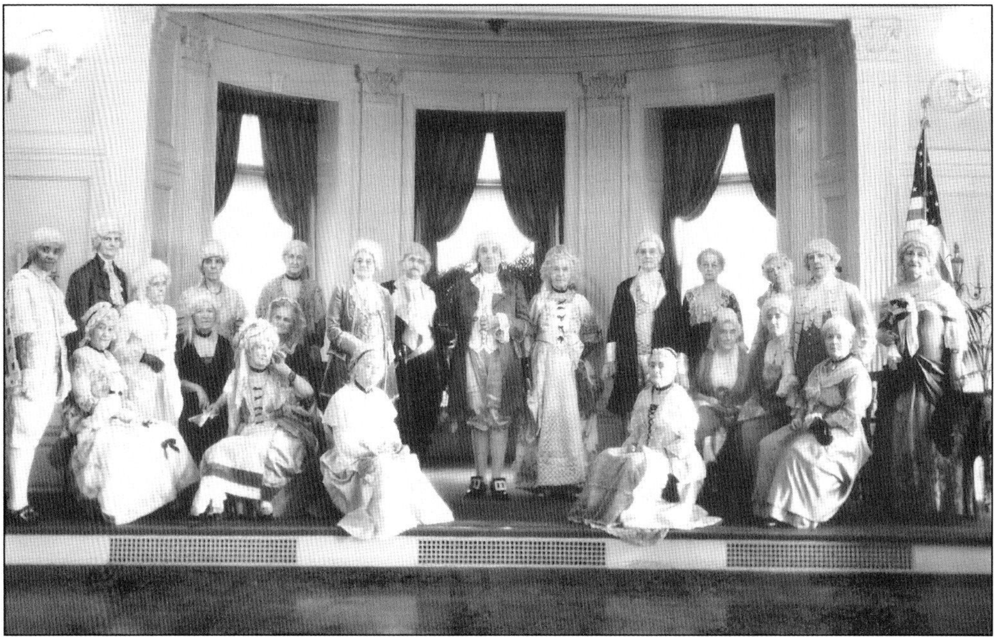

In 1932, plans were underway for the Sterling Building. The Mount Stephen-Strathcona Infirmary building opened in April 1929, three years before. The George Washington party was celebrated on February 22, 1933, in the new dining pavilion that was part of that building improvement. The east dining room doubled as an auditorium when necessary. The custom of George Washington parties lasted over 20 years.

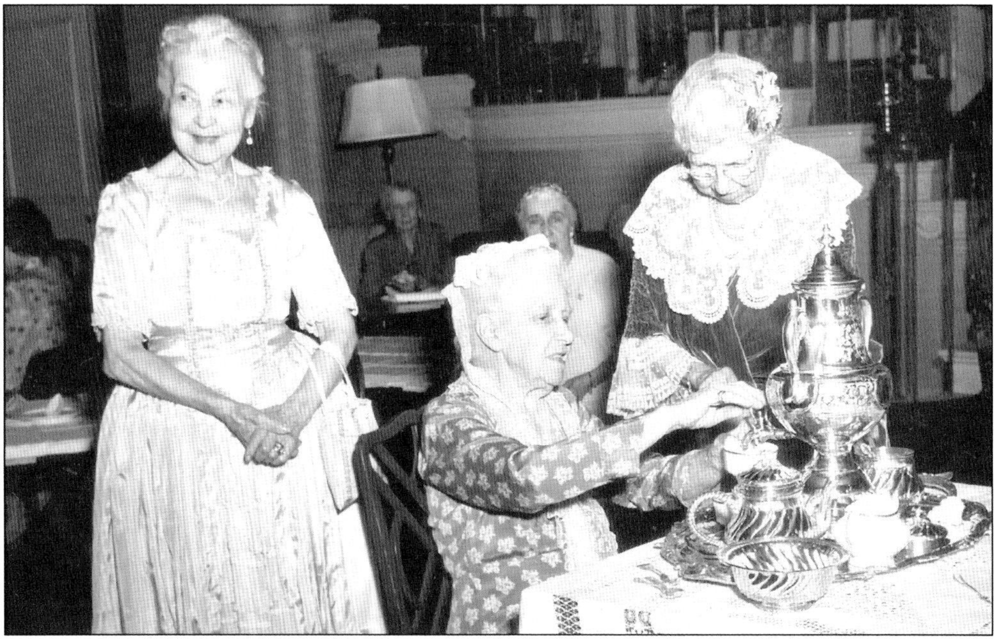

Miriam Osborn's silver tea service in this photograph traditionally is used on special occasions. The residents looked forward to the Matron's Tea, each New Year's Day. Later it was called Miss Jones' Tea and then Miss Cole's Tea to honor the matron at the time. Afternoon tea was served every Thursday, and movies were shown every Tuesday.

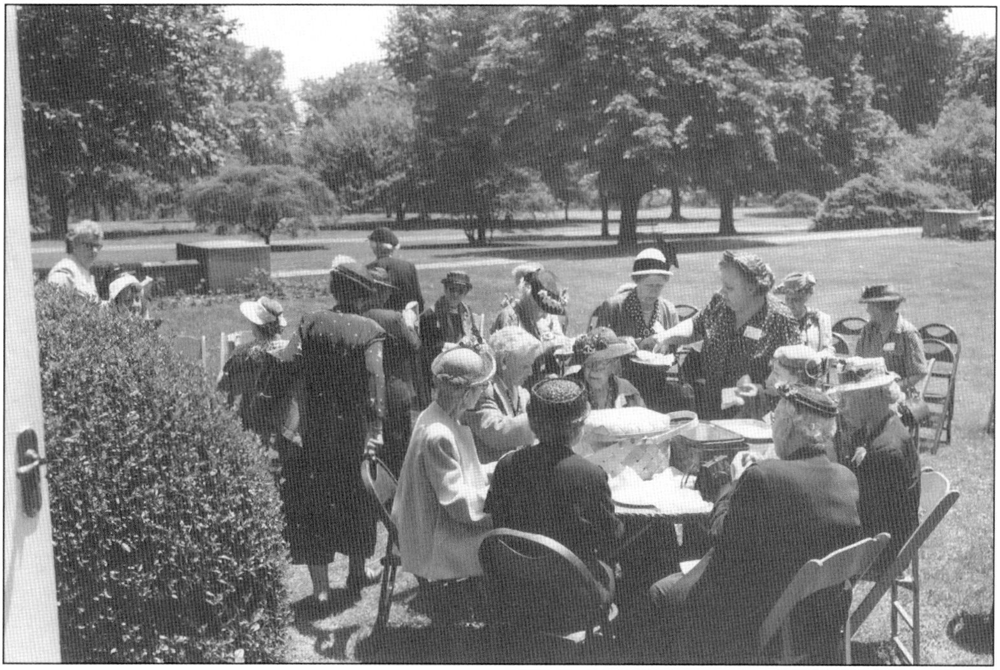

Ladies of the home enjoy a picnic on the grounds. Note their attire, more formal than in later years, that includes flowered hats, purses, seamed stockings, pearl necklaces, and earrings. The basket lunches seem to feature sandwiches.

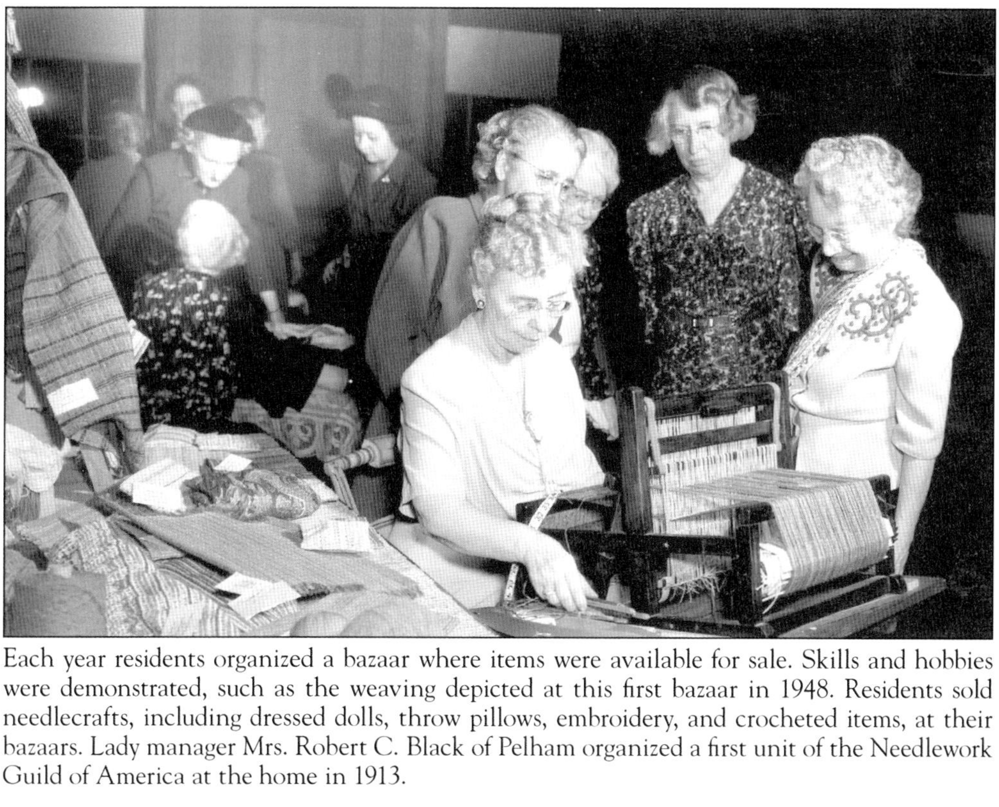

Each year residents organized a bazaar where items were available for sale. Skills and hobbies were demonstrated, such as the weaving depicted at this first bazaar in 1948. Residents sold needlecrafts, including dressed dolls, throw pillows, embroidery, and crocheted items, at their bazaars. Lady manager Mrs. Robert C. Black of Pelham organized a first unit of the Needlework Guild of America at the home in 1913.

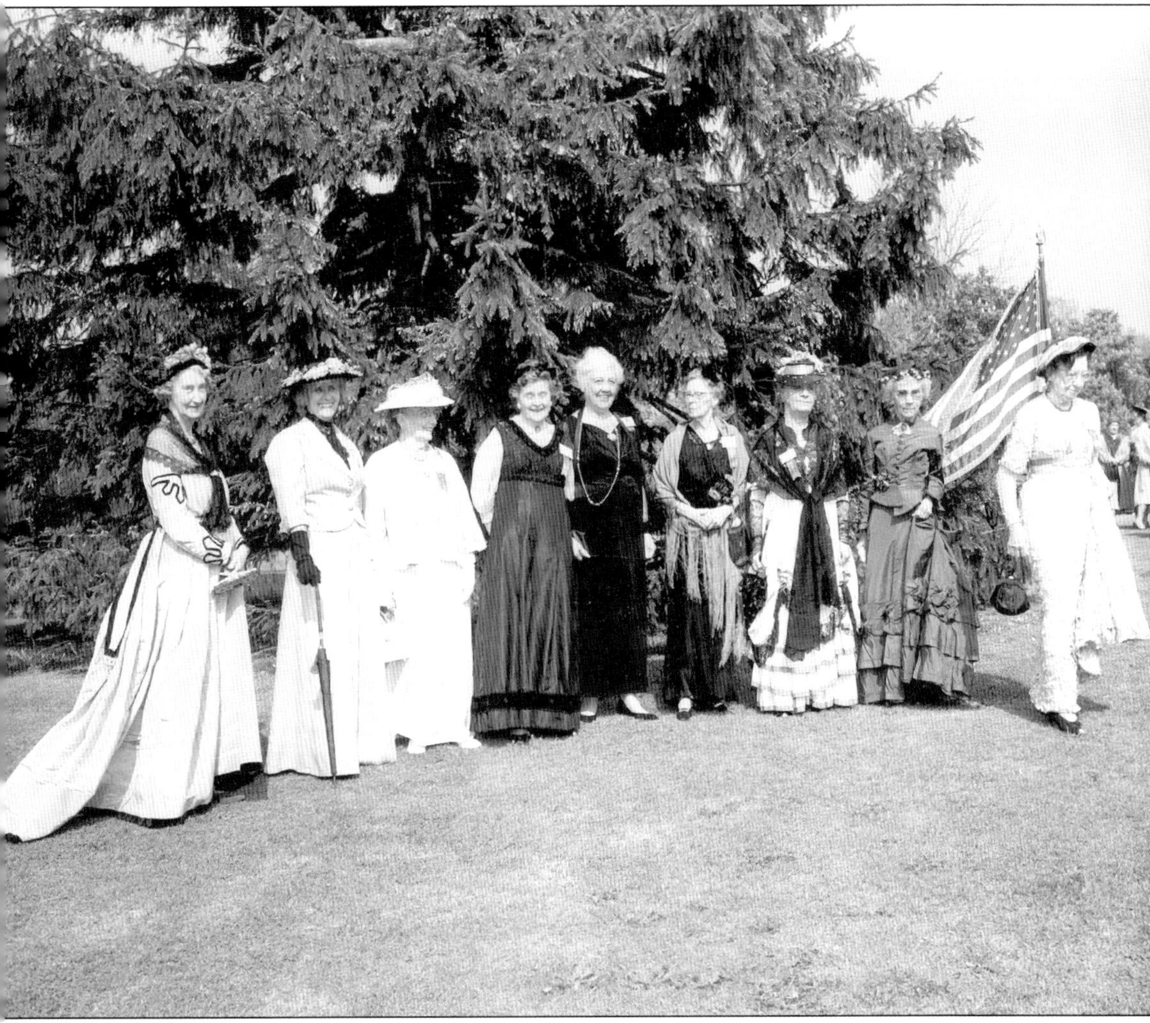

The hostesses for the 50th anniversary party of The Osborn, on May 17, 1958, are dressed in attire like that worn by residents who entered the home 50 years before. By 1958, 190 residents lived at The Osborn. Mechanization transformed the once busy farm life of the home. Cars replaced the horse-drawn carriages of the volunteers and lady managers who took residents for rides. In addition, the ladies drove their own cars as noted by board president Joseph W. Drake, in keeping with the mores of the times. In a program for Old Timers' Day, May 12, 1965, Drake reminisced about a lecture given in the early days of the home by Henry Marquand about the Panama Canal that was being built. Marquand used a stereopticon to show his pictures to the residents. Known as a "magic lantern," it provided entertainment before moving pictures. The Victor Talking Machine with the large horn and the slogan "His Master's Voice" donated by Mrs. Robert C. Black provided other early entertainment.

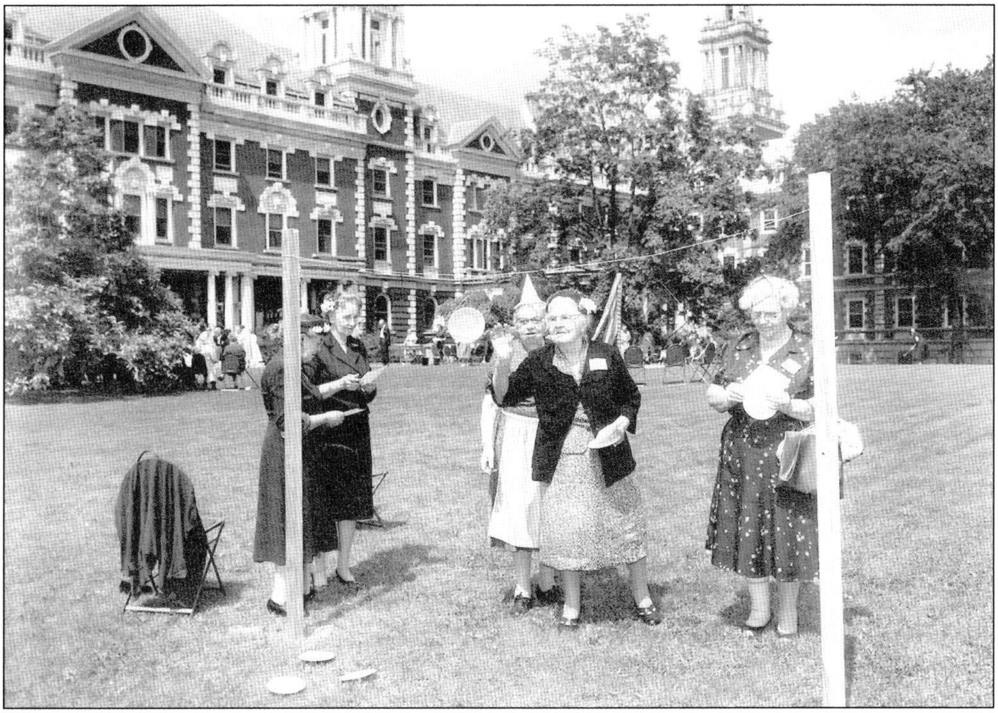

Country fairs were popular at the home for several years in the late 1950s and early 1960s. Note the beautiful architecture of The Osborn building viewed from the south lawn.

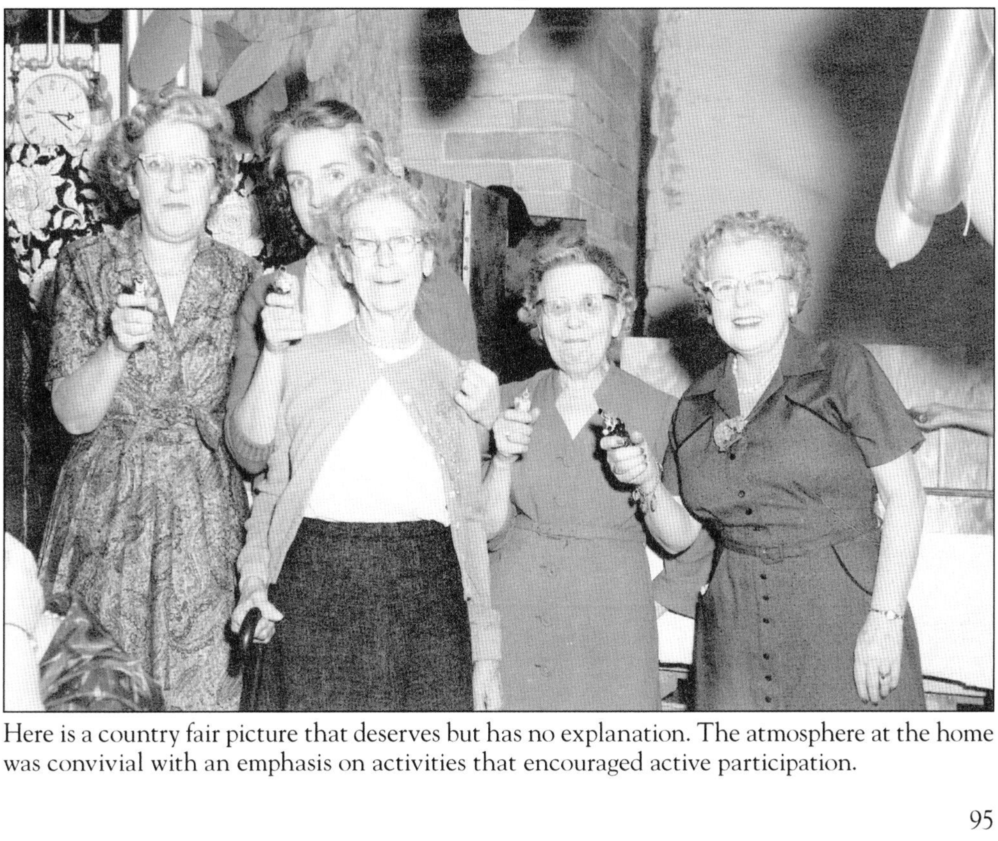

Here is a country fair picture that deserves but has no explanation. The atmosphere at the home was convivial with an emphasis on activities that encouraged active participation.

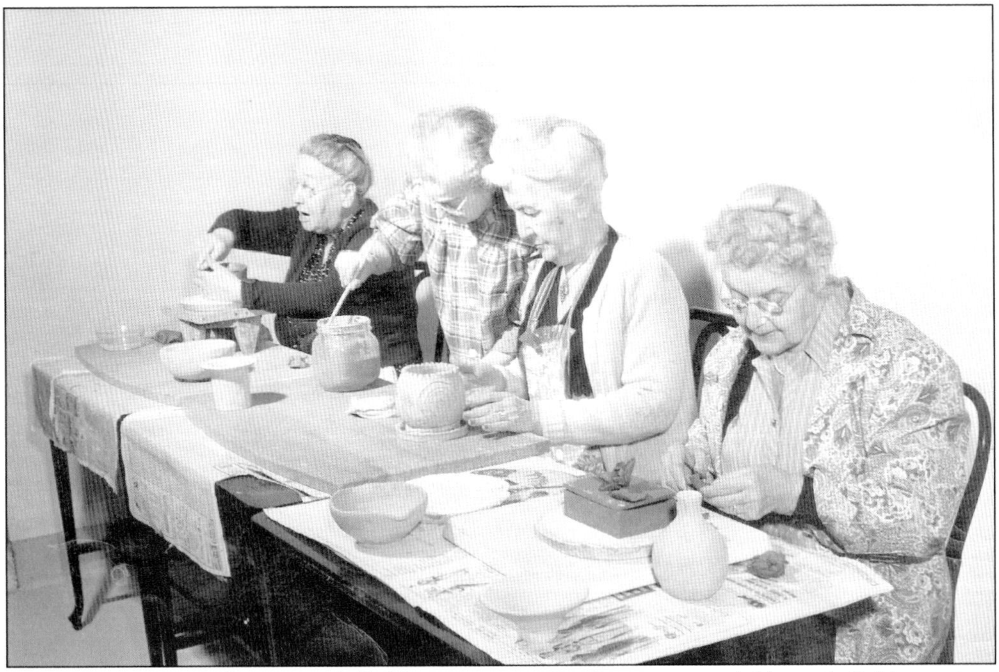

Activities taught residents new skills like ceramics or let them practice lifelong skills like sewing. Since the home required residents to be well at the time of admission, the activity program was of particular importance. Residents enjoyed the many concerts given willingly by those who wanted to play the Steinway piano donated by Olive Trowbridge in 1908. Recorded dates allow insights into the home's lifestyle. For example, Victrola records were donated to the home at Christmas 1912, and the first television was purchased in 1949. Telephones were installed in all rooms in 1955. At the time of the 60th anniversary in 1968, a color television was placed in the Dalphin Room. In 1971, a 12-month activities program was organized with trips and weekly croquet, golf, and picnics.

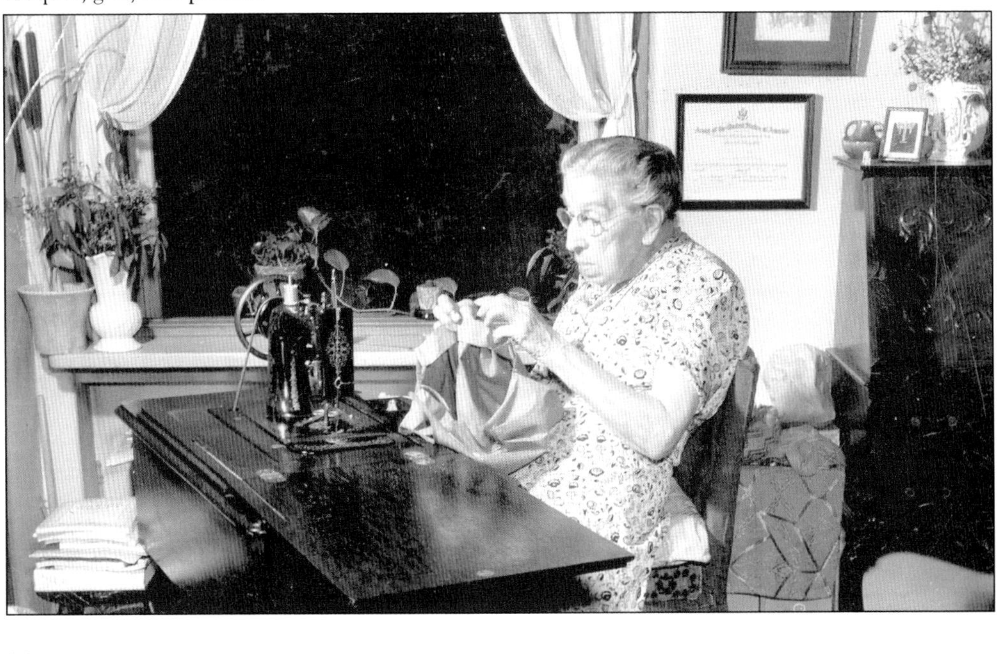

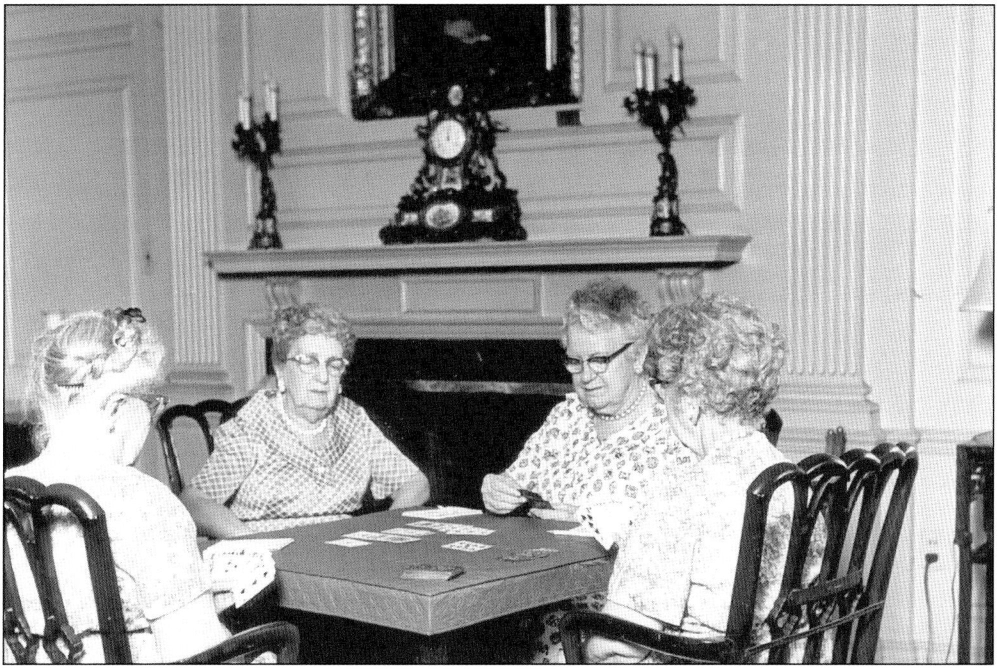

Several time-honored activities enjoyed through the years are part of the home's traditions. Residents still are avid bridge players and gardeners. In the early days of The Osborn, any resident who wanted to enjoy horticulture could work in the shared "ladies garden." In 1946, residents were given individual plots to raise vegetables and flowers.

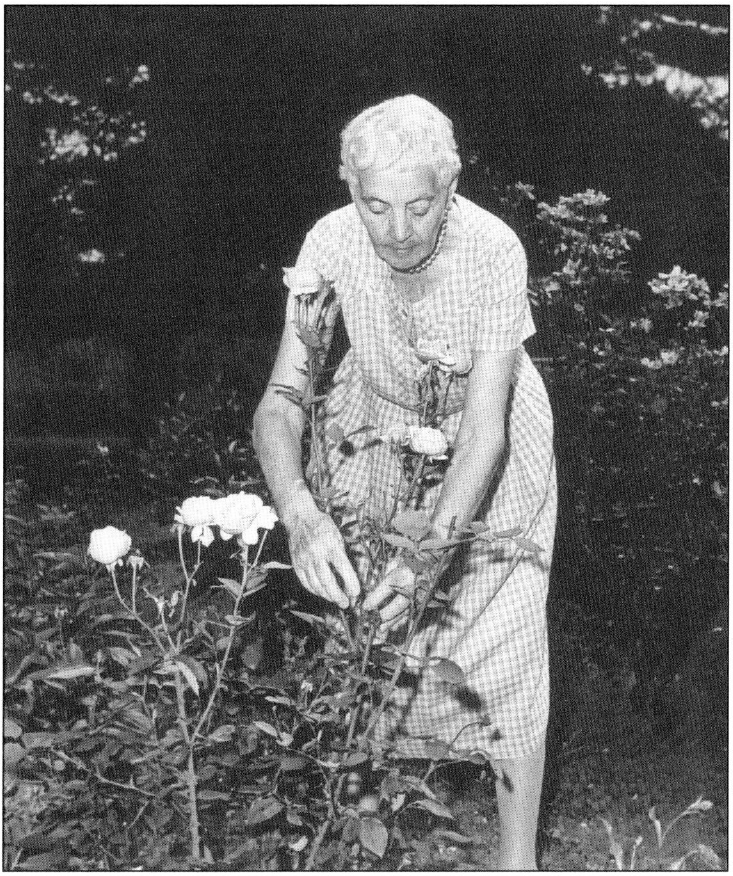

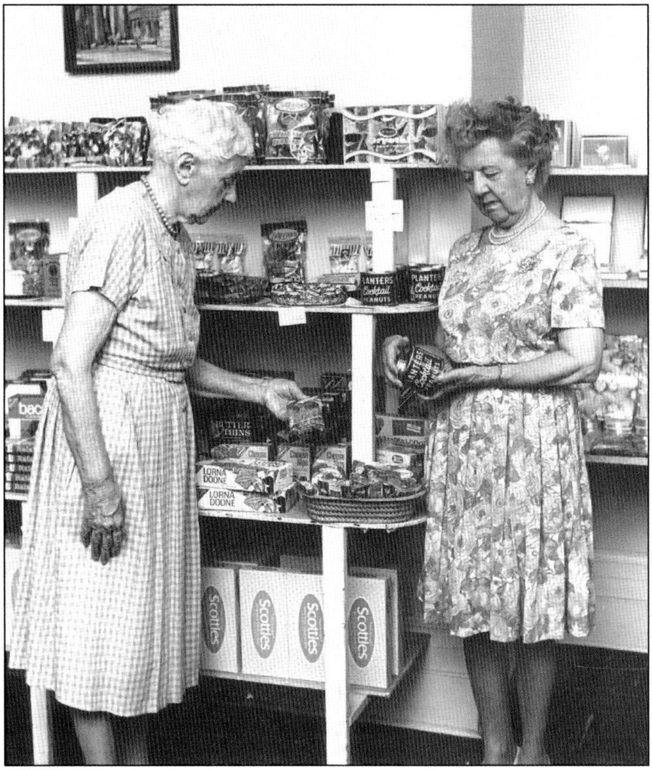

The Osborn store opened in 1951. Residents volunteered to manage the store and act as shopkeepers. Another important volunteer opportunity that continues today is the "pink cart," in fact painted pink, which brings items from the store to residents who cannot get out shopping. Today's store is called the Marketplace.

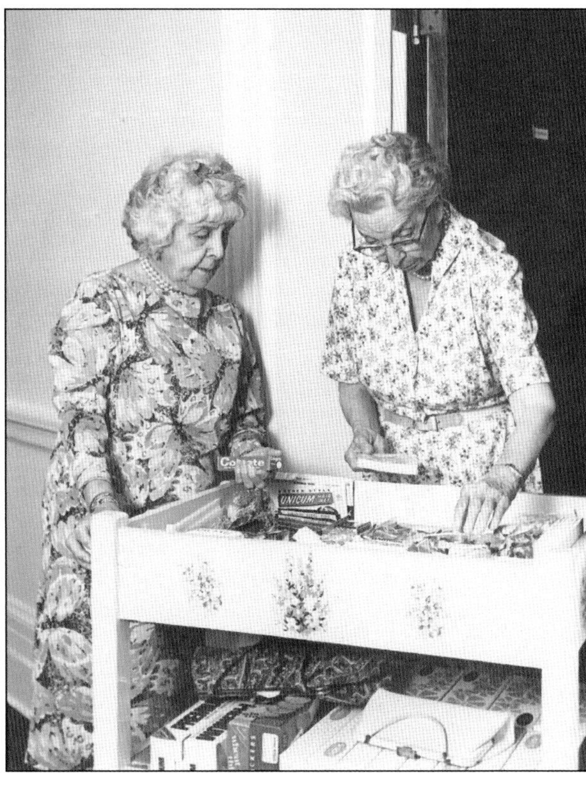

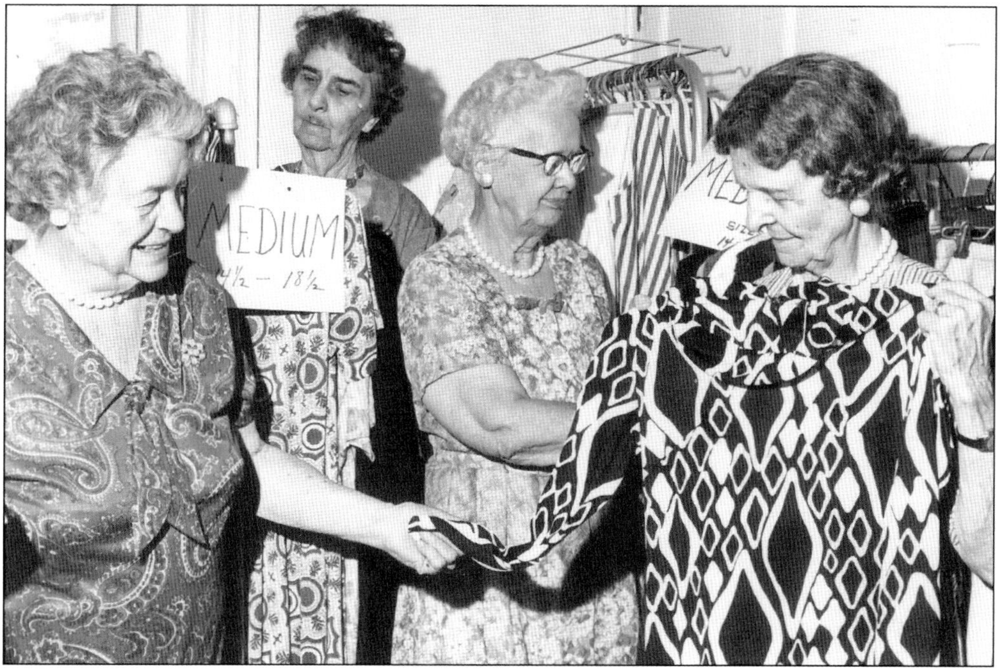

Residents ran the thrift shop and sold their lightly used items of jewelry, clothing, and accessories to each other and to staff. They donated the money to The Osborn. The thrift shop operated through the 1990s.

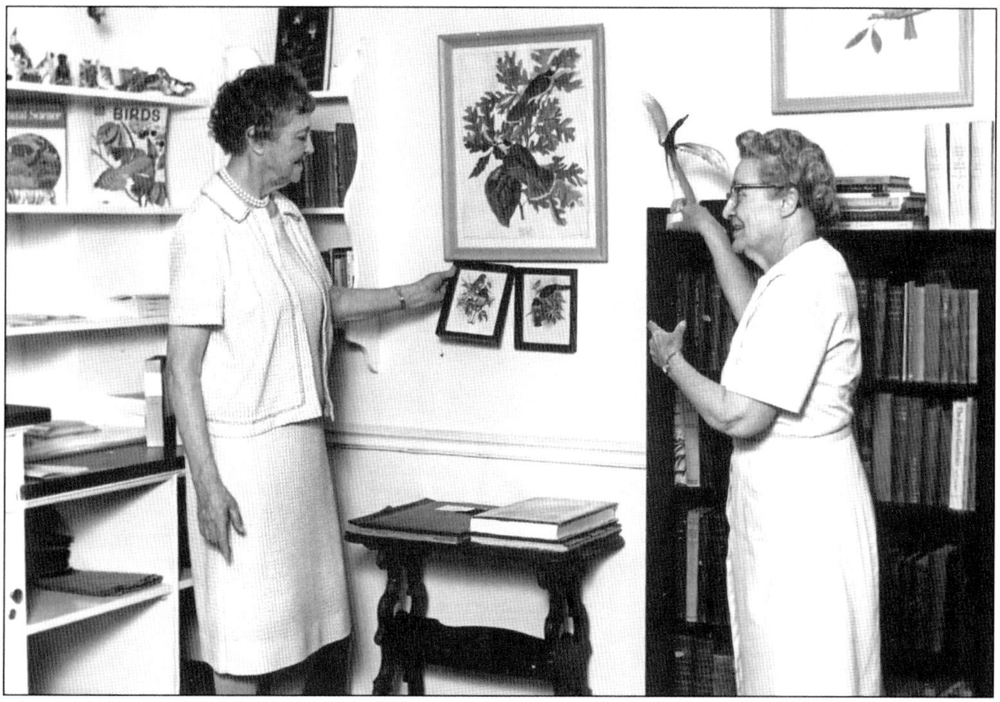

The Audubon Room, dedicated to all things avian, was a favorite spot for residents until it closed in 1995. Resident volunteers maintained the room and informed other residents who had an interest in birding.

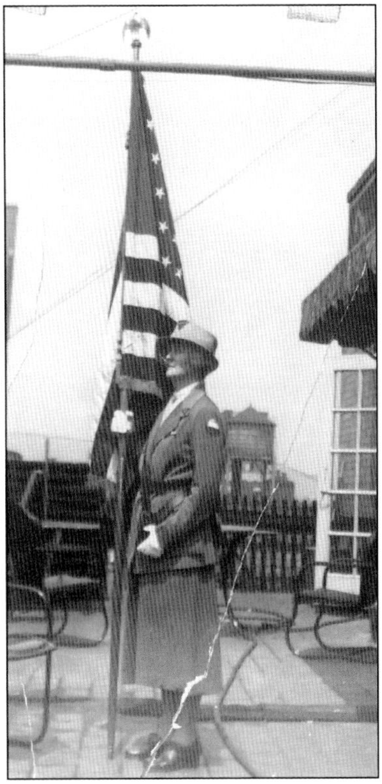

Arletta Crump is dressed in the uniform of the World War I Color Squad of the Woman's Overseas Service League on Memorial Day 1945. In the 1920s, Crump was proprietor of the Crumperie, a tearoom at 104 Washington Place in New York City's Greenwich Village. The fame of the Crumperie extended to Europe because of Crump's talent playing the ukulele. She was famous for entertaining patrons with her music and song. Later in life on May 6, 1954, Crump appeared as a contestant on the popular quiz show *$64,000 Question* with emcee Hal March. Her category was "New York." The sponsor's "Revlon isolation booth" is in the background. Many residents of The Osborn were well known or had interesting personal experiences.

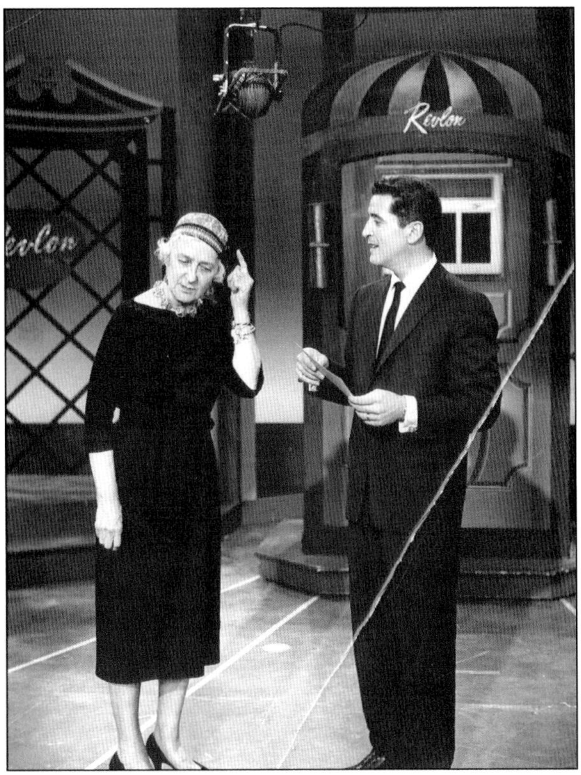

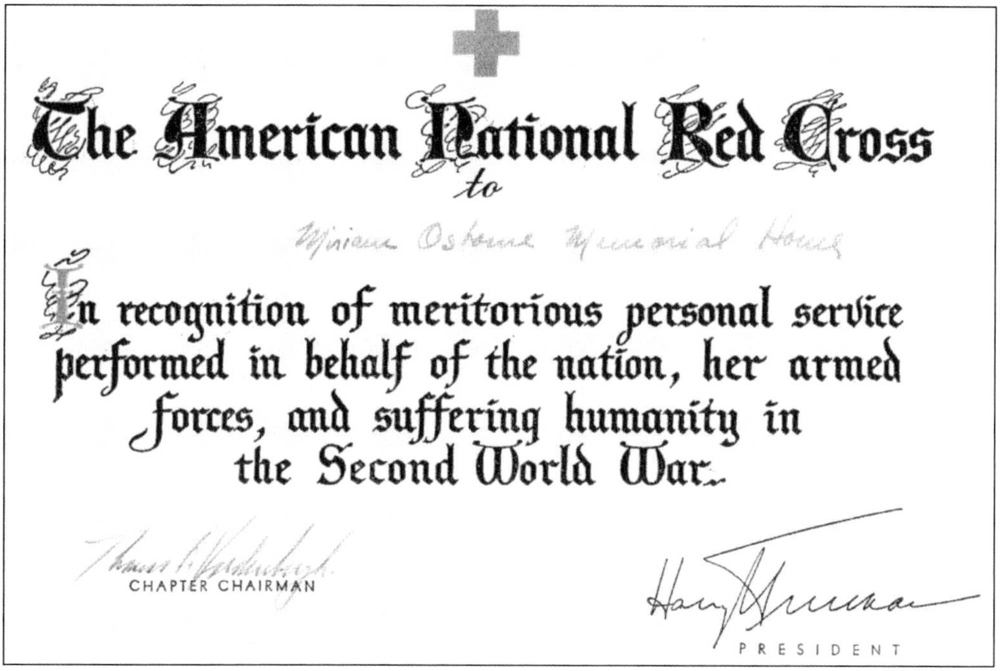
The American National Red Cross

to

Miriam Osborne Memorial Home

In recognition of meritorious personal service performed in behalf of the nation, her armed forces, and suffering humanity in the Second World War.

CHAPTER CHAIRMAN

PRESIDENT

During the years of World War II, blackouts were common at the home. The halls and stairways were fitted with curtains, and small red or blue bulbs lit residents' rooms so they would not fall. R. Eugene Curry, the director, enlisted in the navy and served from 1942 until 1945. Due to the shortage of help, residents volunteered for light work in the infirmary; they washed dishes and helped in the kitchen, preparing vegetables, stringing beans, and shelling peas. In the photograph below, the Red Cross Motor Corp arranged to drive two residents to the Veterans Administration Hospital in Montrose. The women were donating paintings they had done to be placed in the dining hall and lounge at the hospital.

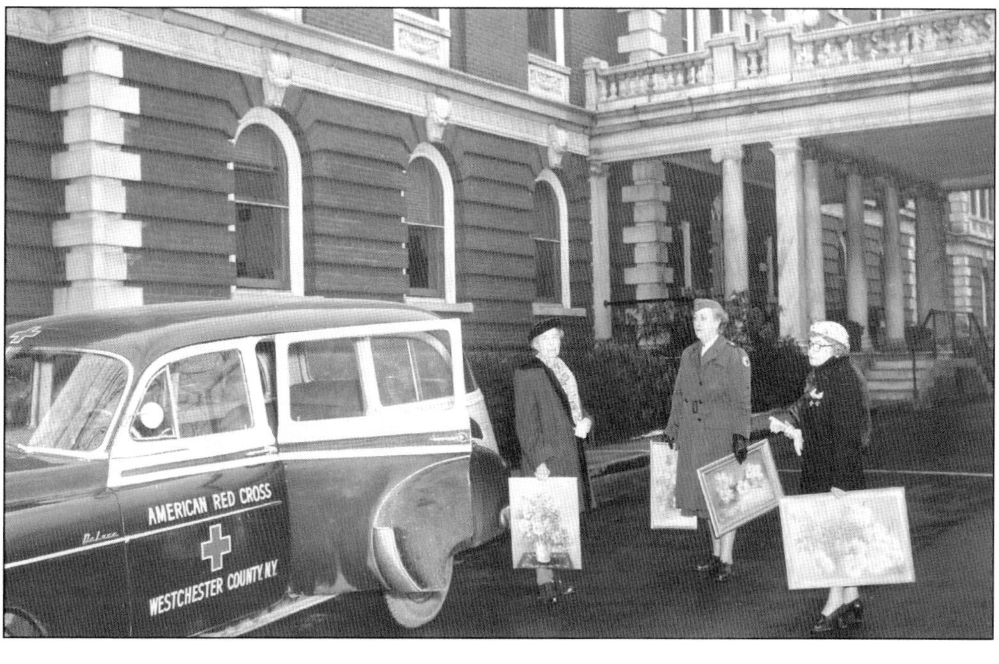

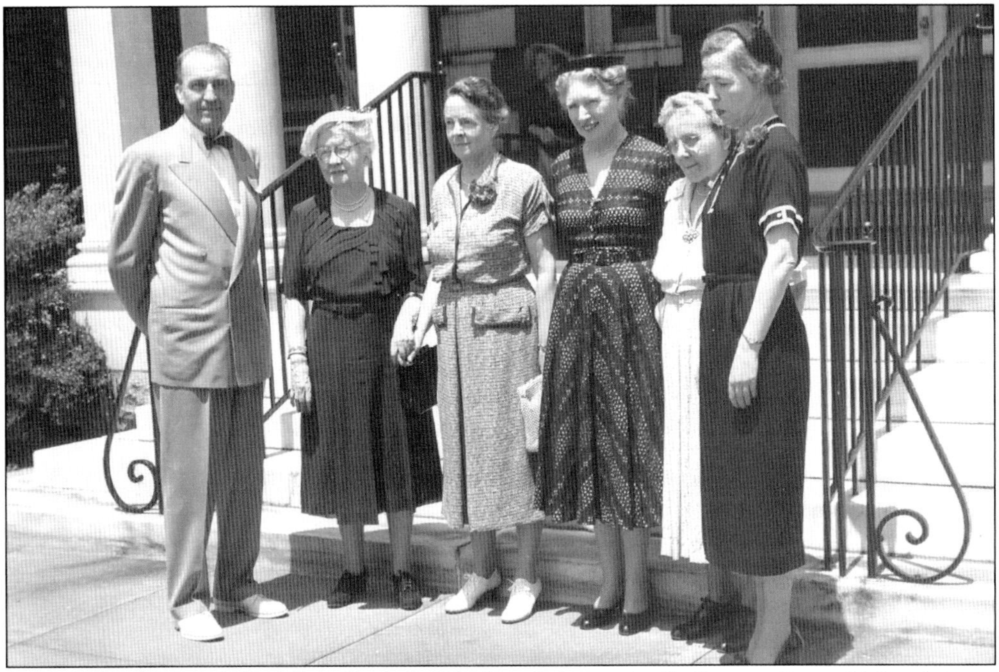

Ruth Taylor (pictured third from the left with, from left to right, R. Eugene Curry, Helen Adams, unidentified, Nancy Cole, and unidentified) was a pioneer in social work and was responsible for the operation of Grasslands Hospital in Westchester County, now the Westchester County Medical Center. In planning for the infirmary, Adams sought the advice of Taylor and Dr. S. S. Goldwater, the New York City commissioner of hospitals, an expert advisor for many institutions in the United States. Goldwater Memorial Hospital on Roosevelt Island is named for him. Taylor was known for developing quality standards for nursing homes. Taylor's signature appears in the guest book on February 12, 1952. She lived many years at The Osborn and died at age 99. The Osborn has been home to significant personalities, including cosmetics giant Hazel Bishop and Nina Hellman, wife of the mayonnaise magnate.

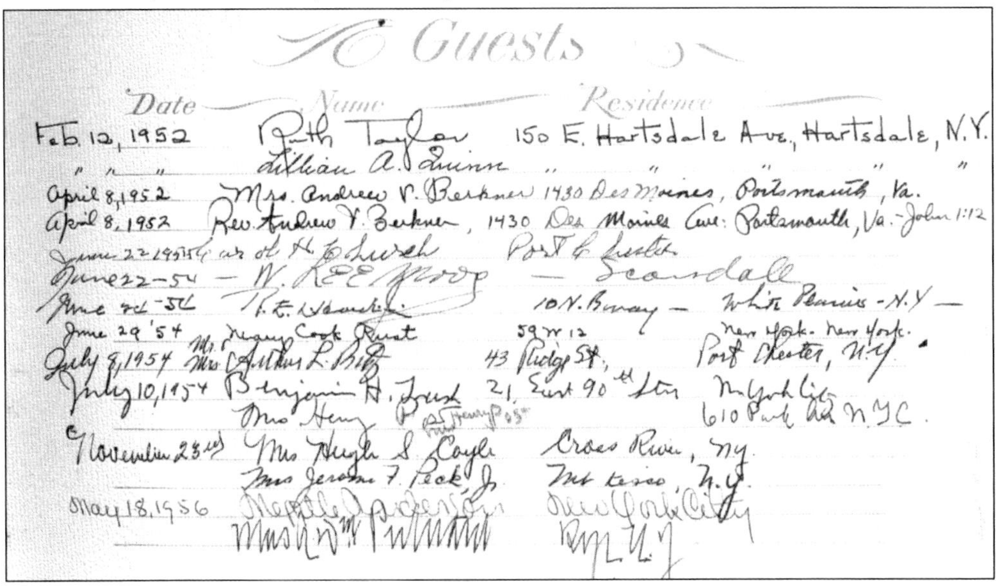
Guests

Date	Name	Residence
Feb. 12, 1952	Ruth Taylor	150 E. Hartsdale Ave., Hartsdale, N.Y.
" " "	Lillian A. Quinn	" " " " "
April 8, 1952	Mrs. Andrew V. Berkner	1430 Des Moines, Portsmouth, Va.
April 8, 1952	Rev. Andrew V. Berkner	1430 Des Moines Ave. Portsmouth, Va. - John 1:12
June 22 1954	[illegible]	Port Chester
June 22-54	W. Lee [illegible]	Scarsdale
June 22-54	[illegible]	10 N. Broadway - White Plains - N.Y.
June 29 '54	Mary Cook Rust	59 W 12 New York. New York.
July 8, 1954	Mr. Mrs. Arthur L. [illegible]	43 Ridge St., Port Chester, N.Y.
July 10, 1954	Benjamin H. [illegible]	21, East 90th Str. New York City
	Mrs. Henry [illegible]	610 Park Ave N.Y.C.
November 23rd	Mrs Hugh S. Coyle	Cross River, N.Y.
	Mrs Jerome F. Peck Jr.	Mt Kisco, N.Y.
May 18, 1956	[illegible]	New York City
	Mrs. [illegible]	[illegible]

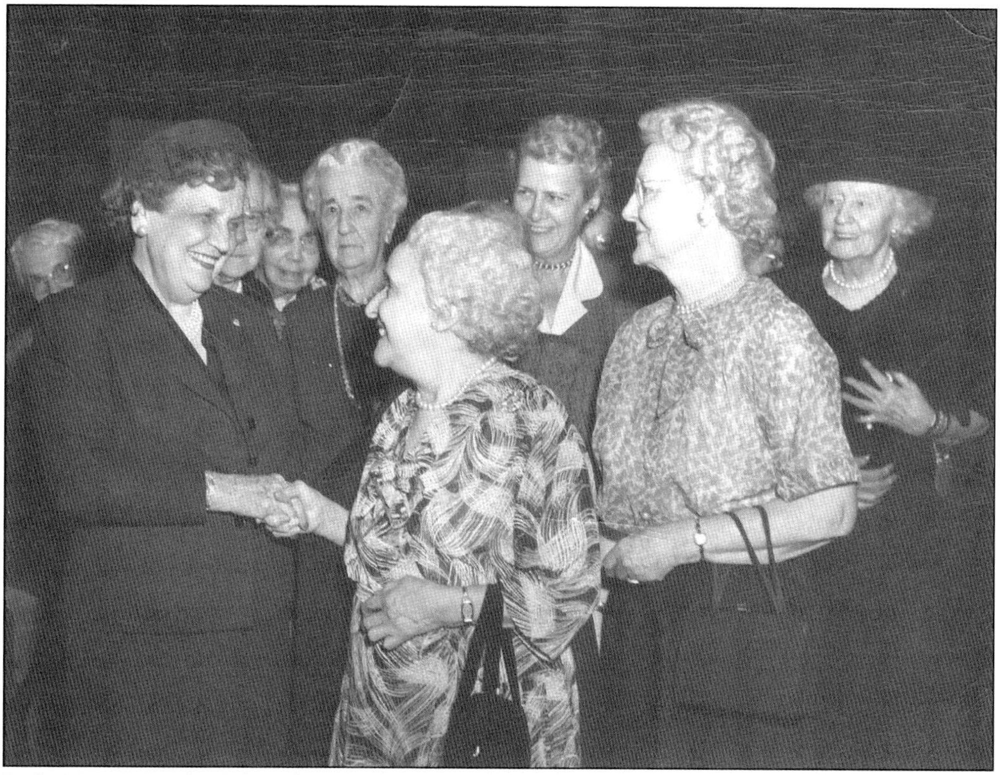

Perle Mesta, on the left with a group of The Osborn residents, was known for her glamorous parties attended by Washington's finest. She visited The Osborn on October 15, 1956. Her lecture topic was "The World Today." Mesta was the United States ambassador to Luxembourg from 1949 until 1953. Irving Berlin based his musical *Call Me Madame* on Mesta. Her signature, indicating another visit, appears in the guest book on September 4, 1961.

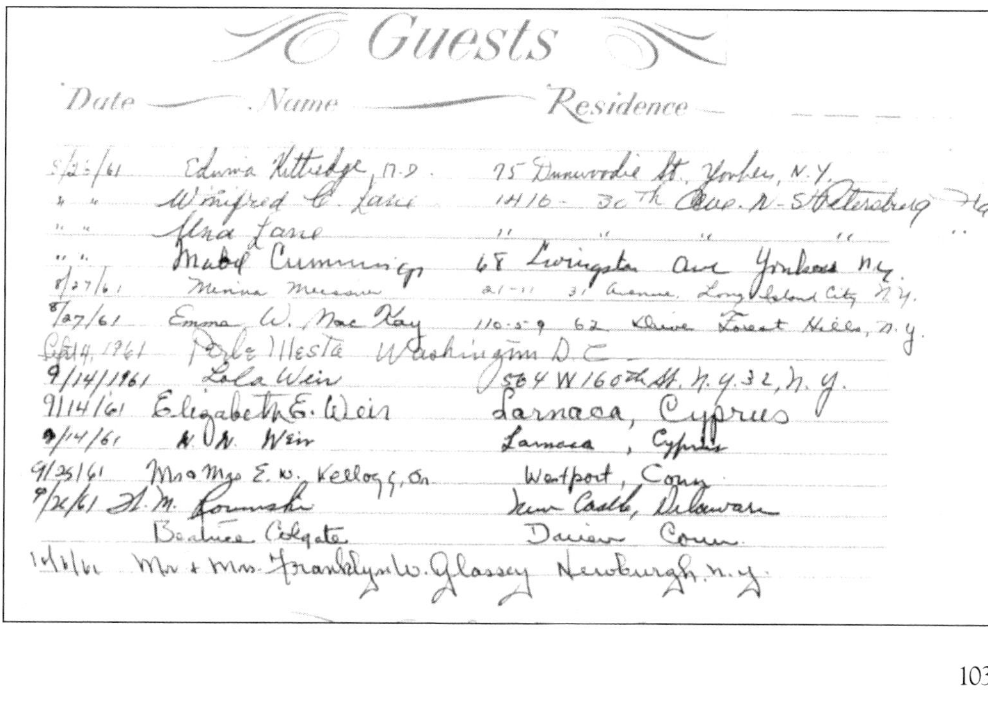

Guests

Date	Name	Residence
5/22/61	Edwina Kittredge, M.D.	75 Dunwoodie St. Yonkers, N.Y.
" "	Winifred C. Lane	1416 - 30th Ave. N. St. Petersburg Fla
" "	Alma Lane	" " " " "
" "	Mabel Cummings	68 Livingston Ave Yonkers N.Y.
8/27/61	Minna Meisner	21-11 31 Avenue, Long Island City N.Y.
8/27/61	Emma W. MacKay	110-59 62 Drive Forest Hills, N.Y.
Sept 4, 1961	Perle Mesta	Washington D.C.
9/14/1961	Lola Weir	564 W 160th St. N.Y. 32, N.Y.
9/14/61	Elizabeth E. Weir	Larnaca, Cyprus
9/14/61	N. N. Weir	Larnaca, Cyprus
9/25/61	Mr & Mrs E. W. Kellogg, Jr.	Westport, Conn
9/26/61	H. M. [illegible]	New Castle, Delaware
	Beatrice Colgate	Darien Conn.
10/1/61	Mr + Mrs. Franklyn W. Glassey	Newburgh, N.Y.

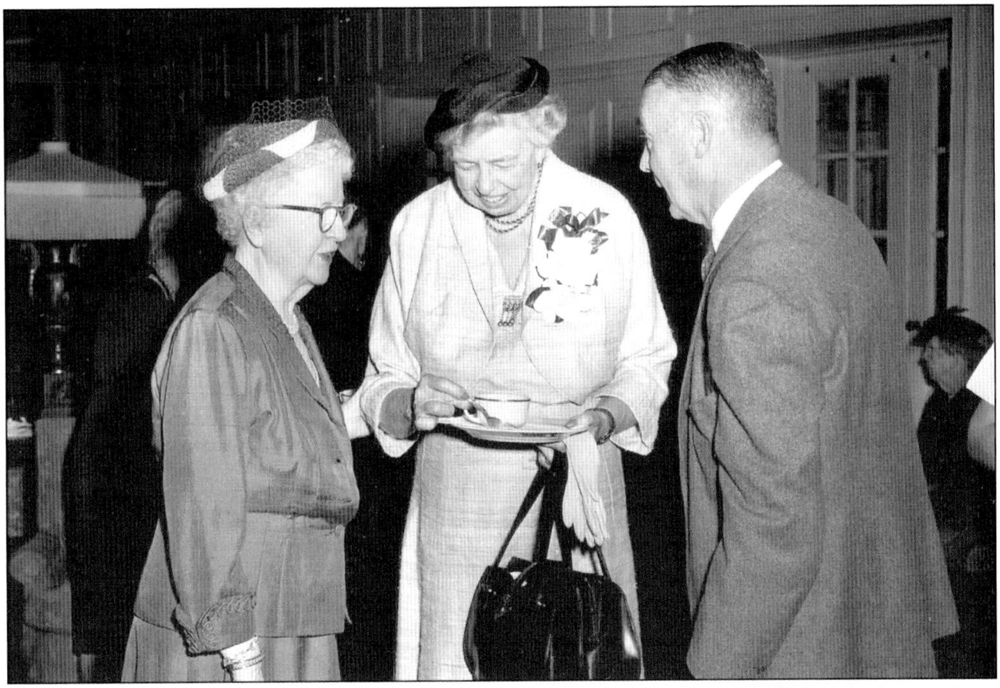

Eleanor Roosevelt visited The Osborn on May 18, 1956. She spoke to a filled auditorium about the United Nations. She enjoys a cup of tea in the Sterling Lounge while chatting with Helen Adams and Chauncey B. Garver. Below, she is pictured with the board president Garver as they leave the auditorium. Note the fur stole martin, a popular fashion statement at the time, held by the person behind the woman in the foreground.

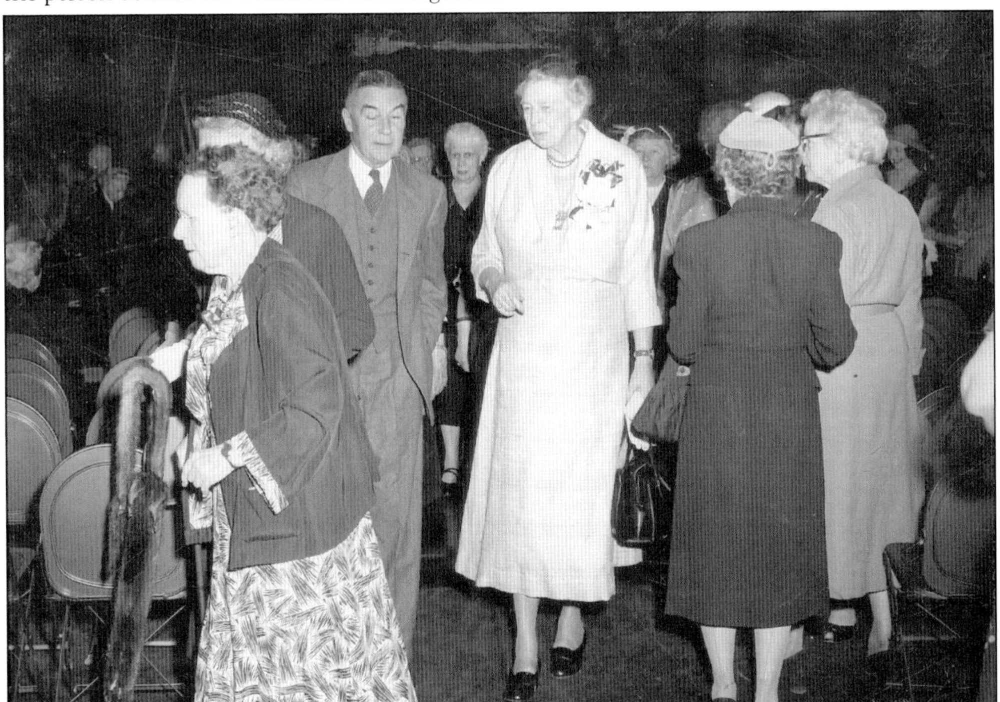

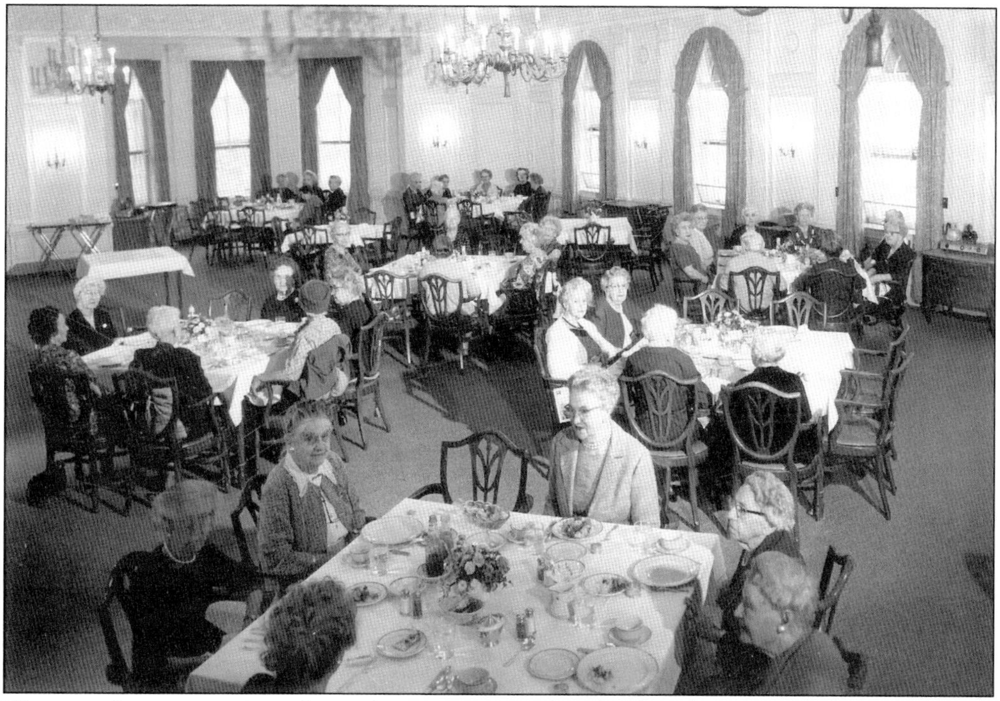

The new dining complex of two dining rooms with a kitchen below and serving pantry in between was added with the Mount Stephen-Strathcona building in 1929. Visitors from many institutions came to look and were generous in their praise according to Helen Adams because the layout was considered an advance in institutional planning. She wrote that the decorations were copied by architect Wick from those in an authentic Adam room in one of the great houses of England. Dining guidelines required residents to sit in assigned places. This allowed staff to be alert to any absences. Below is the architect's photograph of the completed room. At the end of 1929, there were 88 residents. The number of residents did not require the use of the east dining room so it was used as an auditorium when necessary.

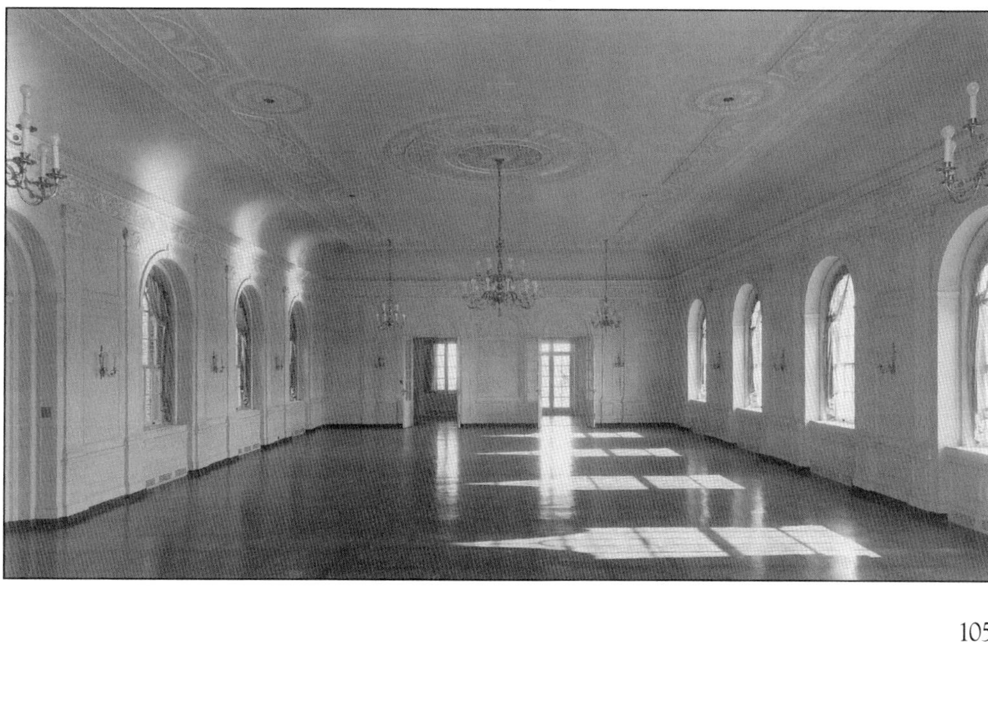

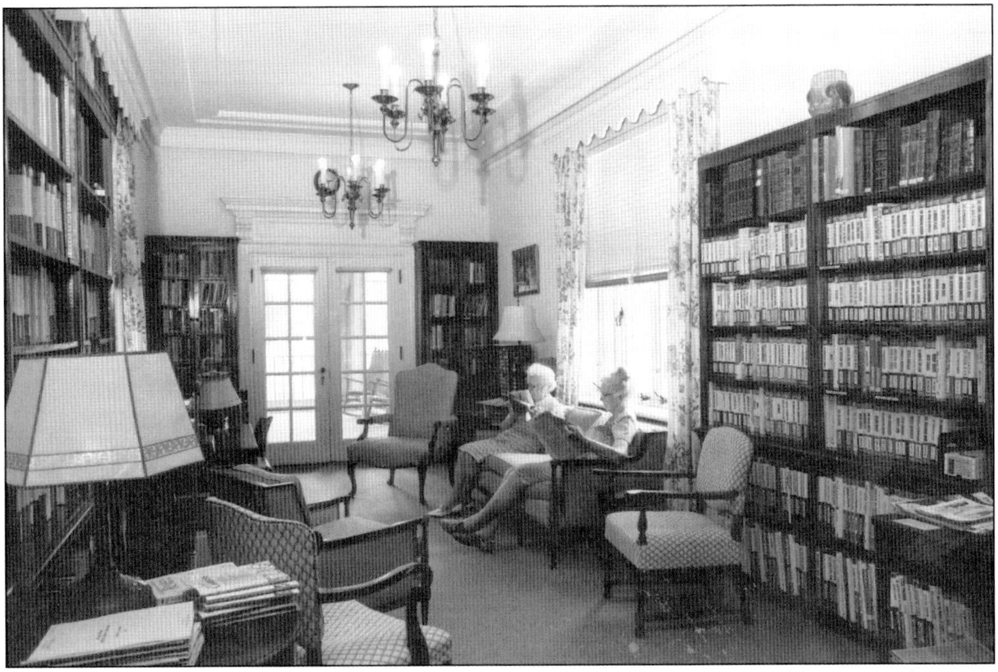

Other rooms important to resident life at the home include the Dalphin library on the main floor, located in the 1908 Osborn building, and the chapel built in 1961 across from the dining rooms.

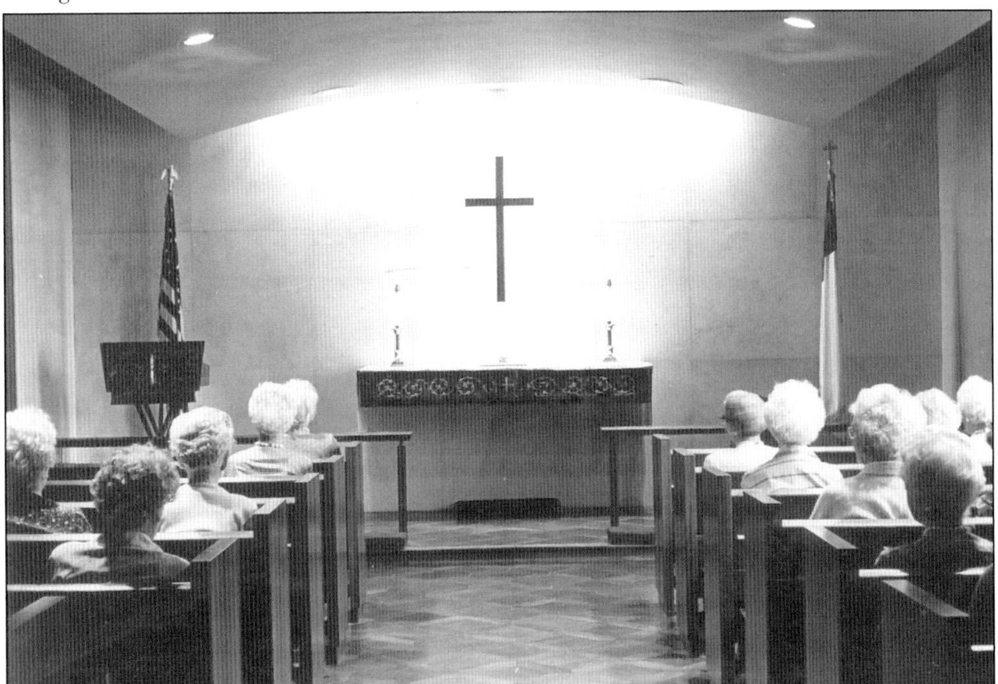

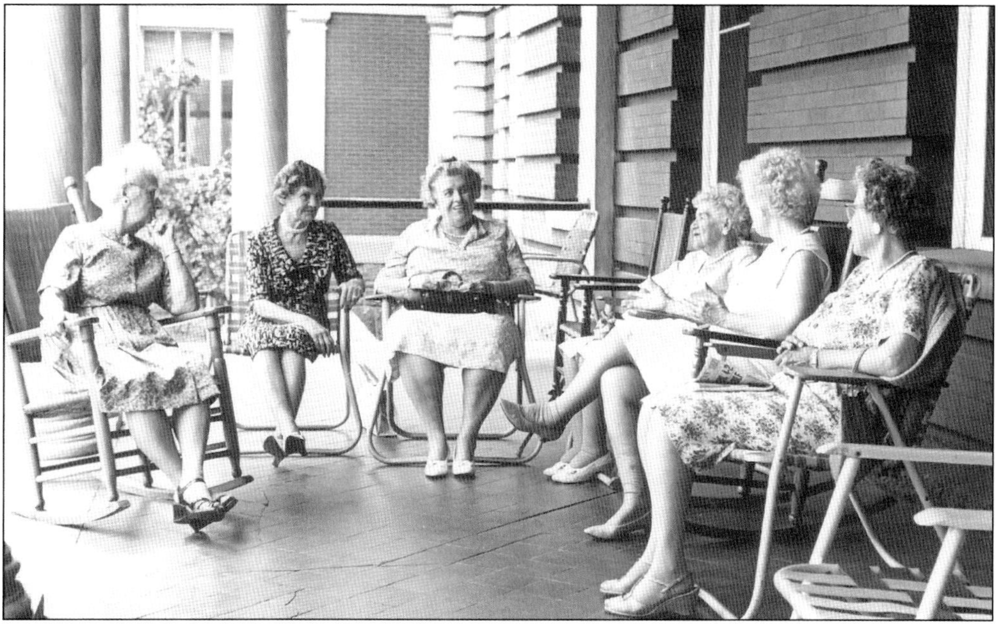

Enduring friendships developed between residents who shared their lifestyles and life stories. The public spaces such as the porch on the south lawn and the parlor, which are pictured, encourage conversation. In the parlor, two residents sit under a picture of R. Eugene Curry, director from 1948 until 1970. Note the Sevres vases in the corner in front of a mirrored screen, exactly as they were arranged in 1908 so that the beauty of the vases could be seen from all sides. When the home opened in 1908, residents' rooms did not have running water but all rooms had a fireplace. At the end of 1909, the "family" was small with 25 residents. By 1913, there were 52 residents. By 1938, there were 168 residents. Today the resident family numbers 416.

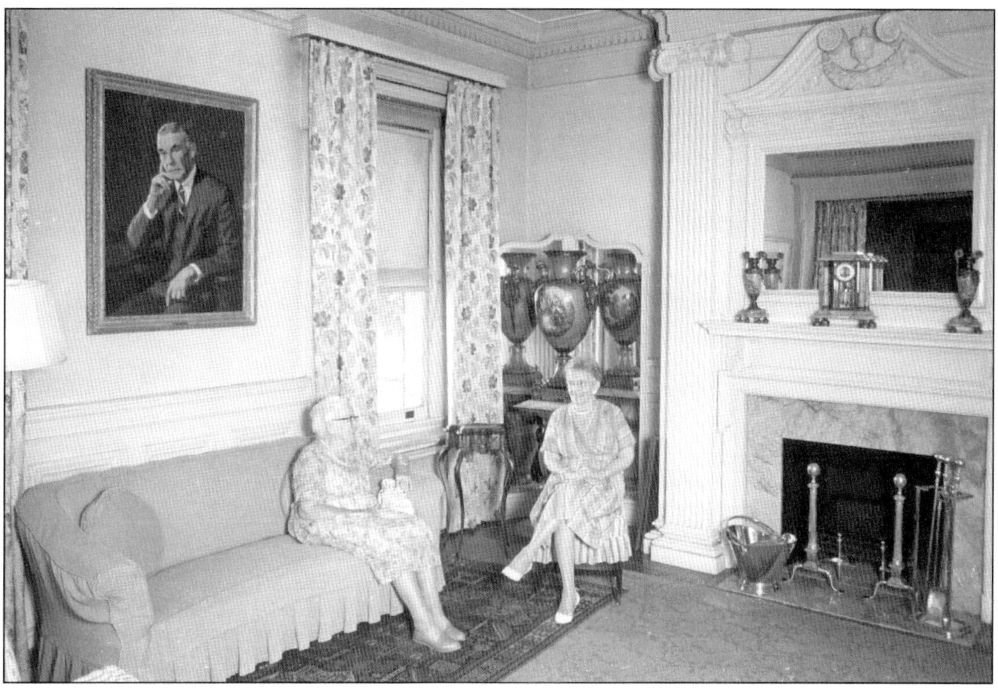

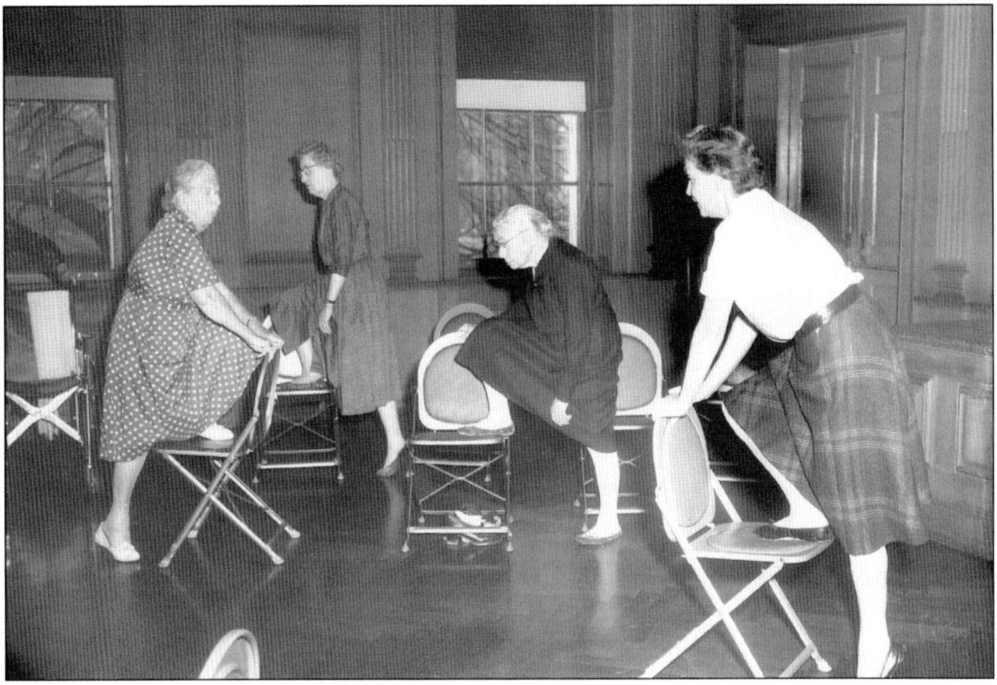

Betty Meredith Jones led exercise classes to encourage fitness and relaxation. Interestingly, even in this setting the women wore dresses for the activity. Trousers for women were not the accepted attire at The Osborn in 1960. Change came, but slowly. A most dramatic change occurred in 1991 when the first male resident, Stanley Martin, was admitted to The Osborn.

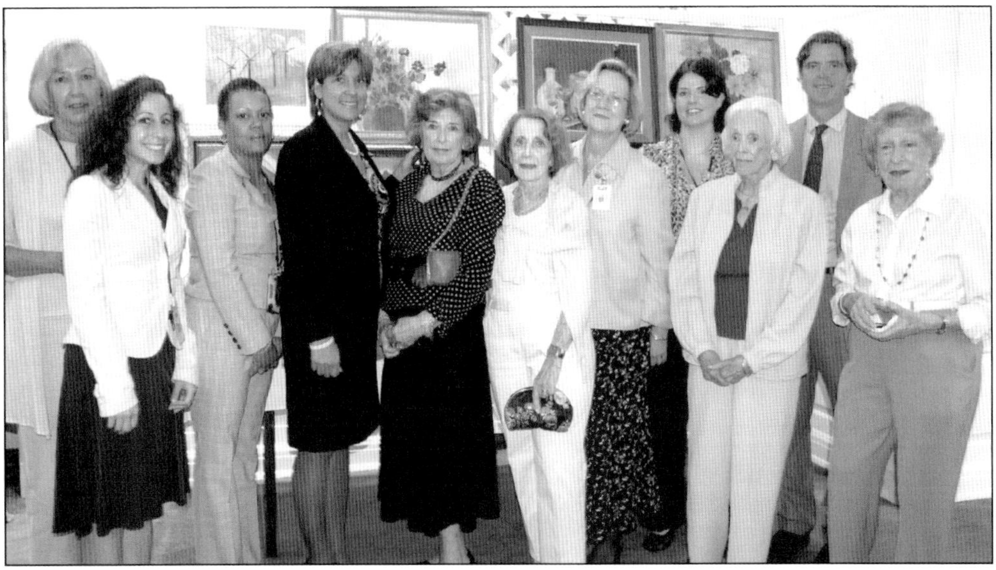

Above from left to right, Sterling Park staff members Susan Bertolacci, Daniela Marini, Ana Maria Lopez, and Debbie Curcio, residents Barbara Ucci and Rose Nackman, Sterling Park manager Janet M. Malang, resident services director Susan Keating, resident Jane Waters, dining director Andrew F. Horn, and resident Dottie Peisinger are pictured at a September 2007 art display reception. Today's elders enjoy a social life enhanced by programs such as art and computer instruction.

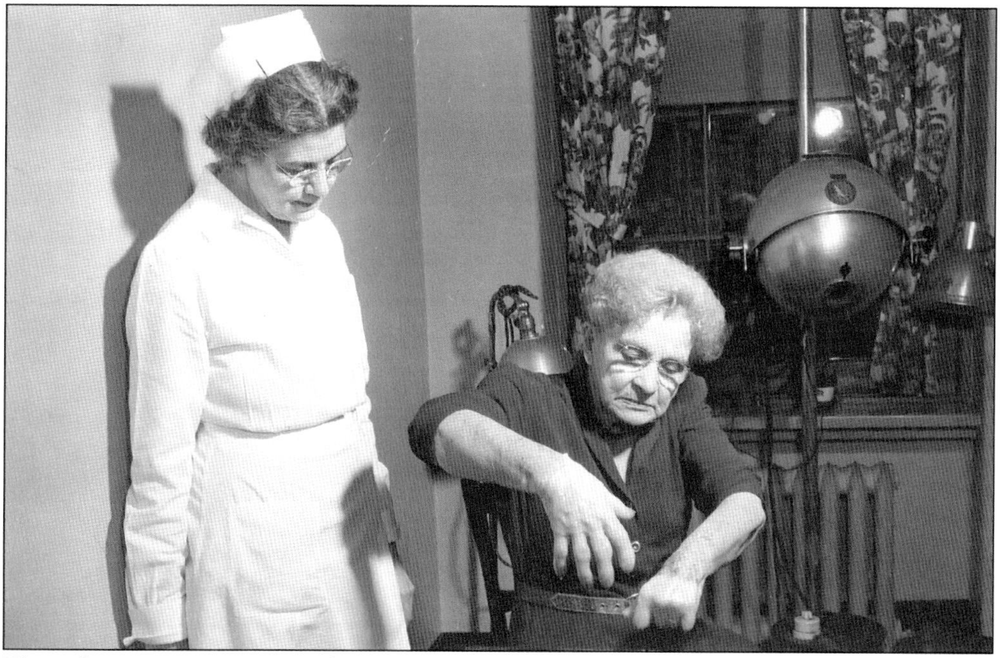

The infirmary, an important advancement at The Osborn in caring for sick elders, opened in 1929 in the Strathcona building. It had 64 single rooms, large enough to allow residents to bring some of their cherished belongings. There was an office for the doctor and head nurse on the third floor and a treatment room with a sterilizing alcove. A portable X-ray machine allowed X-rays on the site. It had electric call lights in the bedrooms and bathrooms, and floor lights illuminated the corridors. The resident pictured with the nurse in the physical therapy department is using a warm paraffin dip to treat arthritis. Below, Kate Loree, a current pavilion resident, assisted by a volunteer, enjoys therapy of a more spirited nature, participating in the 2007 Golden Olympics, a competition of physical activities for elders residing in nursing homes.

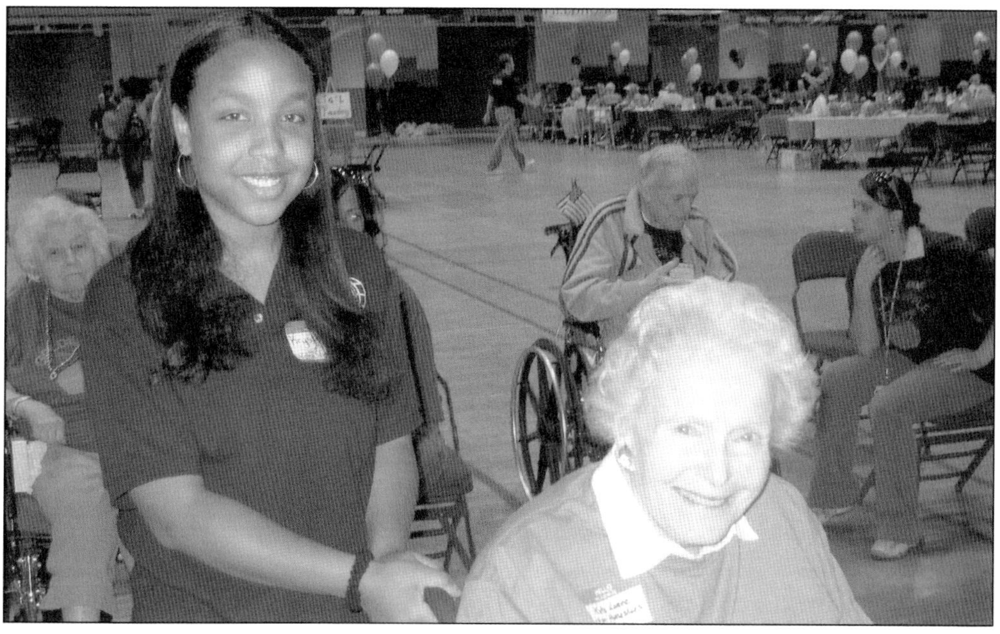

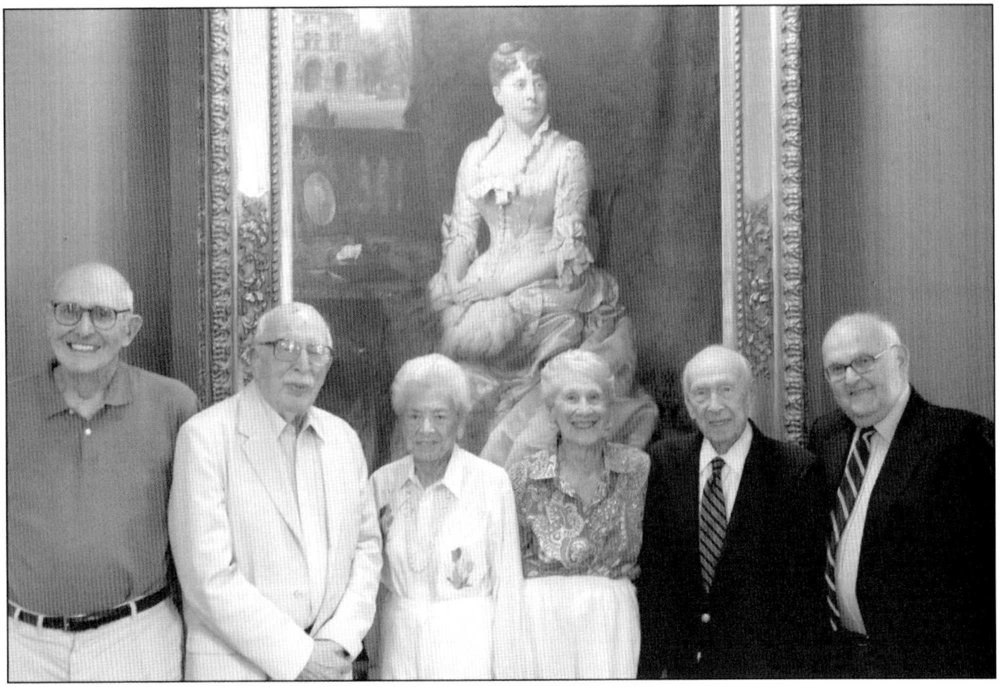

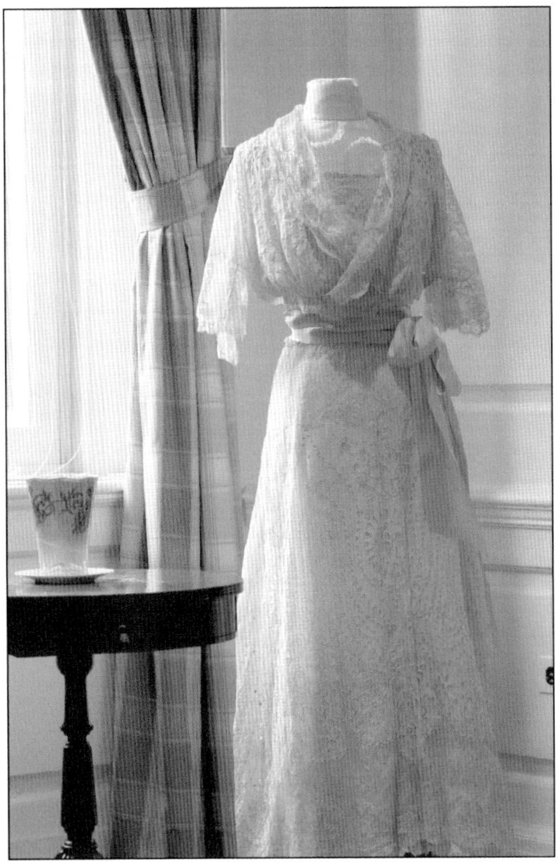

The formality that characterized The Osborn 100 years ago gradually gave way to new practices. The six residents pictured above are the current and past presidents of the Sterling Park Residents Association, organized after the opening of the new buildings. Pictured from left to right are current president Ned Pugh and past presidents Arthur Jacobs, Betty Menke, Sylvia Greenberg, Sol Himmelman, and Arnold "Korky" Kaulakis, the first president elected when the association was formed in 1996. These people were instrumental in providing opportunities for residents to be decision makers in the programs and practices at The Osborn through a committee structure. The association's Costume Group of residents, Louise Lowry, Helen O'Connor, Dorothy Morrison, Evy Greenberg, and Gloria Rennert, preserve and display historic garments donated to The Osborn by past residents. This young woman's party dress was handmade around 1901.

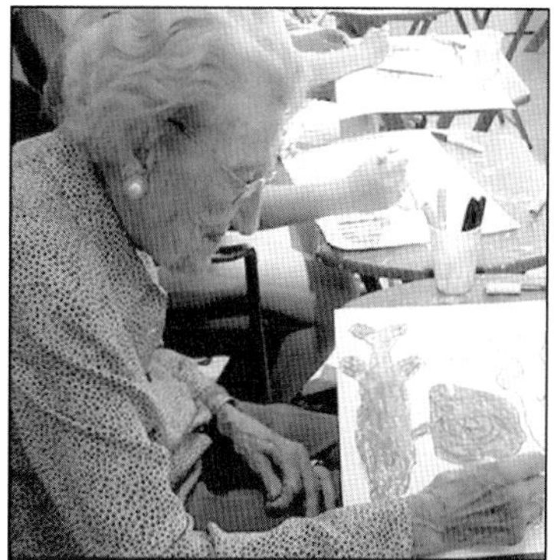

Resident Sarah Weisse (top right) participates in Partners in Art, an art course pairing Osborn residents with high school students. The program uses art to build communication between generations. The art studio in the Strathcona building was funded by a gift from the Horace W. Goldsmith Foundation and the Menschel family of resident MacClaire Arlt, in memory of her husband Paul Arlt, a noted artist and Osborn resident. He was an editorial cartoonist for the *New York Herald Tribune*. The United States government commissioned his work for various public purposes. His art appears at several museums, including the National Air and Space Museum. His *Saturday in Enterprise* hangs in the Enterprise, Alabama, public library. MacClaire Arlt is pictured on the bottom right with Mark R. Zwerger at the opening of the studio. There are regularly scheduled art classes for residents. Works of residents are pictured below.

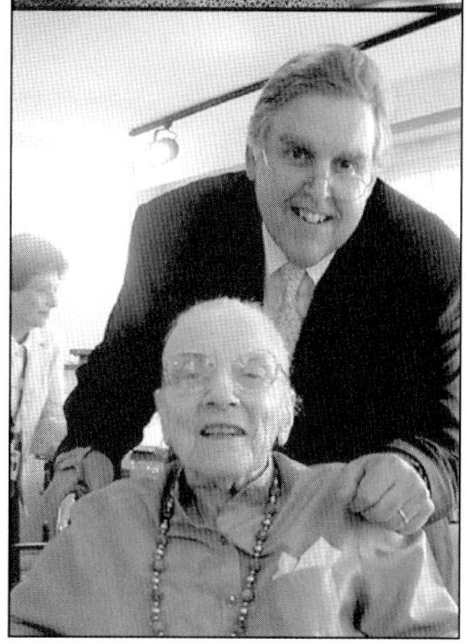

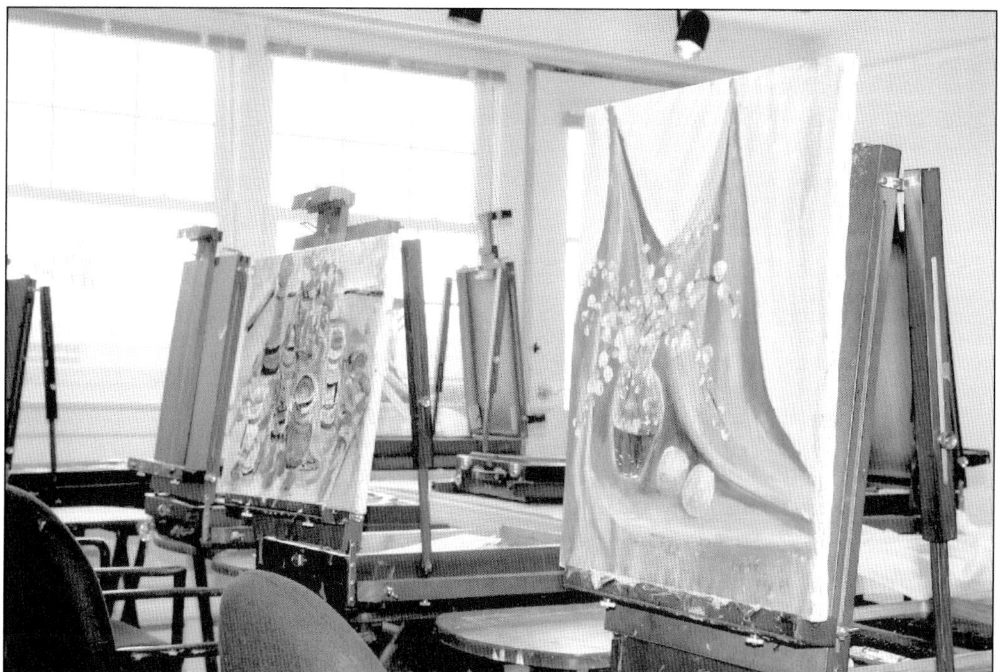

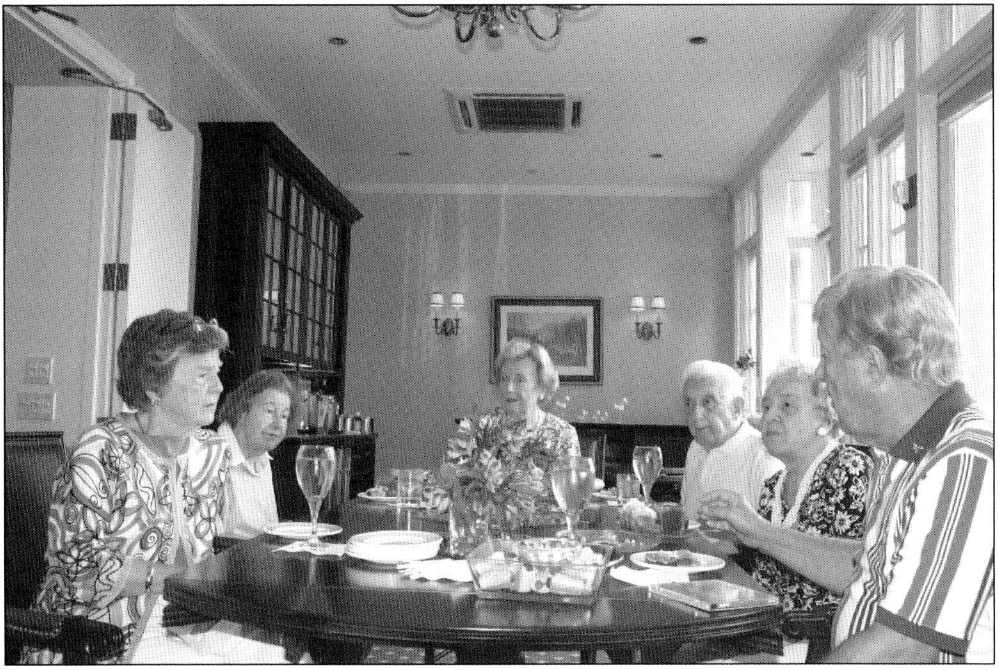

While many things change, some remain the same. Costumed performances are enjoyed as much as the George Washington party of 1933. The photograph above shows some of the cast of the 2007 Murder Mystery Dinner. The residents from left to right are Bibs Reville, Sis Fortune, Ruth Ruth, Vito Rossi, Frances Capici, and Ed Pasciuti. The residents work with Andrew F. Horn, dining director, to create a whodunit that entertains other residents while they dine and try to detect who is the murderer. The photograph below shows residents enjoying an exercise session in the expanded fitness center donated by Osborn residents Marion and Sam Galewitz. Exercise has become part of many residents' routines, like 102 year-old Minnie Lobl in the center of the photograph. Gabrielle Lofaro chats while she works out.

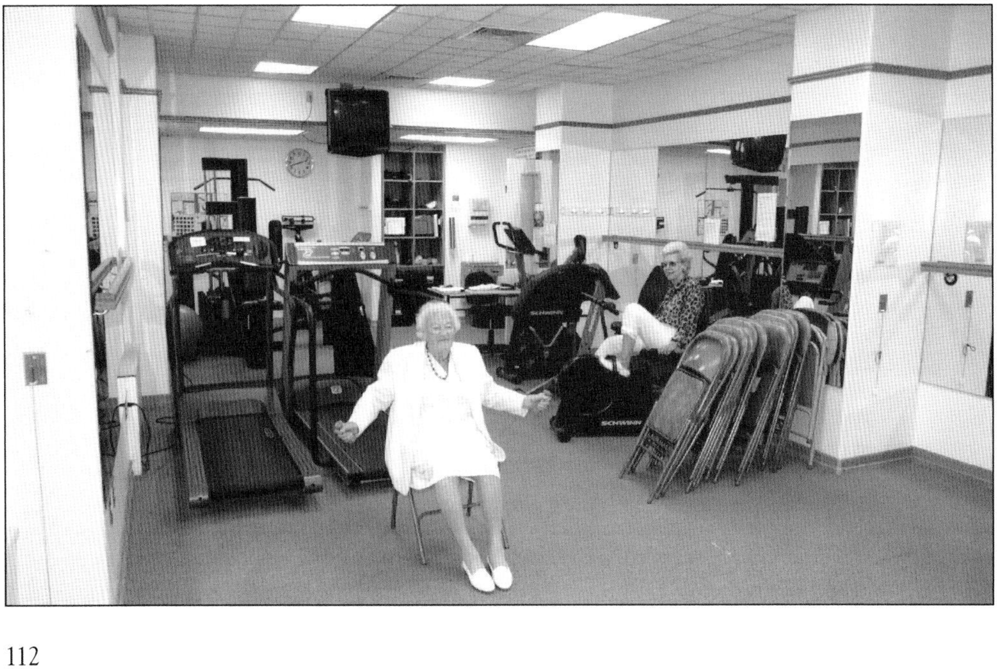

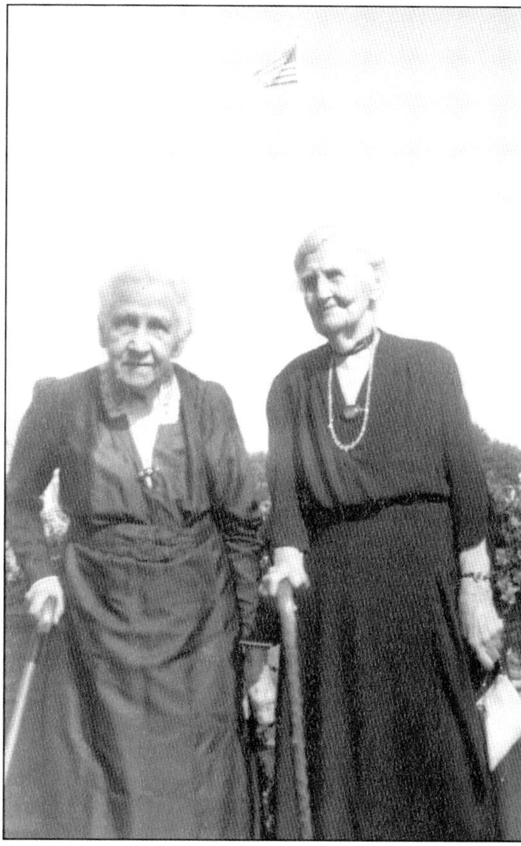

Throughout the years, residents at The Osborn reach wonderful ages. It is not uncommon for many residents to enjoy their 100th birthdays. To the right, two residents, Anne H. Wells (left), age 100, and Jennie Smith, age 101, are pictured on the south lawn in September 1955. In the September 1989 photograph below, chief executive Mark R. Zwerger wishes Elsa Cash happy 100th birthday.

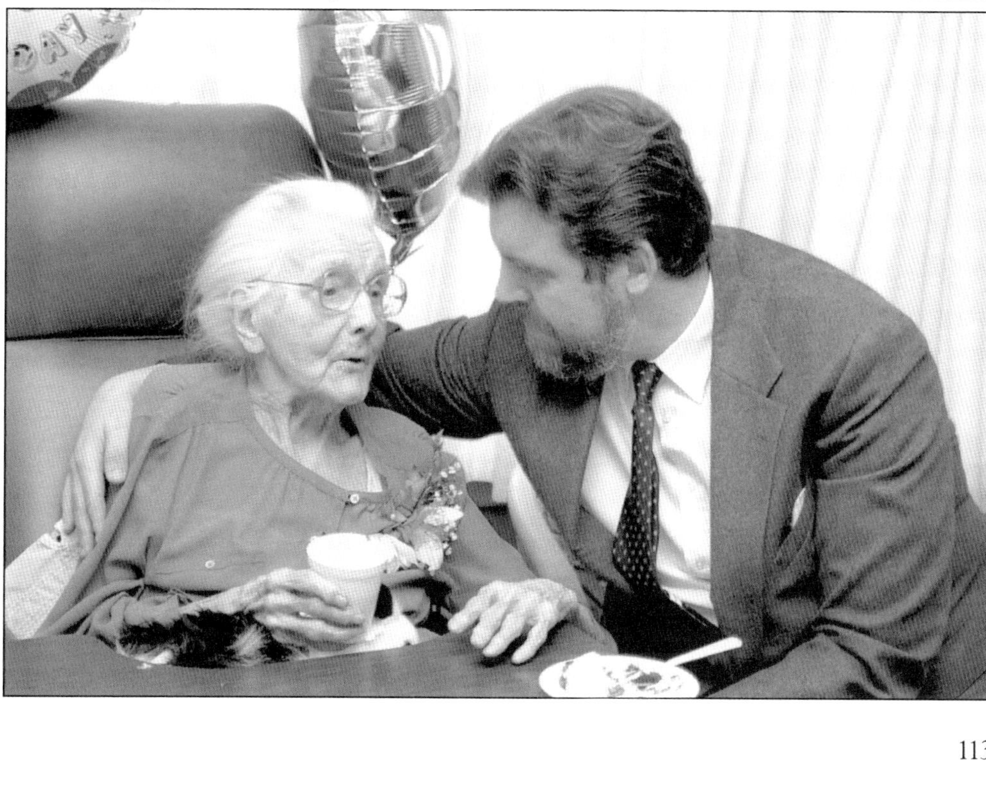

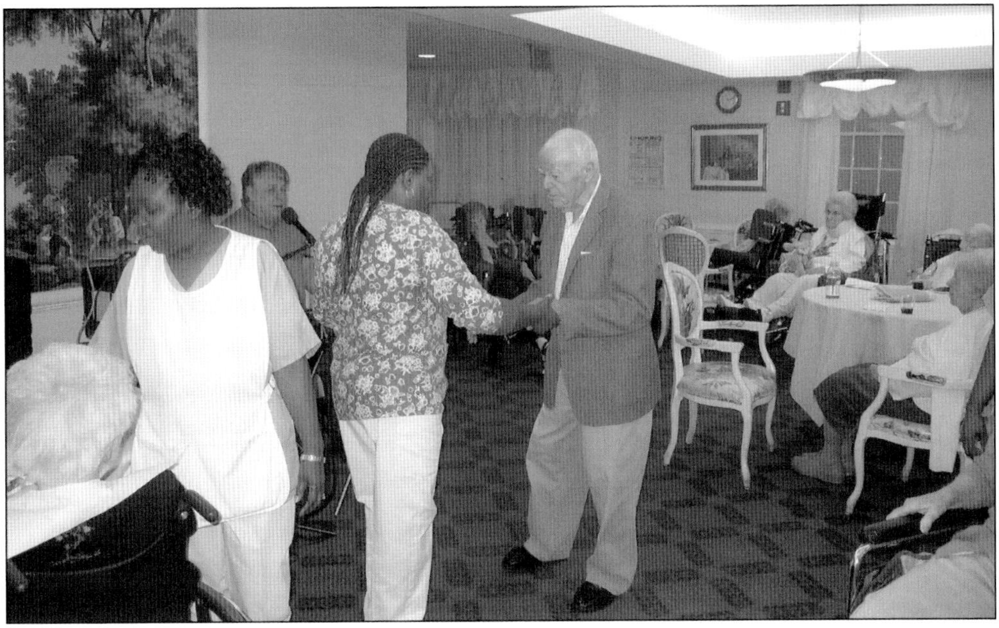

In the photograph above, resident Dr. Austin Murphy is dancing with Beatrice Cameron in the pavilion dining room. Below, Kathleen Pearson (left) and Esther Flowers enjoy a special luncheon with other pavilion residents, families, and staff on the lawn under a tent. The Osborn is a retirement community that has always offered continuing care to the elderly. The opportunity to receive support services personalized to one's level of ability is fundamental to The Osborn. Residents may move into the fully independent program and transition to the pavilion for skilled care or to assisted living for lesser needs. Additionally, home care services are available to support residents in any level of care for as long as possible before requiring care at a higher level. Residents enjoy quality services today just as when the home opened according to the same high-quality standards.

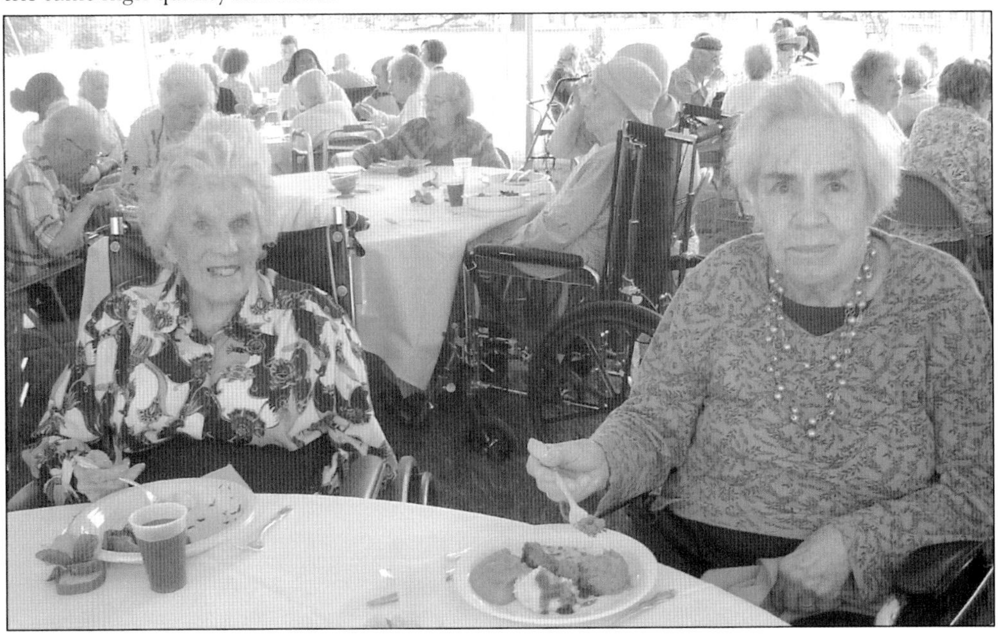

Six

Planning for the Second Century

The operations of The Osborn Home remained unchanged from its 1908 opening until 1975. Beginning in the late 1960s, a series of events revolutionized the field of aging services and the regulation of care of the aged. The passage of Titles XVIII and XIX of the Social Security Act established the Medicare and Medicaid programs and created regulations that govern the establishment and operation of nursing homes in the United States. Over the next two decades, the regulations governing nursing homes became increasingly more stringent.

All of these forces conspired to render The Osborn essentially obsolete in 20 years. As a result, occupancy declined precipitously and the board of trustees began to ask the difficult questions about the future of the institution. The trustees decided on a course of action to restore The Osborn to its original vision and mission. This plan, titled Pathway 2000, was adopted by the board on May 14, 1991. It called for the construction of 26 buildings, including 20 garden homes, 3 multistory apartment buildings, a natatorium, a gatehouse, and a new nursing home, The Osborn Pavilion. The project also included the renovation of the existing three buildings into rental accommodations for seniors. Constructed in phases between 1995 and 2001, Pathway 2000 cost approximately $120 million. The project was financed through two sources: the proceeds of the sale of tax-exempt bonds and the accumulation of 100 percent refundable entrance fees paid by Sterling Park residents. Those fees added up to about $80 million, and the balance of bonds remaining at the completion of the project was about $45 million.

The goal of Pathway 2000, to restore The Osborn to Miriam Osborn and John Sterling's vision and create a sustainable charitable operation into perpetuity, has been accomplished. The Osborn stands as one of the premier facilities of its kind anywhere, providing over $2 million annually in free care to seniors in need. Over 400 residents call The Osborn "home" while 300 others annually come to The Osborn Pavilion for rehabilitation. Hundreds of seniors residing in the community have availed themselves of the care provided by Osborn Home Care.

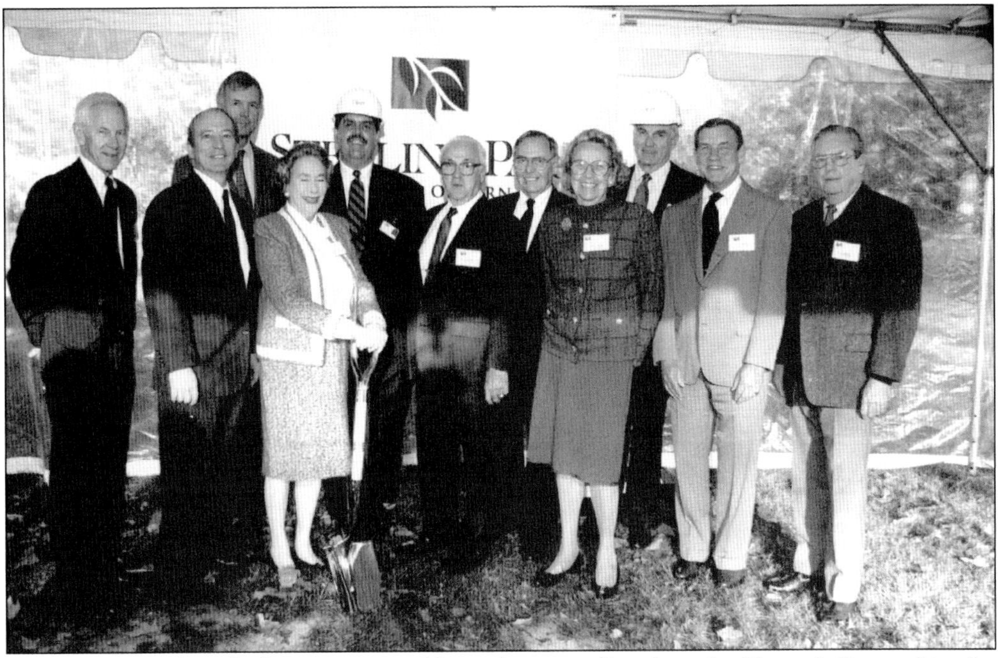

Members of the board of trustees assemble at the groundbreaking for Phase I. Pictured in the photograph from left to right are Arne Hovdesven, Bill Mauritz, mayor of Rye Ted Dunn, Ginny Hutton, chief executive officer Mark R. Zwerger, Ed Grainger, George Reader, M.D., Betty Neagle, chairman of the board Jack Bowen, Dan deMenocal, and Bert Jamison.

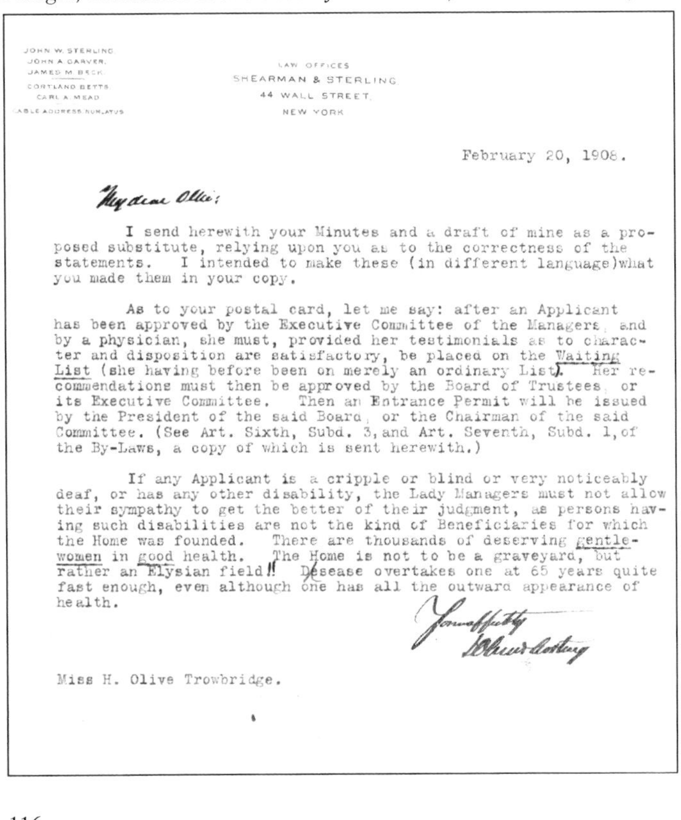

JOHN W. STERLING
JOHN A. GARVER.
JAMES M. BECK.
CORTLANDT BETTS.
CARL A. MEAD.
CABLE ADDRESS NUMLATUS

LAW OFFICES
SHEARMAN & STERLING
44 WALL STREET
NEW YORK

February 20, 1908.

My dear Ollie:

I send herewith your Minutes and a draft of mine as a proposed substitute, relying upon you as to the correctness of the statements. I intended to make these (in different language) what you made them in your copy.

As to your postal card, let me say: after an Applicant has been approved by the Executive Committee of the Managers, and by a physician, she must, provided her testimonials as to character and disposition are satisfactory, be placed on the Waiting List (she having before been on merely an ordinary List). Her recommendations must then be approved by the Board of Trustees, or its Executive Committee. Then an Entrance Permit will be issued by the President of the said Board, or the Chairman of the said Committee. (See Art. Sixth, Subd. 3, and Art. Seventh, Subd. 1, of the By-Laws, a copy of which is sent herewith.)

If any Applicant is a cripple or blind or very noticeably deaf, or has any other disability, the Lady Managers must not allow their sympathy to get the better of their judgment, as persons having such disabilities are not the kind of Beneficiaries for which the Home was founded. There are thousands of deserving gentlewomen in good health. The Home is not to be a graveyard, but rather an Elysian field!! Disease overtakes one at 65 years quite fast enough, even although one has all the outward appearance of health.

Yours affectly
J.W. Sterling

Miss H. Olive Trowbridge.

In his 1908 letter to Olive Trowbridge, John Sterling explains his vision for the home. "There are thousands of deserving gentlewomen in good health. The Home is not to be a graveyard, but rather an Elysian Field. Disease overcomes one at 65 years quite fast enough, even although one has all the outward appearance of health." The letter demonstrates that Pathway 2000 was consistent with the wishes of the founders.

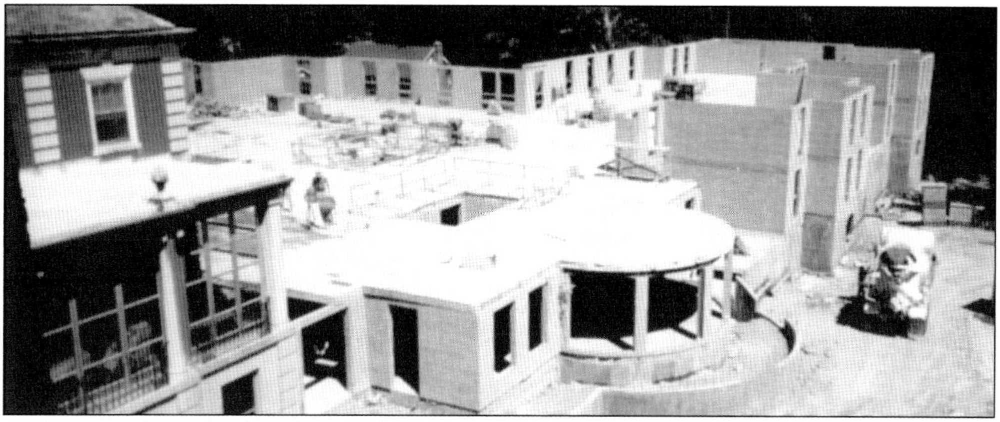

Work proceeds on the foundation of The Osborn Pavilion in the fall of 1995.

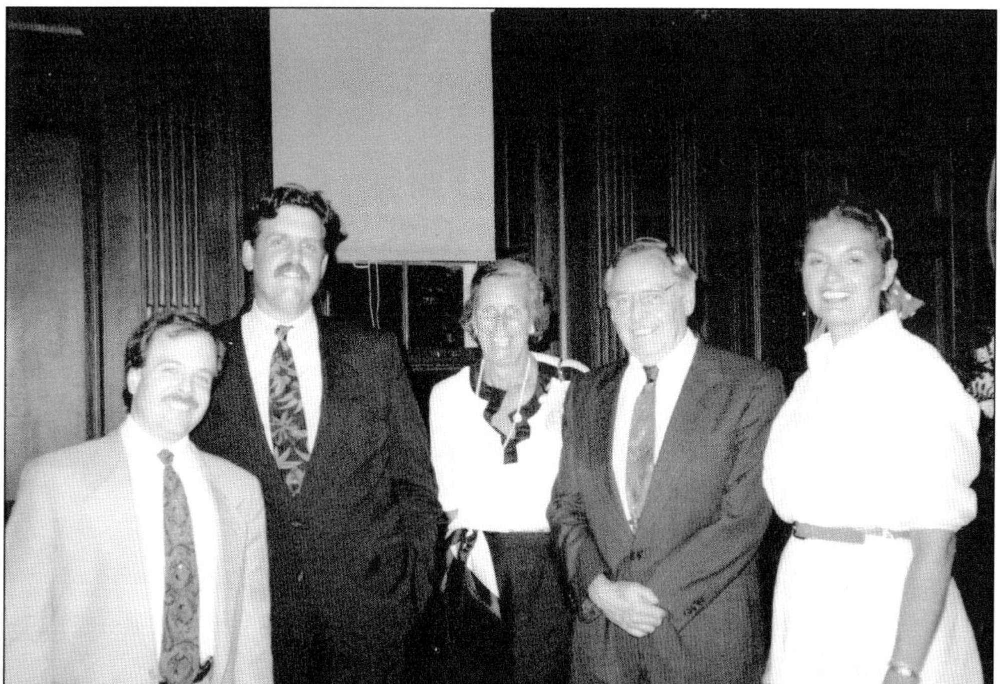

Medical director William Martimucci, M.D., chief executive officer Mark R. Zwerger, Carrie Burns, George Reader, M.D., and Carole Edelman, R.N., are pictured from left to right at the inaugural Lincoln Burns Lecture in 1991 honoring former board chairman the late Lincoln Burns.

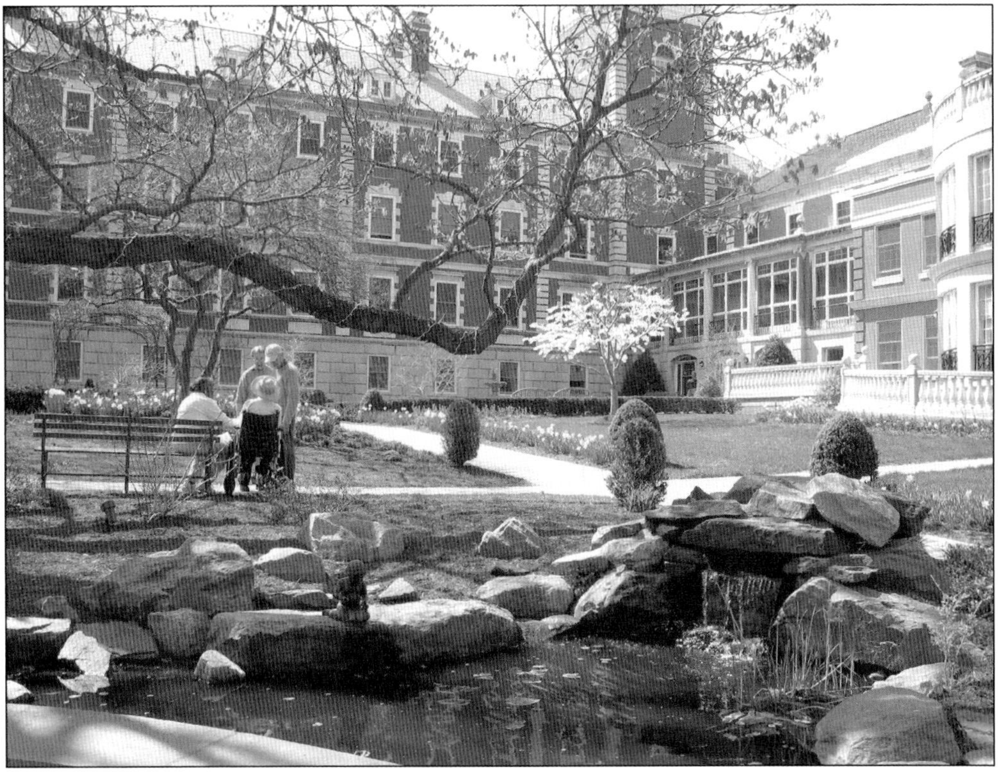

The Betty Neagle Perennial Garden was constructed in 1999 in honor of Betty Neagle, who served on the board of managers and board of trustees for 37 years.

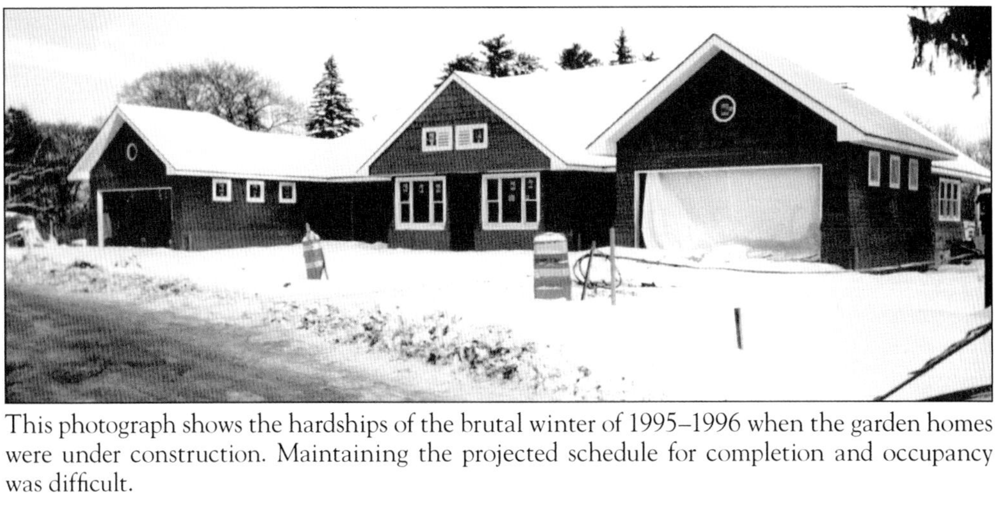

This photograph shows the hardships of the brutal winter of 1995–1996 when the garden homes were under construction. Maintaining the projected schedule for completion and occupancy was difficult.

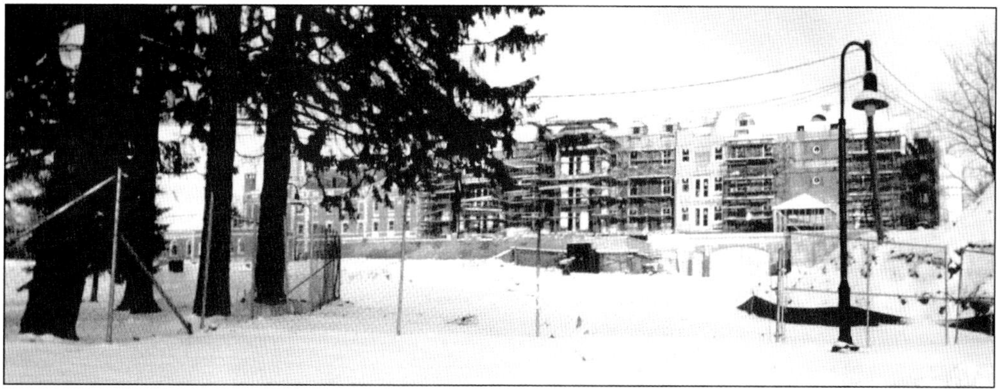

The 2000 building, the first Sterling Park apartment building, was also under construction during one of the many blizzards of 1996.

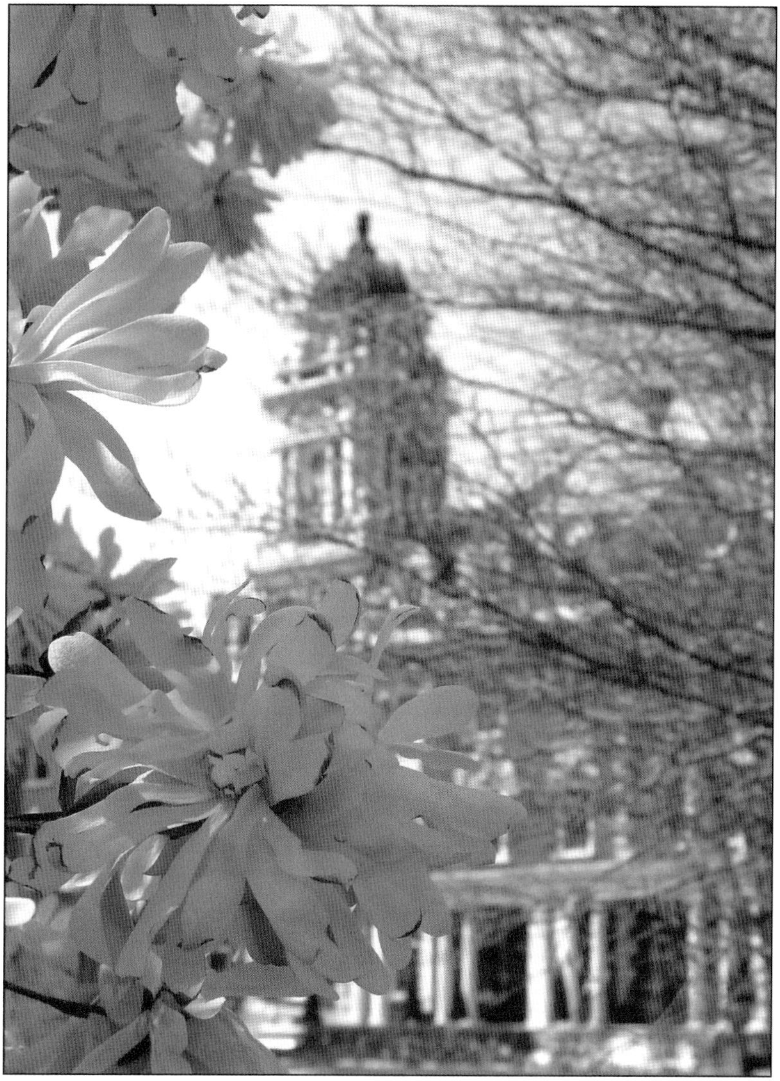

The beauty of the campus is evident in the photograph in which magnolias frame the original 1908 Osborn building. As The Osborn looks forward to its second century, the traditions of the past provide a sound foundation for continued excellence in caring for the aged.

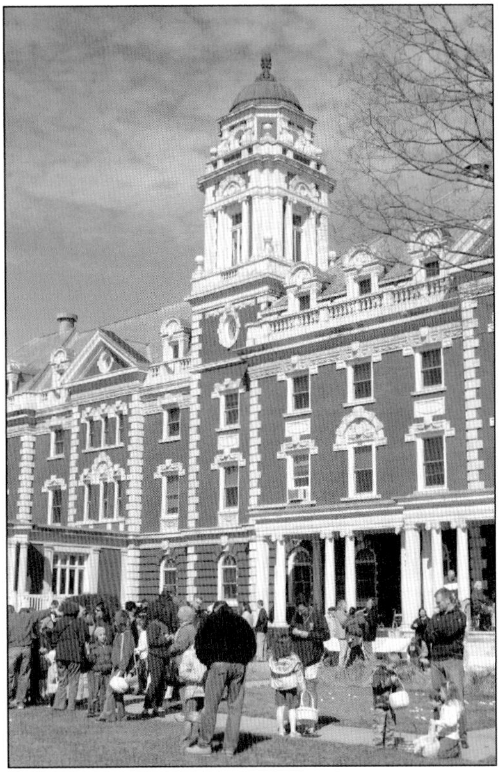

Local children enjoy the annual Easter egg hunt. The Osborn invites the community to many events, including summer outdoor concerts and a yearly Halloween parade of schoolchildren from nearby Osborn Elementary School. Yearly, when other facilities close for vacation, The Osborn opens its pool to the Rye Association for the Handicapped. Each summer local disadvantaged children spend a morning reading, swimming, and feasting at a pizza party.

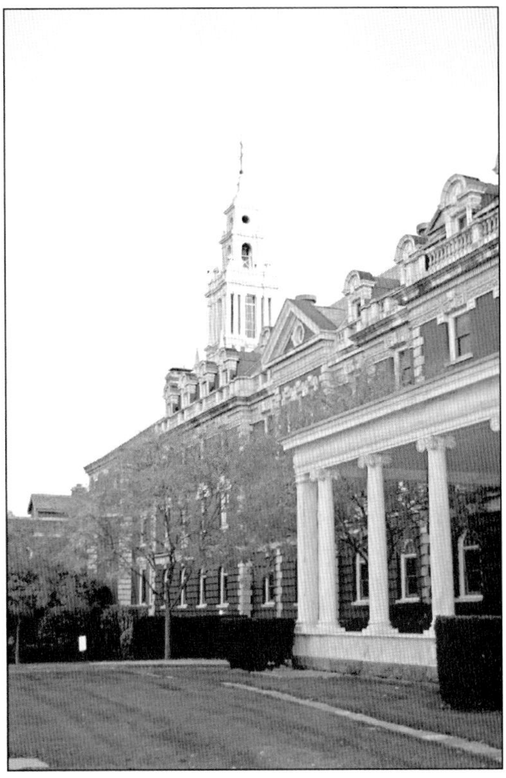

The major renovation of the Strathcona and Sterling buildings in 1998 did not include any exterior changes. The grandeur of these buildings appears today as it did in 1929 and 1932, when they were completed.

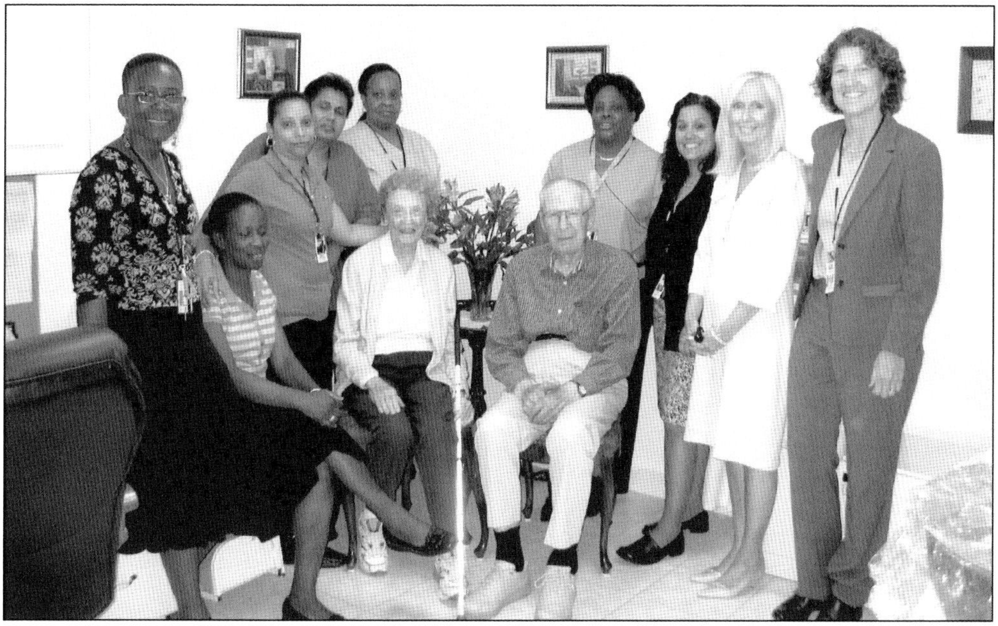

Assisted living staff and residents Kathleen and Peter Krey gather for the grand opening of the new assisted living wellness center. Assisted living offers an ideal setting for residents who need some assistance but are not in need of the pavilion nursing facility. From left to right are Emily Minott, Claudette McLean, Sophe Mitchener, Anita Aban, Sonia Goldson, Kathleen and Peter Krey, Janett Carter, Adrienne Rynne, Eileen Killeen, and Kathy Lonergan.

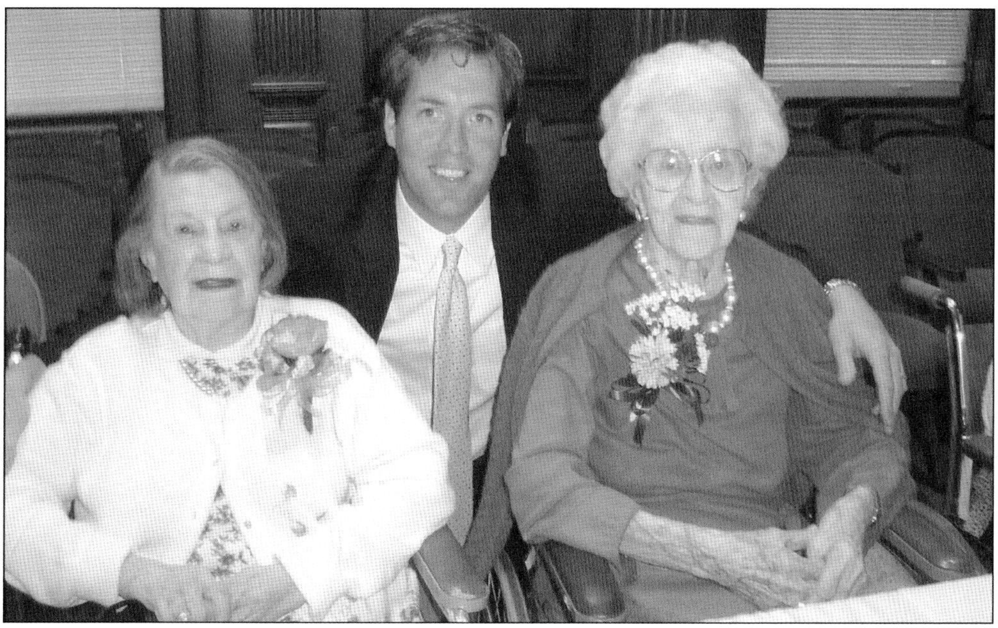

Pavilion administrator Matt Anderson is pictured with Gertrude Miller (right), born on September 26, 1900, and Elizabeth Defaa (left) born on July 13, 1904, at the 2006 Centenarian Celebration. Defaa appeared in the 1921 silent film *Orphans of the Storm*, with Lillian Gish. It is common for The Osborn to be home to a dozen or more centenarians, a testament to the quality of care and the quality of life at The Osborn.

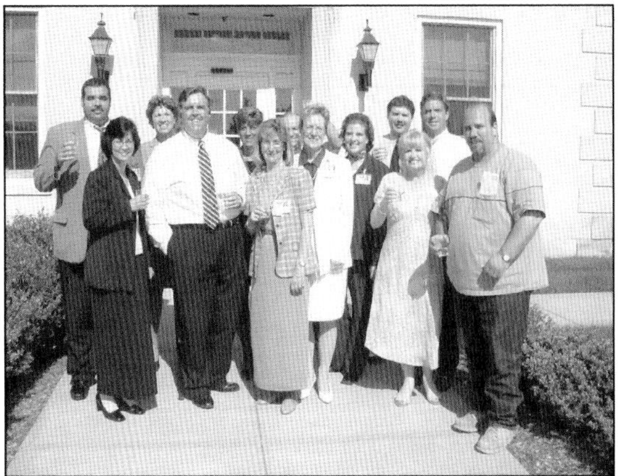

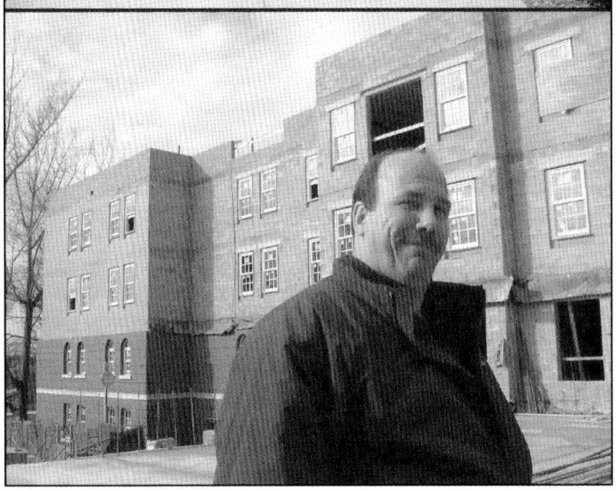

The Osborn team is pictured atop the picture of Mike Pirraglia, The Osborn's construction project manager, from left to right as follows: chief financial officer Nate Soffio, human resources director Elizabeth Rossi, clinical operations manager Kathy Lonergan, chief executive officer Mark R. Zwerger, Sterling Park administrative coordinator Debbie Curcio, environmental services director Dolores Francis, security director Larry Williams, Sterling Park manager Janet M. Malang, resident services director Susan Keating, facilities director Paul Mackey, move-in coordinator Valerie Viapiana, dining director Andrew F. Horn, and construction manager Mike Pirraglia.

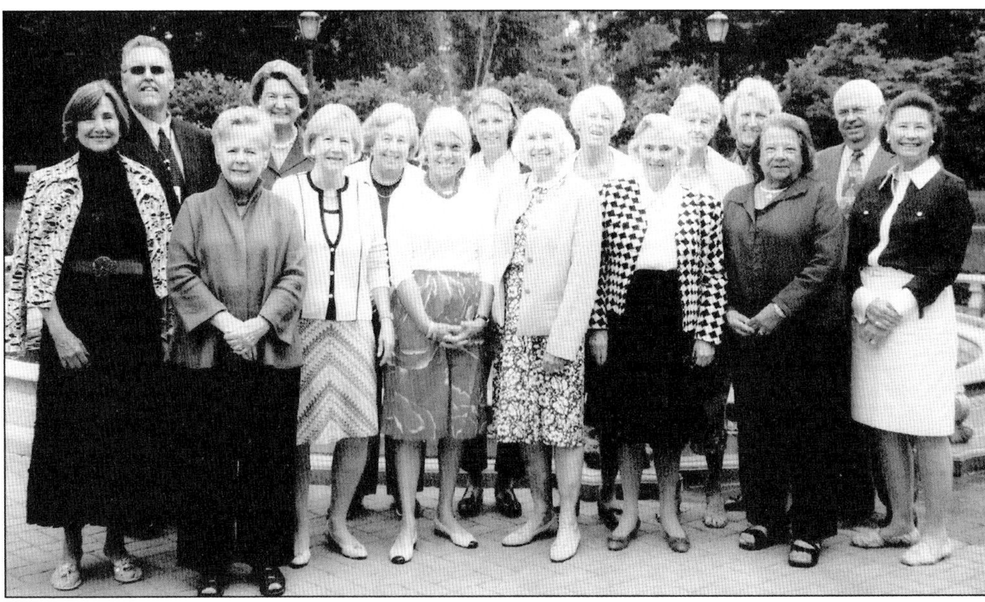

Pictured from left to right are Carol Norton, chief executive officer Mark R. Zwerger, Bess June Lane, Sue Scully, Ann Collins, Peggy Steers, Sue Seitz, Ruth Diefenbach, Ruth Galpin, Anne Kelsey, Molly Rockefeller, Janice Pierce, Angel Morris, Mary Lou Young, board chairman Jack Miller, and Dee Edgar celebrating the 100th anniversary of the board of managers in 2007.

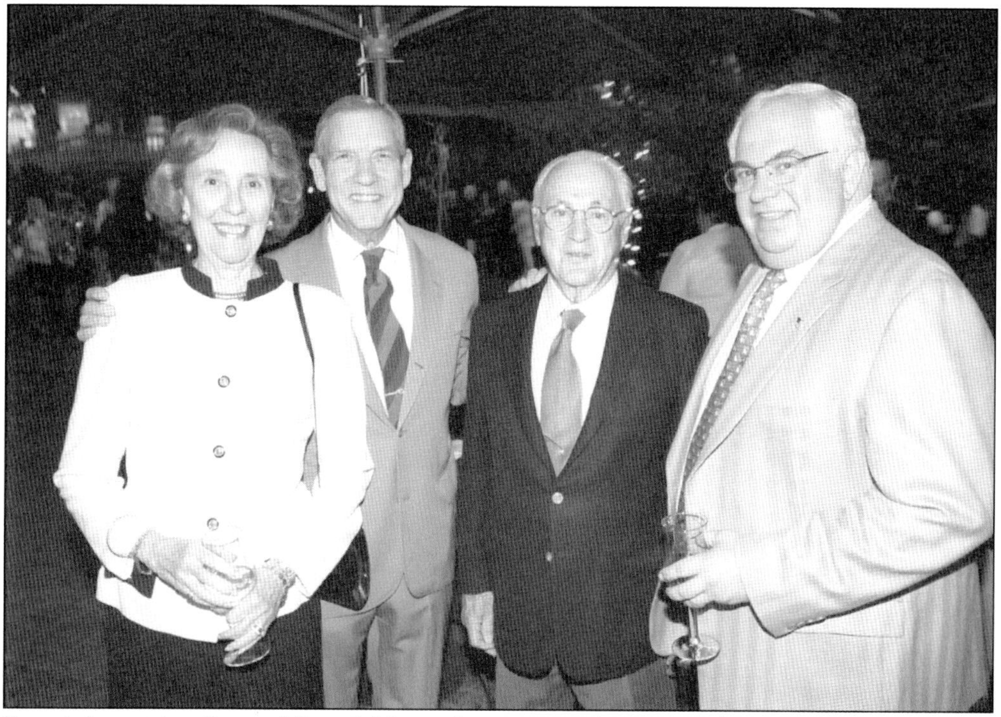

From left to right, Gay and Dan deMenocal, trustee, and trustees Ed Grainger and Jack Miller enjoy the festivities at the dedication ceremony marking the completion of Pathway 2000.

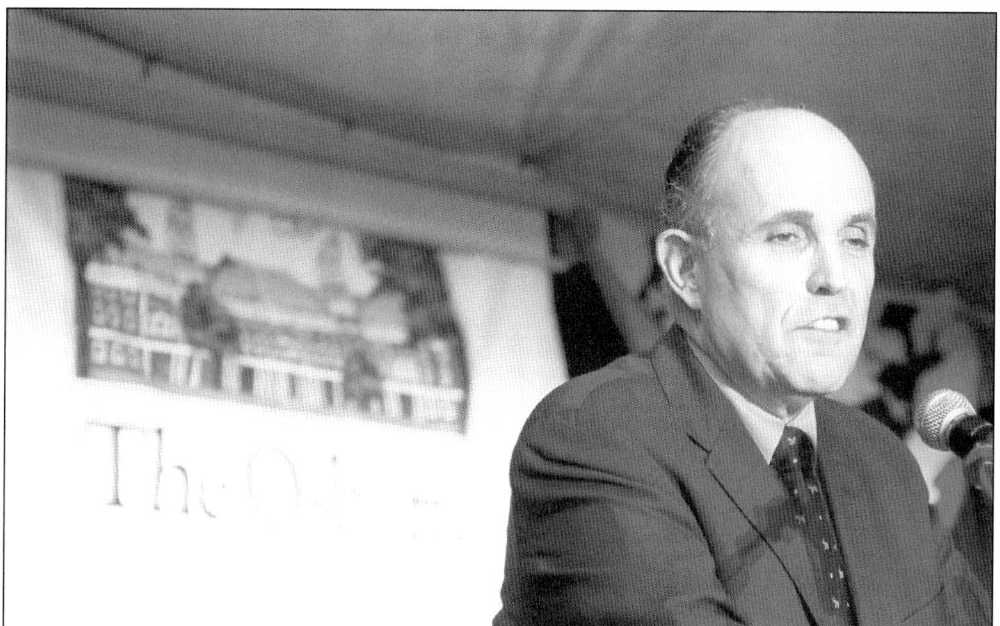

New York City mayor Rudolph Giuliani speaks at the dedication of Pathway 2000 on September 28, 2002.

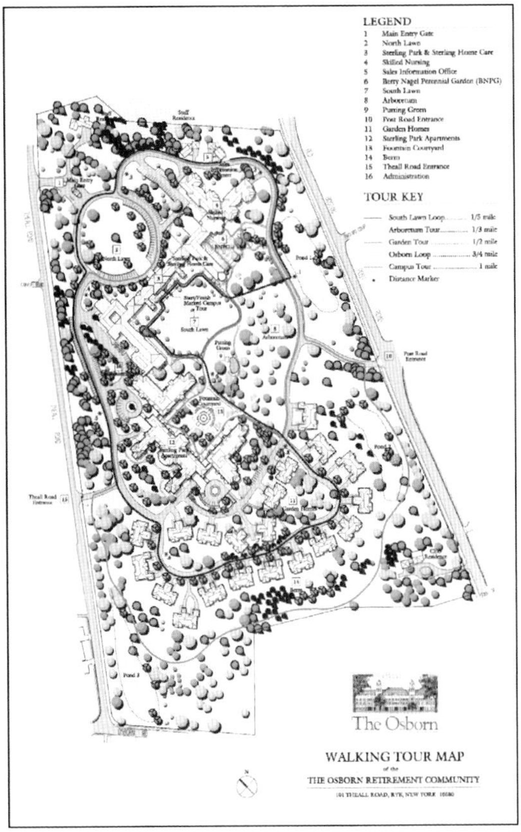

The site plan for Pathway 2000 illustrates how the Boston Post Road view corridor was preserved, a key to securing approval of the project. Encompassing 56 acres, the campus master plan resulted in more than 50 percent of the campus devoted to open space. Over 1,000 trees, many specimens, adorn the campus. Trees removed during construction were replaced at a 3 to 1 ratio.

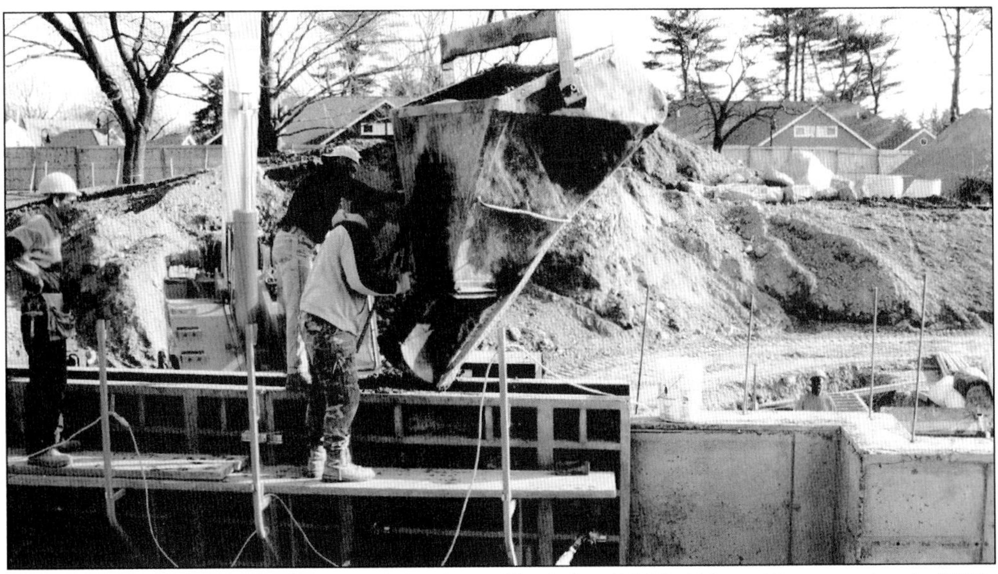

Cement is poured into the framework for the walls of the 4000 building. Commencing in 2000, the project resulted in the creation of 94 apartments, including underground parking for each apartment; the Bistro restaurant, with its beautiful artist painted murals; the campus's third library; a game room; offices for the Sterling Park management team; and a state-of-the-art screening room, Cinema 3000.

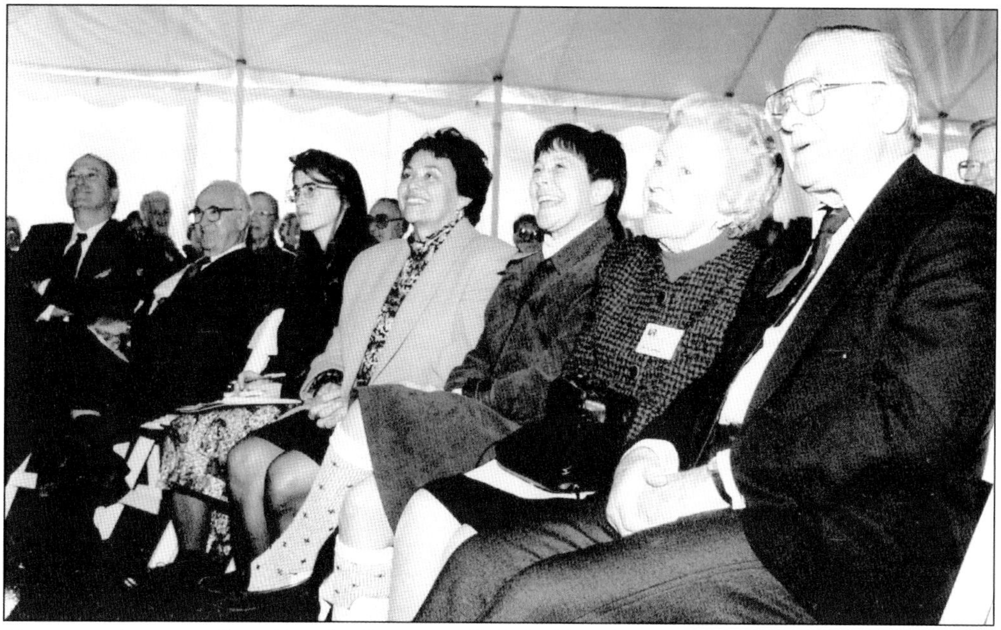

Guests at the groundbreaking for Pathway 2000, held on November 6, 1994, featured speaker Congresswoman Nita Lowey, who is seated fourth from the right. Seated next to her on the right of the photograph are New York State senator Susie Oppenheimer of Mamaroneck and resident Evan Johnson and his late wife, Midge.

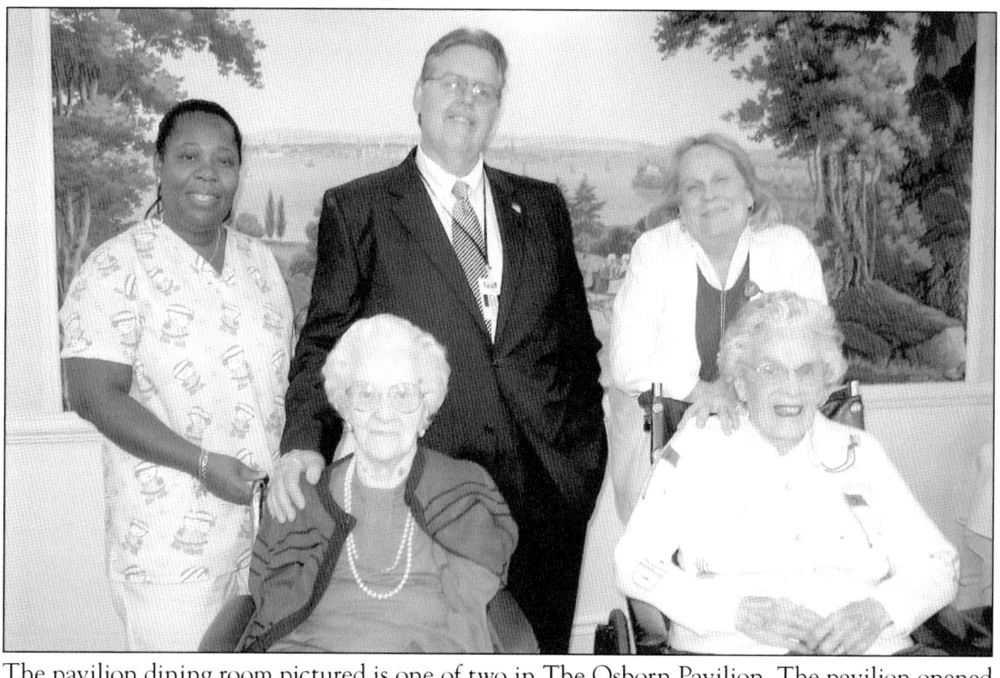

The pavilion dining room pictured is one of two in The Osborn Pavilion. The pavilion opened in 1996. Each resident has a private room, and the cluster design allows greater personalization of care to residents. From left to right are certified nursing assistant Monica Ellis, resident Gertrude Miller, chief executive officer Mark R. Zwerger, pavilion unit 1 manager Susan Brancato, R.N., and resident Kathleen Pearson.

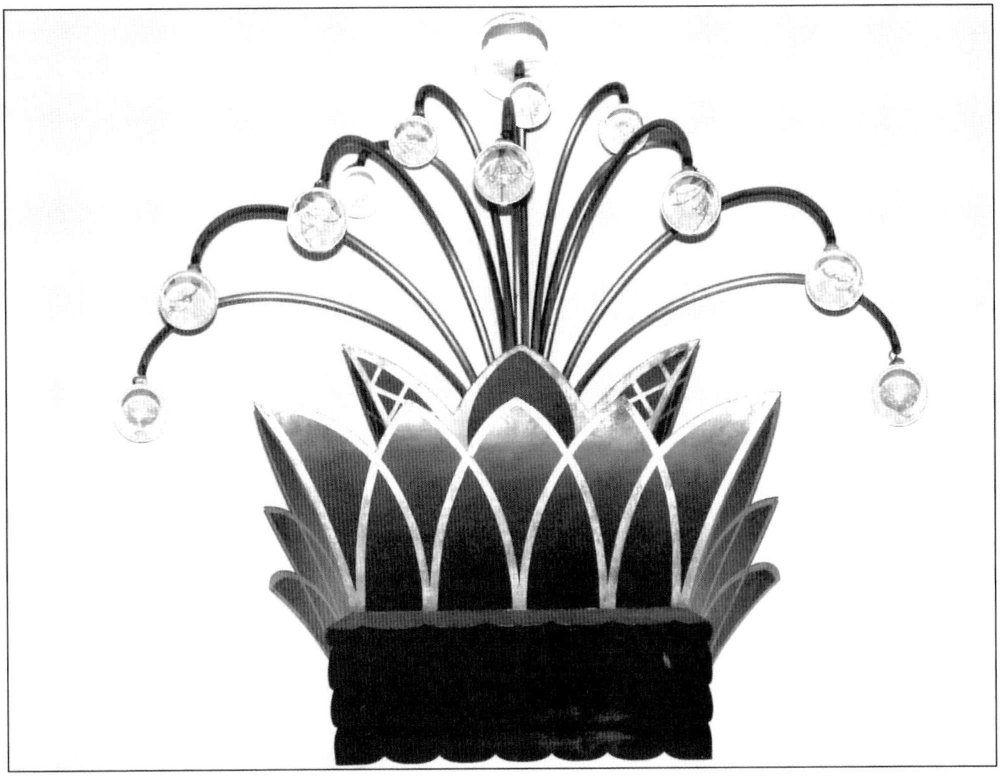

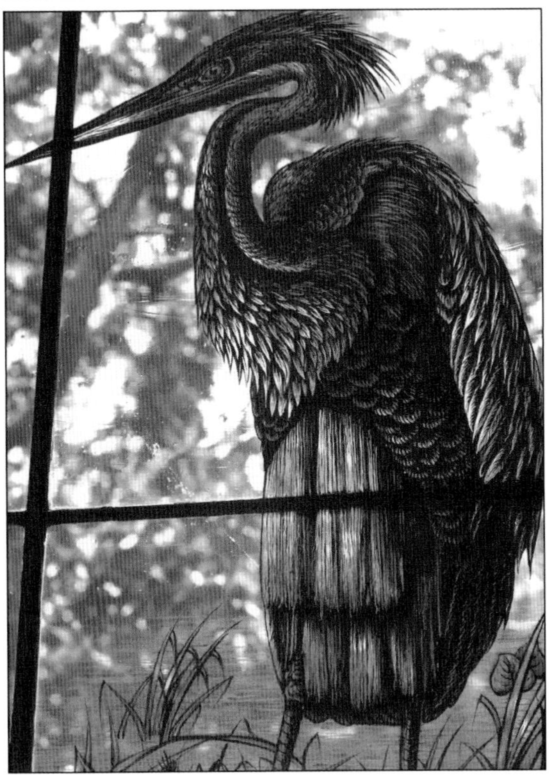

Two of the Catherine Sterling building's remarkable decorative features are the art deco light fixture in the Sterling Theater and, at left, an etching of a great blue heron in the solarium window glass. The same careful attention to detail seen here is present in all the newer buildings.

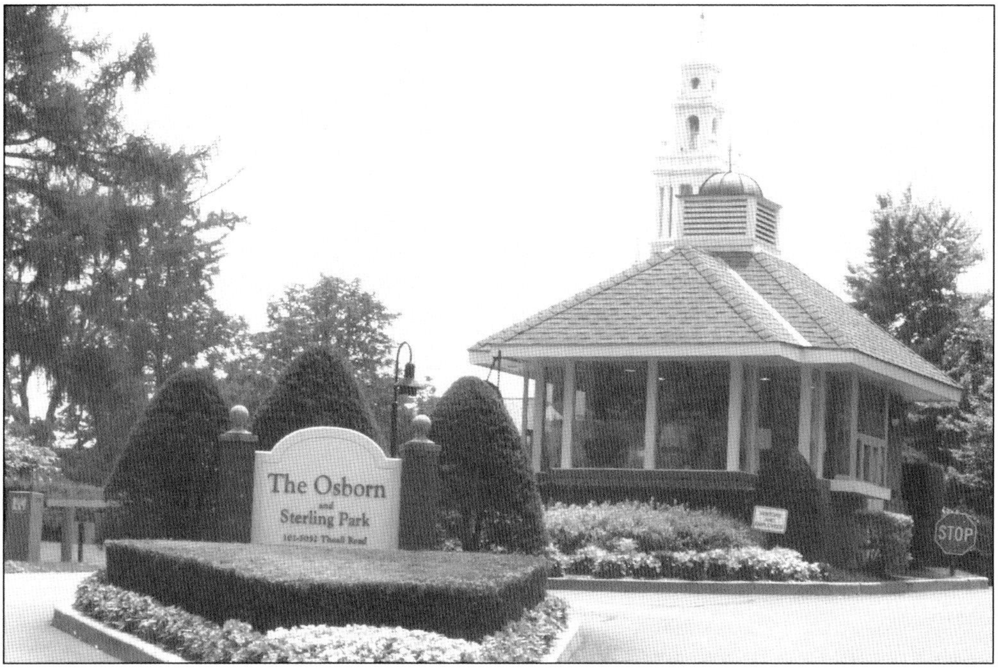

The main entrance on Theall Road welcomes visitors to the campus. As the campus expanded, it was not practical to continue to use the main reception area in The Osborn building rotunda for announcing guests and giving directions. The gatehouse allows a central entrance for all visitors.

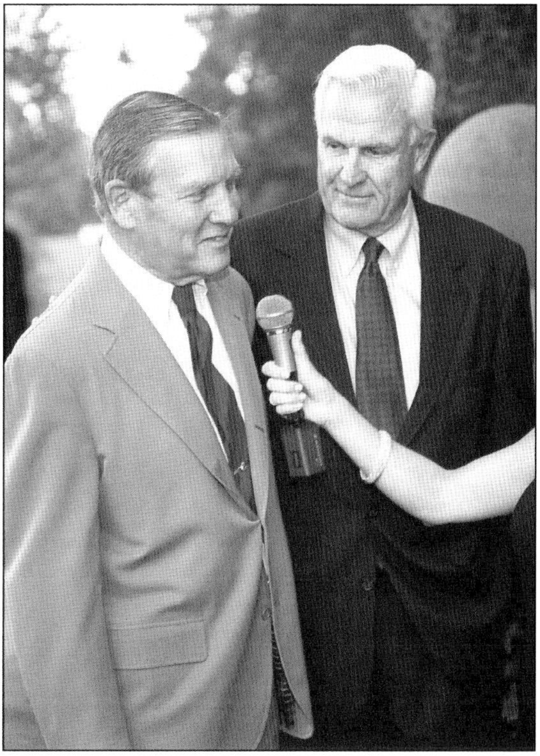

Jack Bowen (right) and Dan deMenocal were special guests at the Pathway 2000 dedication. Longtime Rye resident deMenocal joined the board in 1983 and served as vice president until he retired in 2005. Bowen was recruited by deMenocal in 1991, serving as chairman from 1992 until he retired in 2006. Both were instrumental in the success of Pathway 2000, providing leadership and wise counsel throughout the 10-year project.